AF553448

# EVOLUTION OF PLANTS

# EVOLUTION OF PLANTS

*By*

**Dr. Shubhrata R. Mishra**

*Deptt. of Botany*
*Vikram University*
*Ujjain (M.P.)*
*(India)*

**DISCOVERY PUBLISHING HOUSE PVT. LTD.**
**NEW DELHI-110 002**

*Published by:*
**Tilak Wasan**
**DISCOVERY PUBLISHING HOUSE PVT. LTD.**
4383/4B, Ansari Road, Darya Ganj
New Delhi-110 002 (India)
*Phone* : +91-11-23279245, 43596064-65
*Fax* : +91-11-23253475
*E-mail* : discoverypublishinghouse@gmail.com
sales@discoverypublishinggroup.com
*web* : www.discoverypublishinggroup.com

***First Edition:* 2013**

***Reprinted:* 2017**

**ISBN: 978-93-5056-265-9**

**Evolution of Plants**



*Printed at:*
Infinity Imaging Systems
Delhi

# Preface

Evolution of plants has resulted in increasing levels of complexity, from the earliest algal mats, through bryophytes, lycopods, ferns to the complex gymnosperms and angiosperms of today. While the groups which appeared earlier continue to thrive, especially in the environments in which they evolved, each new grade of organisation has eventually become more 'successful' than its predecessors by most measures.

Probably an algal scum formed on land 1,200 million years ago. In the Ordovician period, around 450 million years ago, the first land plants appeared. These began to diversify in the late Silurian Period, around 420 million years ago, and the fruits of their diversification are displayed in remarkable detail in an early Devonian fossil assemblage from the Rhynie chert. This chert preserved early plants in cellular detail, petrified in volcanic springs. By the middle of the Devonian Period most of the features recognised in plants today are present, including roots, leaves and secondary wood, and by late Devonian times seeds had evolved. Late Devonian plants had thereby reached a degree of sophistication that allowed them to form forests of tall trees. Evolutionary innovation continued after the Devonian period. Most plant groups were relatively unscathed by the Permo-Triassic extinction event, although the structures of communities changed. This may have set the scene for the evolution of flowering plants in the Triassic (~200 million years ago), which exploded in the Cretaceous and Tertiary. The latest major group of plants to evolve were the grasses, which became important in the mid Tertiary, from around 40 million years ago. The grasses, as well as many other groups, evolved new mechanisms of metabolism to survive the low $CO_2$ and warm, dry conditions of the tropics over the last 10 million years.

Land plants evolved from chlorophyte algae, perhaps as early as 510 million years ago; their closest living relatives are the charophytes, specifically Charales. Assuming that the Charales' habit has changed little since the divergence of lineages, this means that the land plants evolved from a branched, filamentous, haplontic alga, dwelling in shallow fresh water, perhaps at the edge of seasonally desiccating pools. Co-operative interactions with fungi may have helped early plants adapt to the stresses of the terrestrial realm.

Plants were not the first photosynthesisers on land, though: consideration of weathering rates suggests that organisms were already living on the land 1,200 million years ago, and microbial fossils have been found in freshwater lake deposits from 1,000 million years ago, but the carbon isotope record suggests that they were too scarce to impact the atmospheric composition until around 850 million years were probably small and simple, forming little more than an 'algal scum'.

The first evidence of plants on land comes from spores of Mid-Ordovician age (early Llanvirn, ~470 million years ago). These spores, known as cryptospores, were produced either singly (monads), in pairs (diads) or groups of four (tetrads), and their microstructure resembles that of modern liverwort spores, suggesting they share an equivalent grade of organisation. They are composed of sporopollenin — further evidence of an embryophytic affinity. It could be that atmospheric 'poisoning' prevented eukaryotes from colonising the land prior to this, or it could simply have taken a great time for the necessary complexity to evolve.

**—Author**

# Contents

# 1 Introduction

Evolution of plants has resulted in increasing levels of complexity, from the earliest algal mats, through bryophytes, lycopods, ferns to the complex gymnosperms and angiosperms of today. While the groups which appeared earlier continue to thrive, especially in the environments in which they evolved, each new grade of organisation has eventually become more 'successful' than its predecessors by most measures.

Probably an algal scum formed on land 1,200 million years ago. In the Ordovician period, around 450 million years ago, the first land plants appeared. These began to diversify in the late Silurian Period, around 420 million years ago, and the fruits of their diversification are displayed in remarkable detail in an early Devonian fossil assemblage from the Rhynie chert. This chert preserved early plants in cellular detail, petrified in volcanic springs. By the middle of the Devonian Period most of the features recognised in plants today are present, including roots, leaves and secondary wood, and by late Devonian times seeds had evolved. Late Devonian plants had thereby reached a degree of sophistication that allowed them to form forests of tall trees. Evolutionary innovation continued after the Devonian period. Most plant groups were relatively unscathed by the Permo-Triassic extinction event, although the structures of communities changed. This may have set the scene for the evolution of flowering plants in the Triassic (~200 million years ago), which exploded in the Cretaceous and Tertiary. The latest major group of plants to evolve were the grasses, which became important in the mid Tertiary, from around 40 million years ago. The grasses, as well as many other groups, evolved new mechanisms of metabolism to survive the low $CO_2$ and warm, dry conditions of the tropics over the last 10 million years.

Land plants evolved from chlorophyte algae, perhaps as early as 510 million years ago; their closest living relatives are the charophytes, specifically Charales. Assuming that the Charales' habit has changed little since the divergence of lineages, this means that the land plants evolved from a branched, filamentous, haplontic alga, dwelling in shallow fresh water, perhaps at the edge of seasonally desiccating pools. Co-operative interactions with fungi may have helped early plants adapt to the stresses of the terrestrial realm.

Plants were not the first photosynthesisers on land, though: consideration of weathering rates suggests that organisms were already living on the land 1,200 million years ago, and microbial fossils have been found in freshwater lake deposits from 1,000 million years ago, but the carbon isotope record suggests that they were too scarce to impact the atmospheric composition until around 850 million years were probably small and simple, forming little more than an 'algal scum'.

The first evidence of plants on land comes from spores of Mid-Ordovician age (early Llanvirn, ~470 million years ago). These spores, known as cryptospores, were produced either singly (monads), in pairs (diads) or groups of four (tetrads), and their microstructure resembles that of modern liverwort spores, suggesting they share an equivalent grade of organisation. They are composed of sporopollenin — further evidence of an embryophytic affinity. It could be that atmospheric 'poisoning' prevented eukaryotes from colonising the land prior to this, or it could simply have taken a great time for the necessary complexity to evolve.

Trilete spores similar to those of vascular plants appear soon afterwards, in Upper Ordovician rocks. Depending exactly when the tetrad splits, each of the four spores may bear a 'trilete mark', a *Y*-shape, reflecting the points at which each cell squashed up against its neighbours. However, this requires that the spore walls be sturdy and resistant at an early stage. This resistance is closely associated with having a desiccation-resistant outer wall—a trait only of use when spores must survive out of water. Indeed, even those embryophytes that have returned to the water lack a resistant wall, thus don't bear trilete marks. A close examination of algal spores shows that none have trilete spores, either because their walls are not resistant enough, or in those rare cases where it is, the spores disperse before they are squashed enough to develop the mark, or don't fit into a tetrahedral tetrad.

The earliest megafossils of land plants were thalloid organisms, which dwelt in fluvial wetlands and are found to have covered most of an early Silurian flood plain. They could only survive when the land was waterlogged. There were also microbial mats.

Once plants had reached the land, there were two approaches to dealing with desiccation. The bryophytes avoid it or give in to it, restricting their ranges to moist settings, or drying out and putting their metabolism 'on hold' until more water arrives. Tracheophytes resist desiccation. They all bear a waterproof outer cuticle layer wherever they are exposed to air (as do some bryophytes), to reduce water loss, but—since a total covering would cut them off from $CO_2$ in the atmosphere—they rapidly evolved stomata, small openings to allow gas exchange. Tracheophytes also developed vascular tissue to aid in the movement of water within the organisms and moved away from a gametophyte dominated life cycle.

Vascular tissue also facilitated upright growth without the support of water and paved the way for the evolution of larger plants on land.

The establishment of a land-based flora caused increased accumulation of oxygen in the atmosphere, as the plants produced oxygen as a waste product. When this concentration rose above 13 per cent, wildfires became possible. This is first recorded in the early Silurian fossil record by charcoalified plant fossils. Apart from a controversial gap in the Late Devonian, charcoal is present ever since.

Charcoalification is an important taphonomic mode. Wildfire drives off the volatile compounds, leaving only a shell of pure carbon. This is not a viable food source for herbivores or detritovores, so is prone to preservation; it is also robust, so can withstand pressure and display exquisite, sometimes sub-cellular, detail.

All multicellular plants have a life cycle comprising two generations or phases. One is termed the gametophyte, has a single set of chromosomes (denoted 1N), and produces gametes (sperm and eggs). The other is termed the sporophyte, has paired chromosomes (denoted 2N), and produces spores. The gametophyte and sporophyte may appear identical – homomorphy – or may be very different – heteromorphy.

The pattern in plant evolution has been a shift from homomorphy to heteromorphy. The algal ancestors to land plants were almost certainly haplobiontic, being haploid for all their life cycles, with a unicellular zygote providing the 2N stage. All land plants (*i.e.* embryophytes) are diplobiontic — that is, both the haploid and diploid stages are multicellular. Two trends are apparent: bryophytes (liverworts, mosses and hornworts) have developed the gametophyte, with the sporophyte becoming almost entirely dependent on it; vascular plants have developed the sporophyte, with the gametophyte being particularly reduced in the seed plants.

There are two competing theories to explain the appearance of a diplobiontic lifecycle.

The interpolation theory (also known as the antithetic or intercalary theory) holds that the sporophyte phase was a fundamentally new invention, caused by the mitotic division of a freshly germinated zygote, continuing until meiosis produces spores. This theory implies that the first sporophytes bore a very different morphology that the gametophyte they depended on. This seems to fit well with what we know of the bryophytes, in which a vegetative thalloid gametophyte is parasitised by simple sporophytes, which often comprise no more than a sporangium on a stalk. Increasing complexity of the ancestrally simple sporophyte, including the eventual acquisition of photosynthetic cells, would free it from its dependence on a gametophyte, as we see in some hornworts (*Anthoceros*), and eventually result in the sporophyte developing organs and vascular tissue, and becoming the dominant phase, as in the tracheophytes (vascular plants). This theory may be supported by observations that smaller *Cooksonia* individuals must have been supported by a gametophyte generation. The observed appearance of larger axial sizes, with room for photosynthetic tissue and thus self-sustainability, provides a possible route for the development of a self-sufficient sporophyte phase.

The alternative hypothesis is termed the transformation theory (or homologous theory). This posits that the sporophyte appeared suddenly by a delay in the occurrence of meiosis after the zygote germinated. Since the same genetic material would be employed, the haploid and diploid phases would look the same. This explains the behaviour of some algae, which produce alternating phases of identical sporophytes and gametophytes. Subsequent adaption to the desiccating land environment, which makes sexual reproduction difficult, would result in the simplification of the sexually active gametophyte, and elaboration of the sporophyte phase to better disperse the waterproof spores. The tissue of sporophytes and gametophytes preserved in the Rhynie chert is of similar complexity, which is taken to support this hypothesis.

## Morphology

### *Xylem*

To photosynthesise, plants must absorb $CO_2$ from the atmosphere. However, this comes at a price: while stomata are open to allow $CO_2$ to enter, water can evaporate. Water is lost much faster than $CO_2$ is absorbed, so plants need to replace it, and have developed systems to transport water from the moist soil to the site of photosynthesis. Early plants sucked water between the walls of their cells, then evolved the ability to control water loss (and $CO_2$ acquisition) through the use of stomata. Specialised water transport tissues soon evolved in the form of hydroids, tracheids, then secondary xylem, followed by an endodermis and ultimately vessels.

The high $CO_2$ levels of Silurian-Devonian times, when plants were first colonising land, meant that the need for water was relatively low. As $CO_2$ was withdrawn from the atmosphere by plants, more water was lost in its capture, and more elegant transport mechanisms evolved. As water transport mechanisms, and waterproof cuticles, evolved, plants could survive without being continually covered by a film of water. This transition from poikilohydry to homoiohydry opened up new potential for colonisation. Plants then needed a robust internal structure that held long narrow channels for transporting water from the soil to all the different parts of the above-soil plant, especially to the parts where photosynthesis occurred.

During the Silurian, $CO_2$ was readily available, so little water needed expending to acquire it. By the end of the Carboniferous, when $CO_2$ levels had lowered to something approaching today's, around 17 times more water was lost per unit of $CO_2$ uptake. However, even in these 'easy' early days, water was at a premium, and had to be transported to parts of the plant from the wet soil to avoid desiccation. This early water transport took advantage of the cohesion-tension mechanism inherent in water. Water has a tendency to diffuse to areas that are drier, and this process is accelerated when water can be wicked along a fabric with small spaces. In small passages, such as that between the plant cell walls (or in tracheids), a column of water behaves like rubber — when molecules evaporate from one end, they literally pull the molecules behind them along the channels. Therefore transpiration alone provided the driving force for water transport in early plants. However, without dedicated transport vessels, the cohesion-tension mechanism cannot transport water more than about 2 cm, severely limiting the size of the earliest plants. This process demands a steady supply of water from one end, to maintain the chains; to avoid exhausing it, plants developed a waterproof cuticle. Early cuticle may not have had pores but did not cover the entire plant surface, so that gas exchange could continue. However, dehydration at times was inevitable; early plants cope with this by having a lot of water stored between their cell walls, and when it comes to it sticking out the tough times by putting life 'on hold' until more water is supplied.

A banded tube from the late Silurian/early Devonian. The bands are difficult to see on this specimen, as an opaque carbonaceous coating conceals much of the tube. Bands are just visible in places on the left half of the image.

To be free from the constraints of small size and constant moisture that the parenchymatic transport system inflicted, plants needed a more efficient water transport system. During the early Silurian, they developed specialized cells, which were lignified (or bore similar chemical compounds) to avoid implosion; this process coincided with cell death, allowing their innards to be emptied and water to be passed through them. These wider, dead, empty cells were a million times more conductive than the inter-cell method, giving the potential for transport over longer distances, and higher $CO_2$ diffusion rates.

The first macrofossils to bear water-transport tubes *in situ* are the early Devonian pretracheophytes *Aglaophyton* and *Horneophyton*, which have structures very similar to the hydroids of modern mosses. Plants continued to innovate new ways of reducing the resistance to flow within their cells, thereby increasing the efficiency of their water transport. Bands on the walls of tubes, in fact apparent from the early Silurian onwards, are an early improvisation to aid the easy flow of water. Banded tubes, as well as tubes with pitted ornamentation on their walls, were lignified and, when they form single celled conduits, are considered to be tracheids. These, the 'next generation' of transport cell design, have a more rigid structure than hydroids, allowing them to cope with higher levels of water pressure. Tracheids may have a single evolutionary origin, possibly within the hornworts, uniting all tracheophytes (but they may have evolved more than once).

Water transport requires regulation, and dynamic control is provided by stomata. By adjusting the amount of gas exchange, they can restrict the amount of water lost through transpiration. This is an important role where water supply is not constant, and indeed stomata appear to have evolved before tracheids, being present in the non-vascular hornworts.

An endodermis probably evolved during the Silu-Devonian, but the first fossil evidence for such a structure is Carboniferous. This structure in the roots covers the water transport tissue and regulates ion exchange (and prevents unwanted pathogens etc. from entering the water transport system). The endodermis can also provide an upwards pressure, forcing water out of the roots when transpiration is not enough of a driver.

Once plants had evolved this level of controlled water transport, they were truly homoiohydric, able to extract water from their environment through root-like organs rather than relying on a film of surface moisture, enabling them to grow to much greater size. As a result of their independence from their surroundings, they lost their ability to survive desiccation — a costly trait to retain.

During the Devonian, maximum xylem diameter increased with time, with the minimum diameter remaining pretty constant. By the middle Devonian, the tracheid diameter of some plant lineages had plateaued. Wider tracheids allow water to be transported faster, but the overall transport rate depends also on the overall cross-sectional area of the xylem bundle itself. The increase in vascular bundle thickness further seems to correlate with the width of plant axes, and plant height; it is also closely related to the appearance of leaves and increased stomatal density, both of which would increase the demand for water.

While wider tracheids with robust walls make it possible to achieve higher water transport pressures, this increases the problem of cavitation. Cavitation occurs when a bubble of air forms within a vessel, breaking the bonds between chains of water molecules and preventing them from pulling more water up with their cohesive tension. A tracheid, once cavitated, cannot have its embolism removed and return to service (except in a few advanced angiosperms which have developed a mechanism of doing so). Therefore it is well worth plants' while to avoid cavitation occurring. For this reason, pits in tracheid walls have very small diametres, to prevent air entering and allowing bubbles to nucleate. Freeze-thaw cycles are a major cause of cavitation. Damage to a tracheid's wall almost inevitably leads to air leaking in and cavitation, hence the importance of many tracheids working in parallel.

Cavitation is hard to avoid, but once it has occurred plants have a range of mechanisms to contain the damage. Small pits link adjacent conduits to allow fluid to flow between them, but not air — although ironically these pits, which prevent the spread of embolisms, are also a major cause of them. These pitted surfaces further reduce the flow of water through the xylem by as much as 30 per cent. Conifers, by the Jurassic, developed an ingenious improvement, using valve-like structures to isolate cavitated elements. These torus-margo structures have a blob floating in the middle of a donut; when one side depressurises the blob is sucked into the torus and blocks further flow. Other plants simply accept cavitation; for instance, oaks grow a ring of wide vessels at the start of each spring, none of which survive the winter frosts. Maples use root pressure each spring to force sap upwards from the roots, squeezing out any air bubbles.

Growing to height also employed another trait of tracheids — the support offered by their lignified walls. Defunct tracheids were retained to form a strong, woody stem, produced in most instances by a secondary xylem. However, in early plants, tracheids were too mechanically vulnerable, and retained a central position, with a layer of tough sclerenchyma on the outer rim of the stems. Even when tracheids do take a structural role, they are supported by sclerenchymatic tissue.

Tracheids end with walls, which impose a great deal of resistance on flow; vessel members have perforated end walls, and are arranged in series to operate as if they were one continuous vessel. The function of end walls, which were the default state in the Devonian, was probably to avoid embolisms. An embolism is where an air bubble is created in a tracheid. This may happen as a result of freezing, or by gases dissolving out of solution. Once an embolism is formed, it usually cannot be removed (but see later); the affected cell cannot pull water up, and is rendered useless.

End walls excluded, the tracheids of prevascular plants were able to operate under the same hydraulic conductivity as those of the first vascular plant, *Cooksonia*.

The size of tracheids is limited as they comprise a single cell; this limits their length, which in turn limits their maximum useful diameter to 80 μm. Conductivity grows with the fourth power of diameter, so increased diameter has huge rewards; vessel elements, consisting of a number of cells, joined at their ends, overcame this limit and allowed larger tubes to form, reaching diameters of up to 500 μm, and lengths of up to 10 m.

Vessels first evolved during the dry, low $CO_2$ periods of the late Permian, in the horsetails, ferns and Selaginellales independently, and later appeared in the mid Cretaceous in angiosperms and gnetophytes. Vessels allow the same cross-sectional area of wood to transport around a hundred times more water than tracheids! This allowed plants to fill more of their stems with structural fibres, and also opened a new niche to vines, which could transport water without being as thick as the tree they grew on. Despite these advantages, tracheid-based wood is a lot lighter, thus cheaper to make, as vessels need to be much more reinforced to avoid cavitation.

## Leaves

Leaves today are, in almost all instances, an adaptation to increase the amount of sunlight that can be captured for photosynthesis. Leaves certainly evolved more than once, and probably originated as spiny outgrowths to protect early plants from herbivory.

Leaves are the primary photosynthetic organs of a plant. Based on their structure, they are classified into two types — microphylls, that lack complex venation patterns and megaphylls, that are large and with a complex venation. It has been proposed that these structures arose independently. Megaphylls, according to the Telome hypothesis, have evolved from plants that showed a three dimensional branching architecture, through three transformations—planation, which involved formation of a planar architecture, webbing, or formation of the outgrowths between the planar branches and fusion, where these webbed outgrowths fused to form a proper leaf lamina. All three steps happened multiple times in the evolution of today's leaves.

It has been proposed that the before the evolution of leaves, plants had the photosynthetic apparatus on the stems. Today's megaphyll leaves probably became commonplace some 360mya, about 40my after the simple leafless plants had colonized the land in the early Devonian period. This spread has been linked to the fall in the atmospheric carbon dioxide concentrations in the Late Paleozoic era associated with a rise in density of stomata on leaf surface. This must have allowed for better transpiration rates and gas exchange. Large leaves with less stomata would have gotten heated up in the sun's heat, but an increased stomatal density allowed for a better-cooled leaf, thus making its spread feasible.

The rhyniophytes of the Rhynie chert comprised nothing more than slender, unornamented axes. The early to middle Devonian trimerophytes, therefore, are the first evidence we have of anything that could be considered leafy. This group of vascular plants are recognisable by their masses of terminal sporangia, which adorn the ends of axes which may bifurcate or trifurcate. Some organisms, such as *Psilophyton*, bore enations. These are small, spiny outgrowths of the stem, lacking their own vascular supply.

Around the same time, the zosterophyllophytes were becoming important. This group is recognisable by their kidney-shaped sporangia, which grew on short lateral branches close to the main axes. They sometimes branched in a distinctive H-shape. The majority of this group bore pronounced spines on their axes. However, none of these had a vascular trace, and the first evidence of vascularised enations occurs in the Rhynie genus *Asteroxylon*. The spines of *Asteroxylon* had a primitive vasuclar supply — at the very least, leaf traces could be seen departing from the central protostele towards each individual 'leaf'. A fossil known as *Baragwanathia* appears in the fossil record slightly earlier, in the late Silurian. In this organism, these leaf traces continue into the leaf to form their mid-vein. One theory, the "enation theory", holds that the leaves developed by outgrowths of the protostele connecting with existing enations, but it is also possible that microphylls evolved by a branching axis forming 'webbing'.

*Asteroxylon* and *Baragwanathia* are widely regarded as primitive lycopods. The lycopods are still extant today, familiar as the quillwort *Isoetes* and the club mosses. Lycopods bear distinctive microphylls — leaves with a single vascular trace. Microphylls could grow to some size — the Lepidodendrales boasted microphylls over a meter in length — but almost all just bear the one vascular bundle. (An exception is the branching *Selaginella*).

The more familiar leaves, megaphylls, are thought to have separate origins — indeed, they appeared four times independently, in the ferns, horsetails, progymnosperms, and seed plants. They appear to have originated from dichotomising branches, which first overlapped (or 'overtopped') one another, and eventually developed 'webbing' and evolved into gradually more leaf-like structures. So megaphylls, by this 'teleome theory', are composed of a group of webbed branches — hence the 'leaf gap' left where the leaf's vascular bundle leaves that of the main branch resembles two axes splitting. In each of the four groups to evolve megaphylls, their leaves first evolved during the late Devonian to early Carboniferous, diversifying rapidly until the designs settled down in the mid Carboniferous.

The cessation of further diversification can be attributed to developmental constraints, but why did it take so long for leaves to evolve in the first place? Plants had been on the land for at least 50 million years before megaphylls became significant. However, small, rare mesophylls are known from the early Devonian genus *Eophyllophyton* — so development could not have been a barrier to their appearance. The best explanation so far incorporates observations that atmospheric $CO_2$ was declining rapidly during this time — falling by around 90 per cent during the Devonian. This corresponded with an increase in stomatal density by 100 times. Stomata allow water to evaporate from leaves, which causes them to curve. It appears that the low stomatal density in the early Devonian meant that evaporation was limited, and leaves would overheat if they grew to any size. The stomatal density could not increase, as the primitive steles and limited root systems would not be able to supply water quickly enough to match the rate of transpiration.

Clearly, leaves are not always beneficial, as illustrated by the frequent occurrence of secondary loss of leaves, famously exemplified by cacti and the 'whisk fern' *Psilotum*.

Secondary evolution can also disguise the true evolutionary origin of some leaves. Some genera of ferns display complex leaves which are attached to the pseudostele by an outgrowth of the vascular bundle, leaving no leaf gap. Further, horsetail (*Equisetum*) leaves bear only a single vein, and appear for all the world to be microphyllous; however, in the light of the fossil record and molecular evidence, we conclude that their forbears bore leaves with complex venation, and the current state is a result of secondary simplification.

Deciduous trees deal with another disadvantage to having leaves. The popular belief that plants shed their leaves when the days get too short is misguided; evergreens prospered in the Arctic circle during the most recent greenhouse earth. The generally accepted reason for shedding leaves during winter is to cope with the weather — the force of wind and weight of snow are much more comfortably weathered without leaves to increase surface area. Seasonal leaf loss has evolved independently several times and is exhibited in the ginkgoales, pinophyta and angiosperms. Leaf loss may also have arisen as a response to pressure from insects; it may have been less costly to lose leaves entirely during the winter or dry season than to continue investing resources in their repair.

## Factors Influencing Leaf Architectures

Various physical and physiological forces like light intensity, humidity, temperature, wind speeds etc. are thought to have influenced evolution of leaf shape and size. It is observed that high trees rarely have large leaves, owing to the obstruction they generate for winds. This obstruction car eventually lead to the tearing of leaves, if they are large. Similarly, trees that grow in temperate or taiga regions have pointed leaves, presumably to prevent nucleation of ice onto the leaf surface and reduce water loss due to transpiration. Herbivory, not only by large mammals, but also small insects has been implicated as a driving force in leaf evolution, an example being plants of the genus *Aciphylla*, that are commonly found in New Zealand. The now extinct Moas fed upon these plants, and its seen that the leaves have spines on their bodies, which probably functioned to discourage the moas from feeding on them. Other members of *Aciphylla* that did not co-exist with the moas, do not have these spines.

## Genetic Evidences for Leaf Evolution

At the genetic level, developmental studies have shown that repression of the KNOX genes is required for initiation of the leaf primordium. This is brought about by *ARP* genes, which encode transcription factors. Genes of this type have been found in many plants studied till now, and the mechanism *i.e.* repression of KNOX genes in leaf primordia, seems to be quite conserved. Interestingly, expression of KNOX genes in leaves produces complex leaves. It is speculated that the *ARP* function arose quite early in vascular plant evolution, because members of the primitive group Lycophytes also have a functionally similar gene Other players that have a conserved role in defining leaf primordia are the phytohormone auxin, gibberelin and cytokinin.

One interesting feature of a plant is its phyllotaxy. The arrangement of leaves on the plant body is such that the plant can maximally harvest light under the given constraints, and hence, one might expect the trait to be genetically robust. However, it may not be so. In maize, a mutation in only one gene called *abphyl (ABNORMAL PHYLLOTAXY)* was enough to change the phyllotaxy of the leaves. It implies that sometimes, mutational tweaking of a single locus on the genome is enough to generate diversity. The *abphyl* gene was later on shown to encode a cytokinin response regulator protein.

Once the leaf primordial cells are established from the SAM cells, the new axes for leaf growth are defined, one important (and more studied) among them being the abaxial-adaxial (lower-upper surface) axes. The genes involved in defining this, and the other axes seem to be more or less conserved among higher plants. Proteins of the *HD-ZIPIII* family have been implicated in defining the adaxial identity. These proteins deviate some cells in the leaf primordium from the default abaxial state, and make them adaxial. It is believed that in early plants with leaves, the leaves just had one type of surface — the abaxial one. This is the underside of today's leaves. The definition of the adaxial identity occurred some 200 million years after the abaxial identity was established. One can thus imagine the early leaves as an intermediate stage in evolution of today's leaves, having just arisen from spiny stem-like outgrowths of their leafless ancestors, covered with stomata all over, and not optimized as much for light harvesting. How the infinite variety of plant leaves is generated is a subject of intense research. Some common themes have emerged. One of the most significant is the involvement of KNOX genes in generating compound leaves, as in tomato . But this again is not universal. For example, pea uses a different mechanism for doing the same thing. Mutations in genes affecting leaf curvature can also change leaf form, by changing the leaf from flat, to a crinky shape, like the shape of cabbage leaves. There also exist different morphogen gradients in a developing leaf which define the leaf's axis. Changes in these morphogen gradients may also affect the leaf form. Another very important class of regulators of leaf development are the microRNAs, whose role in this process has just begun to be documented. The coming years should see a rapid development in comparative studies on leaf development, with many EST sequences involved in the process coming online.

### Tree Form

The trunk of early tree fern *Psaronius*, showing internal structure. The top of the plant would have been to the left of the image.

The early Devonian landscape was devoid of vegetation taller than waist height. Without the evolution of a robust vascular system, taller heights could not be attained. There was, however, a constant evolutionary pressure to attain greater height. The most obvious advantage is the harvesting of more sunlight for photosynthesis — by overshadowing competitors — but a further advantage is present in spore distribution, as spores (and, later, seeds) can be blown greater distances if they start higher. This may be demonstrated by *Prototaxites*, thought to be a late Silurian fungus reaching eight metres in height.

To attain arborescence, early plants had to develop woody tissue that provided support and water transport. To understand wood, we must know a little of vascular behaviour. The stele of plants undergoing 'secondary growth' is surrounded by the vascular cambium, a ring of cells which produces more xylem (on the inside) and phloem (on the outside). Since xylem cells comprise dead, lignified tissue, subsequent rings of xylem are added to those already present, forming wood.

The first plants to develop this secondary growth, and a woody habit, were apparently the ferns, and as early as the middle Devonian one species, *Wattieza*, had already reached heights of 8 m and a tree-like habit.

Other clades did not take long to develop a tree-like stature; the late Devonian *Archaeopteris*, a precursor to gymnosperms which evolved from the trimerophytes, reached 30 m in height. These progymnosperms were the first plants to develop true wood, grown from a bifacial cambium, of which the first appearance is in the mid Devonian *Rellimia*. True wood is only thought to have evolved once, giving rise to the concept of a 'lignophyte' clade.

These *Archaeopteris* forests were soon supplemented by lycopods, in the form of lepidodendrales, which topped 50m in height and 2m across at the base. These lycopods rose to dominate late Devonian and Carboniferous coal deposits. Lepidodendrales differ from modern trees in exhibiting determinate growth: after building up a reserve of nutrients at a low height, the plants would 'bolt' to a genetically determined height, branch at that level, spread their spores and die. They consisted of 'cheap' wood to allow their rapid growth, with at least half of their stems comprising a pith-filled cavity. Their wood was also generated by a unifacial vascular cambium — it did not produce new phloem, meaning that the trunks could not grow wider over time.

The horsetail *Calamites* was next on the scene, appearing in the Carboniferous. Unlike the modern horsetail *Equisetum, Calamites* had a unifacial vascular cambium, allowing them to develop wood and grow to heights in excess of 10 m. They also branched multiple times.

While the form of early trees was similar to that of today's, the groups containing all modern trees had yet to evolve.

The dominant groups today are the gymnosperms, which include the coniferous trees, and the angiosperms, which contain all fruiting and flowering trees. It was long thought that the angiosperms arose from within the gymnosperms, but recent molecular evidence suggests that their living representatives form two distinct groups. The molecular data has yet to be fully reconciled with morphological data, but it is becoming accepted that the morphological support for paraphyly is not especially strong. This would lead to the conclusion that both groups arose from within the pteridosperms, probably as early as the Permian.

The angiosperms and their ancestors played a very small role until they diversified during the Cretaceous. They started out as small, damp-loving organisms in the understory, and have been diversifying ever since the mid Cretaceous, to become the dominant member of non-boreal forests today.

## Roots

The roots of lepidodendrales are thought to be functionally equivalent to the stems , as the similar appearance of 'leaf scars' and 'root scars' on these specimens from different species demonstrates.

Roots are important to plants for two main reasons: Firstly, they provide anchorage to the substrate; more importantly, they provide a source of water and nutrients from the soil. Roots allowed plants to grow taller and faster.

The onset of roots also had effects on a global scale. By disturbing the soil, and promoting its acidification (by taking up nutrients such as nitrate and phosphate, they enabled it to weather more deeply, promoting the draw-down of $CO_2$ with huge implications for climate. These effects may have been so profound they led to a mass extinction.

But how and when did roots evolve in the first place? While there are traces of root-like impressions in fossil soils in the late Silurian, body fossils show the earliest plants to be devoid of roots. Many had tendrils which sprawled along or beneath the ground, with upright axes or thalli dotted here and there, and some even had non-photosynthetic subterranean branches which lacked stomata. The distinction between root and specialised branch is developmental; true roots follow a different developmental trajectory to stems. Further, roots differ in their branching pattern, and in possession of a root cap. So while Silu-Devonian plants such as *Rhynia* and *Horneophyton* possessed the physiological equivalent of roots, roots — defined as organs differentiated from stems — did not arrive until later. Unfortunately, roots are rarely preserved in the fossil record, and our understanding of their evolutionary origin is sparse.

Rhizoids — small structures performing the same role as roots, usually a cell in diameter — probably evolved very early, perhaps even before plants colonised the land; they are recognised in the Characeae, an algal sister group to land plants. That said, rhizoids probably evolved more than once; the rhizines of lichens, for example, perform a similar role. Even some animals (*Lamellibrachia*) have root-like structures!

More advanced structures are common in the Rhynie chert, and many other fossils of comparable early Devonian age bear structures that look like, and acted like, roots. The rhyniophytes bore fine rhizoids, and the trimerophytes and herbaceous lycopods of the chert bore root-like structure penetrating a few centimetres into the soil. However, none of these fossils display all the features borne by modern roots. Roots and root-like structures became increasingly more common and deeper penetrating during the Devonian period, with lycopod trees forming roots around 20 cm long during the Eifelian and Givetian. These were joined by progymnosperms, which rooted up to about a metre deep, during the ensuing Frasnian stage. True gymnosperms and zygopterid ferns also formed shallow rooting systems during the Famennian period.

The rhizomorphs of the lycopods provide a slightly different approach to rooting. They were equivalent to stems, with organs equivalent to leaves performing the role of rootlets. A similar construction is observed in the extant lycopod *Isoetes*, and this appears to be evidence that roots evolved independently at least twice, in the lycophytes and other plants.

A vascular system is indispensable to a rooted plants, as non-photosynthesising roots need a supply of sugars, and a vascular system is required to transport water and nutrients from the roots to the rest of the plant. These plants are little more advanced than their Silurian forbears, without a dedicated root system; however, the flat-lying axes can be clearly seen to have growths similar to the rhizoids of bryophytes today.

By the mid-to-late Devonian, most groups of plants had independently developed a rooting system of some nature. As roots became larger, they could support larger trees, and the soil was weathered to a greater depth. This deeper weathering had effects not only on the aforementioned drawdown of $CO_2$, but also opened up new habitats for colonisation by fungi and animals.

Roots today have developed to the physical limits. They penetrate many metres of soil to tap the water table. The narrowest roots are a mere 40 µm in diameter, and could not physically transport water if they were any narrower The earliest fossil roots recovered, by contrast, narrowed from 3 mm to under 700 µm in diameter; of course, taphonomy is the ultimate control of what thickness we can see.

## Arbuscular Mycorrhizae

The efficiency of many plants' roots is increased via a symbiotic relationship with a fungal partner. The most common are arbuscular mycorrhizae (AM), literally 'tree-like fungal roots'. These comprise fungi which invade some root cells, filling the cell membrane with their hyphae. They feed on the plant's sugars, but return nutrients generated or extracted from the soil (especially phosphate), which the plant would otherwise have no access to.

This symbiosis appears to have evolved early in plant history. AM are found in all plant groups, and 80 per cent of extant vascular plants, suggesting an early ancestry; a 'plant'-fungus symbiosis may even have been the step that enabled them to colonise the land,. Such fungi increase the productivity even of simple plants such as liverworts. Indeed, AM are abundant in the Rhynie chert; the association occurred even before there were true roots to colonise, and some have suggested that roots evolved to provide a more comfortable habitat for mycorrhizal fungi.

## Seeds

Early land plants reproduced in the fashion of ferns: spores germinated into small gametophytes, which produced sperm. These would swim across moist soils to find the female organs (archegonia) on the same or another gametophyte, where they would fuse with an ovule to produce an embryo, which would germinate into a sporophyte.

This mode of reproduction restricted early plants to damp environments, moist enough that the sperm could swim to their destination. Therefore, early land plants were constrained to the lowlands, near shores and streams. The development of heterospory freed them from this constraint.

Heterosporic organisms, as their name suggests, bear spores of two sizes — microspores and megaspores. These would germinate to form microgametophytes and megagametophytes, respectively. This system paved the way for seeds: taken to the extreme, the megasporangia could bear only a single megaspore tetrad, and to complete the transition to true seeds, three of the megaspores in the original tetrad could be aborted, leaving one megaspore per megasporangium.

The transition to seeds continued with this megaspore being "boxed in" to its sporangium while it germinates. Then, the megagametophyte is contained within a waterproof integument, which forms the bulk of the seed. The microgametophyte — a pollen grain which has germinated from a microspore — is employed for dispersal, only releasing its desiccation-prone sperm when it reaches a receptive megagametophyte.

Lycopods go a fair way down the path to seeds without ever crossing the threshold. Fossil lycopod megaspores reaching 1 cm in diameter, and surrounded by vegetative tissue, are known — these even germinate into a megagametophyte *in situ*. However, they fall short of being seeds, since the nucellus, an inner spore-covering layer, does not completely enclose the spore. A very small slit remains, meaning that the seed is still exposed to the atmosphere. This has two consequences —*firstly,* it means it is not fully resistant to desiccation, and *secondly,* sperm do not have to 'burrow' to access the archegonia of the megaspore.

The first 'spermatophytes' (literally:seed plants) — that is, the first plants to bear true seeds — are called pteridosperms: literally, 'seed ferns', so called because their foliage consisted of fern-like fronds, although they were not closely related to ferns. The oldest fossil evidence of seed plants is of Late Devonian age and they appear to have evolved out of an earlier group known as the progymnosperms. These early seed plants ranged from trees to small, rambling shrubs; like most early progymnosperms, they were woody plants with fern-like foliage. They all bore ovules, but no cones, fruit or similar. While it is difficult to track the early evolution of seeds, we can trace the lineage of the seed ferns from the simple trimerophytes through homosporous Aneurophytes.

This seed model is shared by basically all gymnosperms (literally: 'naked seeds'), most of which encase their seeds in a woody or fleshy (the yew, for example) cone, but none of which fully enclose their seeds. The angiosperms ('vessel seeds') are the only group to fully enclose the seed, in a carpel.

Fully enclosed seeds opened up a new pathway for plants to follow: that of seed dormancy. The embryo, completely isolated from the external atmosphere and hence protected from desiccation, could survive some years of drought before germinating. Gymnosperm seeds from the late Carboniferous have been found to contain embryos, suggesting a lengthy gap between fertilisation and germination. This period is associated with the entry into a greenhouse earth period, with an associated increase in aridity. This suggests that dormancy arose as a response to drier climatic conditions, where it became advantageous to wait for a moist period before germinating. This evolutionary breakthrough appears to have opened a floodgate: previously inhospitable areas, such as dry mountain slopes, could now be tolerated, and were soon covered by trees.

Seeds offered further advantages to their bearers: they increased the success rate of fertilised gametophytes, and because a nutrient store could be 'packaged' in with the embryo, the seeds could germinate rapidly in inhospitable environments, reaching a size where it could fend for itself more quickly. For example, without an endosperm, seedlings growing in arid environments would not have the reserves to grow roots deep enough to reach the water table before they expired from dehydration. Likewise, seeds germinating in a gloomy understory require an additional reserve of energy to quickly grow high enough to capture sufficient light for self-sustenance. A combination of these advantages gave seed plants the ecological edge over the previously dominant genus *Archaeopteris*, thus increasing the biodiversity of early forests.

## Flowers

Flowers are modified leaves possessed only by the angiosperms, which are relatively late to appear in the fossil record. Flower-like structures first appear in the fossil records some ~130 mya, in the Cretaceous era. Colourful and/or pungent structures surround the cones of plants such as cycads and gnetales, making a strict definition of the term 'flower' elusive.

The main function of a flower is reproduction, which, before the evolution of the flower and angiosperms, was the job of microsporophylls and megasporophylls. A flower can be considered a powerful evolutionary innovation, because its presence allowed the plant world to access new means and mechanisms for reproduction.

The flowering plants have long been assumed to have evolved from within the *gymnosperms*; according to the traditional morphological view, they are closely allied to the gnetales. However, as noted above, recent molecular evidence is at odds to this hypothesis, nd further suggests that gnetales are more closely related to some gymnosperm groups than angiosperms, and that extant gymnosperms form a distinct clade to the angiosperms, the two clades diverging some 300 million years ago.

The relationship of stem groups to the angiosperms is important in determining the evolution of flowers. stem groups provide an insight into the state of earlier 'forks' on the path to the current state. Convergence increases the risk of misidentifying stem groups. Since the protection of the megagametophyte is evolutionarily desirable, probably many separate groups evolved protective encasements independently. In flowers, this protection takes the form of a carpel, evolved from a leaf and recruited into a protective role, shielding the ovules. These ovules are further protected by a double-walled integument.

Penetration of these protective layers needs something more than a free-floating microgametophyte. Angiosperms have pollen grains comprising just three cells. One cell is responsible for drilling down through the integuments, and creating a conduit for the two sperm cells to flow down. The megagametophyte has just seven cells; of these, one fuses with a sperm cell, forming the nucleus of the egg itself, and another joins with the other sperm, and dedicates itself to forming a nutrient-rich endosperm. The other cells take auxiliary roles. This process of 'double fertilisation' is unique and common to all angiosperms.

In the fossil record, there are three intriguing groups which bore flower-like structures. The first is the Permian pteridosperm *Glossopteris*, which already bore recurved leaves resembling carpels. The Triassic *Caytonia* is more flower-like still, with enclosed ovules — but only a single integument. Further, details of their pollen and stamens set them apart from true flowering plants.

The Bennettitales bore remarkably flower-like organs, protected by whorls of bracts which may have played a similar role to the petals and sepals of true flowers; however, these flower-like structures evolved independently, as the Bennettitales are more closely related to cycads and ginkgos than to the angiosperms.

However, no true flowers are found in any groups save those extant today. Most morphological and molecular analyses place *Amborella*, the nymphaeales and Austrobaileyaceae in a basal clade dubbed 'ANA'. This clade appear to have diverged in the early Cretaceous, around 130 million years ago – around the same time as the earliest fossil angiosperm, and just after the first angiosperm-like pollen, 136 million years ago. The magnoliids diverged soon after, and a rapid radiation had produced eudicots and monocots by 125 million years ago. By the end of the Cretaceous 65.5 million years ago, over 50 per cent of today's angiosperm orders had evolved, and the clade accounted for 70 per cent of global species. It was around this time that flowering trees became dominant over conifers.

The features of the basal 'ANA' groups suggest that angiosperms originated in dark, damp, frequently disturbed areas. It appears that the angiosperms remained constrained to such habitats throughout the Cretaceous — occupying the niche of small herbs early in the successional series. This may have restricted their initial significance, but given them the flexibility that accounted for the rapidity of their later diversifications in other habitats.

## Origins of the Flower

The family Amborellaceae is regarded as the sister family of all living flowering plants. That means members of this family were most likely the first flowering plants.

It seems that on the level of the organ, the leaf may be the ancestor of the flower, or at least some floral organs. When we mutate some crucial genes involved in flower development, we end up with a cluster of leaf-like structures. Thus, sometime in history, the developmental programme leading to formation of a leaf must have been altered to generate a flower. There probably also exists an overall robust framework within which the floral diversity has been generated. An example of that is a gene called *LEAFY (LFY)*, which is involved in flower development in *Arabidopsis thaliana*. The homologs of this gene are found in angiosperms as diverse as tomato, snapdragon, pea, maize and even gymnosperms. Expression of *Arabidopsis thaliana* LFY in distant plants like poplar and citrus also results in flower-production in these plants. The *LFY* gene regulates the expression of some gene belonging to the MADS-box family. These genes, in turn, act as direct controllers of flower development.

## Evolution of the MADS-box Family

The members of the MADS-box family of transcription factors play a very important and evolutionarily conserved role in flower development. According to the ABC Model of flower development, three zones — A,B and C — are generated within the developing flower primordium, by the action of some transcription factors, that are members of the

MADS-box family. Among these, the functions of the B and C domain genes have been evolutionarily more conserved than the A domain gene. Many of these genes have arisen through gene duplications of ancestral members of this family. Quite a few of them show redundant functions.

The evolution of the MADS-box family has been extensively studied. These genes are present even in pteridophytes, but the spread and diversity is many times higher in angiosperms. There appears to be quite a bit of pattern into how this family has evolved. Consider the evolution of the C-region gene *AGAMOUS (AG)*. It is expressed in today's flowers in the stamens, and the carpel, which are reproductive organs. It's ancestor in gymnosperms also has the same expression pattern. Here, it is expressed in the strobili, an organ that produces pollens or ovules. Similarly, the B-genes' *(AP3 and PI)* ancestors are expressed only in the male organs in gymnosperms. Their descendants in the modern angiosperms also are expressed only in the stamens, the male reproductive organ. Thus, the same, then-existing components were used by the plants in a novel manner to generate the first flower. This is a recurring pattern in evolution.

### Factors Influencing Floral Diversity

There is enormous variation in the developmental programmes of plants. For example, grasses possess unique floral structures. The carpels and stamens are surrounded by scale-like lodicules and two bracts the lemma and the palea. Genetic evidence and morphology suggest that lodicules are homologous to eudicot petals. The palea and lemma may be homologous to sepals in other groups, or may be unique grass structures. The genetic evidence is not clear.

Variation in floral structure is typically due to slight changes in the MADS-box genes and their expression pattern.

Another example is that of *Linaria vulgaris*, which has two kinds of flower symmetries-radial and bilateral. These symmetries are due to epigenetic changes in just one gene called *CYCLOIDEA*.

*Arabidopsis thaliana* has a gene called *AGAMOUS* that plays an important role in defining how many petals and sepals and other organs are generated. Mutations in this gene give rise to the floral meristem obtaining an indeterminate fate, and many floral organs keep on getting produced. We have flowers like roses, carnations and morning glory, for example, that have very dense floral organs. These flowers have been selected by horticulturists since long for increased number of petals. Researchers have found that the morphology of these flowers is because of strong mutations in the *AGAMOUS* homolog in these plants, which leads to them making a large number of petals and sepals. Several studies on diverse plants like petunia, tomato, Impatiens, maize etc. have suggested that the enormous diversity of flowers is a result of small changes in genes controlling their development.

Some of these changes also cause changes in expression patterns of the developmental genes, resulting in different phenotypes. The Floral Genome Project looked at the EST data from various tissues of many flowering plants. The researchers confirmed that the ABC Model of flower development is not conserved across all angiosperms. Sometimes expression domains change, as in the case of many monocots, and also in some basal angiosperms like *Amborella*. Different models of flower development like the *The fading boundaries model*, or the *Overlapping-boundaries model* which propose non-rigid domains of expression, may explain these architectures. There is a possibility that from the basal to the modern angiosperms, the domains of floral architecture have gotten more and more fixed through evolution.

## Flowering Time

Another floral feature that has been a subject of natural selection is flowering time. Some plants flower early in their life cycle, others require a period of vernalization before flowering. This decision is based on factors like temperature, light intensity, presence of pollinators and other environmental signals. We know that genes like *CONSTANS (CO)*, *Flowering*

*Locus C* (*FLC*) and *FRIGIDA* regulate integration of environmental signals into the pathway for flower development. Variations in these loci have been associated with flowering time variations between plants. For example, *Arabidopsis thaliana* ecotypes that grow in the cold, temperate regions require prolonged vernalization before they flower, while the tropical varieties, and the most common lab strains, don't. We now know that this variation is due to mutations in the *FLC* and *FRIGIDA* genes, rendering them non-functional.

Quite a few players in this process are conserved across all the plants studied. Sometimes though, despite genetic conservation, the mechanism of action turns out to be different. For example, rice is a short-day plant, while *Arabidopsis thaliana* is a long-day plant. Now, in both plants, the proteins *CO* and *FLOWERING LOCUS T (FT)* are present. But in *Arabidopsis thaliana, CO* enhances *FT* production, while in rice, the *CO* homolog represses *FT* production, resulting in completely opposite downstream effects.

## Theories of Flower Evolution

There are many theories that propose how flowers evolved. Some of them are described below.

The *anthophyte theory* was based upon the observation that a gymnospermic group Gnetales has a flower-like ovule. It has partially developed vessels as found in the angiosperms, and the megasporangium is covered by three envelopes, like the ovary structure of angiosperm flowers. However, many other lines of evidence show that Gnetales is not related to angiosperms.

The *male theory* has a more genetic basis. Proponents of this theory point out that the gymnosperms have two very similar copies of the gene *LFY* while angiosperms just one. Molecular clock analysis has shown that the other *LFY* paralog was lost in angiosperms around the same time as flower fossils become abundant, suggesting that this event might have led to floral evolution. According to this theory, loss of one of the *LFY* paralog led to flowers that were more male, with the ovules being expressed ectopically. These ovules initially performed the function of attracting pollinators, but sometime later, may have been integrated into the core flower.

## Advances in Metabolism

Photosynthesis is not quite as simple as adding water to $CO_2$ to produce sugars and oxygen. A complex chemical pathway is involved, facilitated along the way by a range of enzymes and co-enzymes. The enzyme RuBisCO is responsible for 'fixing' $CO_2$ — that is, it attaches it to a carbon-based molecule to form a sugar, which can be used by the plant, releasing an oxygen molecule along the way. However, the enzyme is notoriously inefficient, and just as effectively will also fix oxygen instead of $CO_2$ in a process called photorespiration. This is energetically costly as the plant has to use energy to turn the products of photorepsiration back into a form that can react with $CO_2$.

## Concentrating Carbon

$C_4$ plants evolved carbon concentrating mechanisms. These work by increasing the concentration of $CO_2$ around RuBisCO, thereby facilitating photosynthesis and decreasing photorespiration. The process of concentrating $CO_2$ around RuBisCO requires more energy than allowing gases to diffuse, but under certain conditions — *i.e.* warm temperatures (>25°C), low $CO_2$ concentrations, or high oxygen concentrations — pays off in terms of the decreased loss of sugars through photorespiration.

One type of $C_4$ metabolism employs a so-called Kranz anatomy. This transports $CO_2$ through an outer mesophyll layer, via a range of organic molecules, to the central bundle sheath cells, where the $CO_2$ is released. In this way, $CO_2$ is concentrated near the site of RuBisCO operation. Because RuBisCO is operating in an environment with much more $CO_2$ than it otherwise would be, it performs more efficiently.

A second mechanism, CAM photosynthesis, temporally separates photosynthesis from the action of RuBisCO.

RuBisCO only operates during the day, when stomata are sealed and $CO_2$ is provided by the breakdown of the chemical malate. More $CO_2$ is then harvested from the atmosphere when stomata open, during the cool, moist nights, reducing water loss.

## Evolutionary Record

These two pathways, with the same effect on RuBisCO, evolved a number of times independently — indeed, $C_4$ alone arose in 18 different plant families. The $C_4$ construction is most famously used by a subset of grasses, while CAM is employed by many succulents and cacti. The trait appears to have emerged during the Oligocene, around 25 to 32 million years ago; however, they did not become ecologically significant until the Miocene, -1 million years ago. Remarkably, some charcoalified fossils preserve tissue organised into the Kranz anatomy, with intact bundle sheath cells, allowing the presence $C_4$ metabolism to be identified without doubt at this time. In deducing their distribution and significance, we resort to the use of isotopic markers. $C_3$ plants preferentially use the lighter of two isotopes of carbon in the atmosphere, $^{12}C$, which is more readily involved in the chemical pathways involved in its fixation. Because $C_4$ metabolism involves a further chemical step, this effect is accentuated. Plant material can be analysed to deduce the ratio of the heavier $^{13}C$ to $^{12}C$. This ratio is denoted $d^{13}C$. $C_3$ plants are on average around 14‰ (parts per thousand) lighter than the atmospheric ratio, while $C_4$ plants are about 28‰ lighter. The $d^{13}C$ of CAM plants depends on the percentage of carbon fixed at night relative to what is fixed in the day, being closer to $C_3$ plants if they fix most carbon in the day and closer to $C_4$ plants if they fix all their carbon at night.

It's troublesome procuring original fossil material in sufficient quantity to analyse the grass itself, but fortunately we have a good proxy: horses. Horses were globally widespread in the period of interest, and browsed almost exclusively on grasses. There's an old phrase in isotope palæontology, "you are what you eat (plus a little bit)" — this refers to the fact that organisms reflect the isotopic composition of whatever they eat, plus a small adjustment factor. There is a good record of horse teeth throughout the globe, and their d[13]C has been measured. The record shows a sharp negative inflection around -1 million years ago, during the Messinian, and this is interpreted as the rise of $C_4$ plants on a global scale.

### When is $C_4$ an advantage?

While $C_4$ enhances the efficiency of RuBisCO, the concentration of carbon is highly energy intensive. This means that $C_4$ plants only have an advantage over $C_3$ organisms in certain conditions: namely, high temperatures and low rainfall. $C_4$ plants also need high levels of sunlight to thrive. Models suggest that without wildfires removing shade-casting trees and shrubs, there would be no space for $C_4$ plants. But wildfires have occurred for 400 million years — why did $C_4$ take so long to arise, and then appear independently so many times? The Carboniferous period (~300 million years ago) had notoriously high oxygen levels — almost enough to allow spontaneous combustion — and very low $CO_2$, but there is no $C_4$ isotopic signature to be found. And there doesn't seem to be a sudden trigger for the Miocene rise.

During the Micoene, the atmosphere and climate was relatively stable. If anything, $CO_2$ increased gradually from 14 to 9 million years ago before settling down to concentrations similar to the Holocene. This suggests that it did not have a key role in invoking $C_4$ evolution. Grasses themselves (the group which would give rise to the most occurrences of $C_4$) had probably been around for 60 million years or more, so had had plenty of time to evolve $C_4$, which in any case is present in a diverse range of groups and thus evolved independently. There is a strong signal of climate change in South Asia; increasing aridity — hence increasing fire frequency and intensity — may have led to an increase in the importance of grasslands. However, this is difficult to reconcile with the North American record. It is possible that the signal is entirely biological, forced by the fire-driven acceleration of grass evolution — which, both by increasing weathering and incorporating more carbon into sediments, reduced atmospheric $CO_2$ levels. Finally, there is evidence that the onset of $C_4$ from 9 to 7 million years ago is a biased signal, which only holds true for North America, from where most samples originate; emerging evidence suggests that grasslands evolved to a dominant state at least 15Ma earlier in South America.

## Secondary Metabolism

Although we know many secondary metabolites produced by plants, the extent of the same is still unfathomable. Secondary metabolites are essentially low molecular weight compounds, sometimes having complex structures. They function in processes as diverse as immunity, anti-herbivory, pollinator attraction, communication between plants, maintaining symbiotic associations with soil flora, enhancing the rate of fertilization etc., and hence are significant from the evo-devo perspective. The structural and functional diversity of these secondary metabolites across the plant kingdom is vast; it is estimated that hundreds of thousands of enzymes might be involved in this process in the entire of the plant kingdom, with about 15-25 per cent of the genome coding for these enzymes, and every species having its unique arsenal of secondary metabolites. Many of these metabolites are of enormous medical significance to humans.

What is the purpose of having so many secondary metabolites being produced, with a significant chunk of the metabolome devoted to this activity? It is hypothesized that most of these chemicals help in generating immunity, and in consequence, the diversity of these metabolites is a result of a constant war between plants and their parasites. There is evidence that this may be true in many cases. The big question here is the reproductive cost involved in maintaining such an impressive inventory. Various models have been suggested that probe into this aspect of the question, but a consensus on the extent of the cost is lacking. We still cannot predict whether a plant with more secondary metabolites would be better off than other plants in its vicinity.

Secondary metabolite production seems to have arisen quite early during evolution. Even bacteria possess the ability to make these compounds. But they assume more significant roles in life from fungi onwards to plants. In plants they seem to have spread out using different mechanisms like gene duplications, evolution of novel genes etc. Furthermore, studies have shown that diversity in some of these compounds may be positively selected for.

Although the role of novel gene evolution in the evolution of secondary metabolism cannot be denied, there are several examples where new metabolites have been formed by small changes in the reaction. For example, cyanogen glycosides have been proposed to have evolved multiple times in different plant lineages. There are several such instances of convergent evolution. For example, we now know that enzymes for synthesis of limonene — a terpene — are more similar between angiosperms and gymnosperms than to their own terpene synthesis enzymes. This suggests independent evolution of the limonene biosynthetic pathway in these two lineages.

While environmental factors are significantly responsible for evolutionary change, they act merely as agents for natural selection. Change is inherently brought about via phenomena at the genetic level - mutations, chromosomal rearrangements and epigenetic changes. While the general types of mutations hold true across the living world, in plants, some other mechanisms have been implicated as highly significant.

Polyploidy is a very common feature in plants. It is believed that at least half *(and probably all)* plants are or have been polyploids. Polyploidy leads to genome doubling, thus generating functional redundancy in most genes. The duplicated genes may attain new function, either by changes in expression pattern or changes in activity. Polyploidy and gene duplication are believed to be among the most powerful forces in evolution of plant form. It is not know though, why genome doubling is such a frequent process in plants. One probable reason is the production of large amounts of secondary metabolites in plant cells. Some of them might interfere in the normal process of chromosomal segregation, leading to polypoidy.

In recent times, plants have been shown to possess significant microRNA families, which are conserved across many plant lineages. In comparison to animals, while the number of plant miRNA families are lesser than animals, the size of each family is much larger. The miRNA genes are also much more spread out in the genome than those in animals, where we find them clustered. It has been proposed that these miRNA families have expanded by duplications of chromosomal regions. Many miRNA genes involved in regulation of plant development have been found to be quite conserved between plants studied.

Domestication of plants like maize, rice, barley, wheat etc. has also been a significant driving force in their evolution. Some studies have tried to look at the origins of the maize plant and it turns out that maize is a domesticated derivative of a wild plant from Mexico called teosinte. Teosinte belongs to the genus *Zea*, just as maize, but bears very small inflorescence, 5-10 hard cobs and a highly branched and spread out stem.

Interestingly, crosses between a particular teosinte variety and maize yields fertile offsprings that are intermediate in phenotype between maize and teosinte. QTL analysis has also revealed some loci that when mutated in maize yield a teosinte-like stem or teosinte-like cobs. Molecular clock analysis of these genes estimates their origins to some 9000 years ago, well in accordance with other records of maize domestication. It is believed that a small group of farmers must have selected some maize-like natural mutant of teosinte some 9000 years ago in Mexico, and subjected it to continuous selection to yield the maize plant as we know today.

Another interesting case is that of cauliflower. The edible cauliflower is a domesticated version of the wild plant *Brassica oleracea*, which does not possess the dense undifferentiated inflorescence called the curd, that cauliflower possesses.

Cauliflower possesses a single mutation in a gene called *CAL*, controlling meristem differentiation into inflorescence. This causes the cells at the floral meristem to gain an undifferentiated identity, and instead of growing into a flower, they grow into a lump of undifferentiated cells. This mutation has been selected through domestication at least since the Greek empire.

# Plant Cell

Plant cells are eukaryotic cells that differ in several key respects from the cells of other eukaryotic organisms. Their distinctive features include:

- A large central vacuole, a water-filled volume enclosed by a membrane known as the *tonoplast* maintains the cell's turgor, controls movement of molecules between the cytosol and sap, stores useful material and digests waste proteins and organelles.
- A cell wall composed of cellulose and hemicellulose, pectin and in many cases lignin, are secreted by the protoplast on the outside of the cell membrane. This contrasts with the cell walls of fungi (which are made of chitin), and of bacteria, which are made of peptidoglycan.
- Specialised cell-cell communication pathways known as plasmodesmata, pores in the primary cell wall through which the plasmalemma and endoplasmic reticulum of adjacent cells are continuous.
- Plastids, the notables one being the chloroplasts, which contain chlorophyll and the biochemical systems for light harvesting and photosynthesis, but also amyloplasts specialized for starch storage, elaioplasts specialized for fat storage, and chromoplasts specialized for synthesis

and storage of pigments. As in mitochondria, which have a genome encoding 37 genes, plastids have their own genomes of about 100-120 unique genes and, it is presumed, arose as prokaryotic endosymbionts living in the cells of an early eukaryotic ancestor of the land plants and algae.

- Cell division by construction of a phragmoplast as a template for building a cell plate late in cytokinesis is characteristic of land plants and a few groups of algae, the notable one being the Charophytes and the Order Trentepohliales.
- The sperm of bryophytes have flagellae similar to those in animals, but higher plants, (including Gymnosperms and flowering plants) lack the flagellae and centrioles that are present in animal cells.

## Cell Types

Parenchyma cells are living cells that have diverse functions ranging from storage and support to photosynthesis and phloem loading ( transfer cells). Apart from the xylem and phloem in its vascular bundles, leaves are composed mainly of parenchyma cells. Some parenchyma cells, as in the epidermis, are specialized for light penetration and focussing or regulation of gas exchange, but others are among the least specialized cells in plant tissue, and may remain totipotent, capable of dividing to produce new populations of undifferentiated cells, throughout their lives. Parenchyma cells have thin, permeable primary walls enabling the transport of small molecules between them, and their cytoplasm is responsible for a wide range of biochemical functions such as nectar secretion, or the manufacture of secondary products that discourage herbivory. Parenchyma cells that contain many chloroplasts and are concerned primarily with photosynthesis are called chlorenchyma cells. Others, such as the majority of the parenchyma cells in potato tubers and the seed cotyledons of legumes, have a storage function.

## Collenchyma Cells

Collenchyma cells are alive at maturity and have only a primary wall. These cells mature from meristem derivatives that initially resemble parenchyma, but differences quickly become apparent. Plastids do not develop, and the secretory apparatus (ER and Golgi) proliferates to secrete additional primary wall. The wall is most commonly thickest at the corners, where three or more cells come in contact, and thinnest where only two cells come in contact, though other arrangements of the wall thickening are possible.

Pectin and hemicellulose are the dominant constituents of collenchyma cell walls of dicotyledon angiosperms, which may contain as little as 20 per cent of cellulose in *Petasites*. Collenchyma cells are typically quite elongated, and may divide transversely to give a septate appearance. The role of this cell type is to support the plant in axes still growing in length, and to confer flexibility and tensile strength on tissues. The primary wall lacks lignin that would make it tough and rigid, so this cell type provides what could be called plastic support — support that can hold a young stem or petiole into the air, but in cells that can be stretched as the cells around them elongate. Stretchable support (without elastic snap-back) is a good way to describe what collenchyma does. Parts of the strings in celery are collenchyma.

## Sclerenchyma Cells

Sclerenchyma cells (from the Greek skleros, *hard*) are hard and tough cells with a function in mechanical support. They are of two broad types — sclereids or stone cells and fibres. The cells develop an extensive secondary cell wall that is laid down on the inside of the primary cell wall. The secondary wall is impregnated with lignin, making it hard and impermeable to water. Thus, these cells cannot survive for long' as they cannot exchange sufficient material to maintain active metabolism. Sclerenchyma cells are typically dead at functional maturity, and the cytoplasm is missing, leaving an empty central cavity.

Functions for sclereid cells (hard cells that give leaves or fruits a gritty texture) include discouraging herbivory, by damaging digestive passages in small insect larval stages, and physical protection (a solid tissue of hard sclereid cells form the pit wall in a peach and many other fruits). Functions of fibres include provision of load-bearing support and tensile strength to the leaves and stems of herbaceous plants. Sclerenchyma fibres are not involved in conduction, either of water and nutrients (as in the xylem) or of carbon compounds (as in the phloem), but it is likely that they may have evolved as modifications of xylem and phloem initials in early land plants.

The major classes of cells differentiate from undifferentiated meristematic cells (analogous to the stem cells of animals) to form the tissue structures of roots, stems, leaves, flowers, and reproductive structures.

Xylem cells are elongated cells with lignified secondary thickening of the cell walls. Xylem cells are specialised for conduction of water, and first appeared in plants during their transition to land in the Silurian period more than 425 million years ago . The possession of xylem defines the vascular plants or Tracheophytes. Xylem tracheids are pointed, elongated xylem cells, the simplest of which have continuous primary cell walls and lignified secondary wall thickenings in the form of rings, hoops, or reticulate networks. More complex tracheids with valve-like perforations called bordered pits characterise the gymnosperms. The ferns and other pteridophytes and the gymnosperms have only xylem tracheids, while the angiosperms also have xylem vessels. Vessel members are hollow xylem cells aligned end-to-end, without end walls that are assembled into long continuous tubes. The bryophytes lack true xylem cells, but their sporophytes have a water-conducting tissue known as the hydrome that is composed of elongated cells of simpler construction.

Co... ...em is a specialised tissue for food conduction in higher

Ph... ...onduction of food is a complex process that is

plants. T... he ...

carried in the plant with the help of special cell called phloem cells. These cells conduct inter- and intra-cellular fluid (food-proteins and other essential elements required by the plant for its metabolism) through the process of osmosis. This phenomenon is called ascent of sap in plants. Phloem consists of two cell types, the sieve tubes and the intimately-associated companion cells. The sieve tube elements lack nuclei and ribosomes, and their metabolism and functions are regulated by the adjacent nucleate companion cells. Sieve tubes are joined end-to-end with perforate end-plates between known as *sieve plates*, which allow transport of photosynthate between the sieve elements. The companion cells, connected to the sieve tubes via plasmodesmata, are responsible for loading the phloem with sugars. The bryophytes lack phloem, but moss sporophytes have a simpler tissue with analogous function known as the leptome.

Plant epidermal cells are specialised parenchyma cells covering the external surfaces of leaves, stems and roots. The epidermal cells of aerial organs arise from the superficial layer of cells known as the *tunica* (L1 and L2 layers) that covers the plant shoot apex, whereas the cortex and vascular tissues arise from innermost layer of the shoot apex known as the *corpus* (L3 layer). The epidermis of roots originates from the layer of cells immediately beneath the root cap.

The epidermis of all aerial organs, but not roots, is covered with a cuticle made of waxes and the polyester cutin. Several cell types may be present in the epidermis. Notable among these are the stomatal guard cells, glandular and clothing hairs or trichomes, and the root hairs of primary roots. In the shoot epidermis of most plants, only the guard cells have chloroplasts. The epidermal cells of the primary shoot are thought to be the only plant cells with the biochemical capacity to synthesize cutin.

## Eukaryote

A eukaryote is an organism whose cells contain complex structures enclosed within membranes. The defining membrane-bound structure that sets eukaryotic cells apart from prokaryotic cells is the nucleus, or nuclear envelope, within which the genetic material is carried. The presence of a nucleus gives eukaryotes their name, which comes from the Greek e (*eu*, 'good') and (*karyon*, 'nut' or 'kernel'). Most eukaryotic cells also contain other membrane-bound organelles such as mitochondria, chloroplasts and the Golgi apparatus. All species of large complex organisms are eukaryotes, including animals, plants and fungi, although most species of eukaryotic protists are microorganisms.

Cell division in eukaryotes is different from that in organisms without a nucleus (prokaryotes). It involves separating the duplicated chromosomes, through movements directed by microtubules. There are two types of division processes. In mitosis, one cell divides to produce two genetically identical cells. In meiosis, which is required in sexual reproduction, one diploid cell (having two instances of each chromosome, one from each parent) undergoes recombination of each pair of parental chromosomes, and then two stages of cell division, resulting in four haploid cells (gametes). Each gamete has just one complement of chromosomes, each a unique mix of the corresponding pair of parental chromosomes.

Eukaryotes appear to be monophyletic, and so make up one of the three domains of life. The two other domains, Bacteria and Archaea, are prokaryotes and have none of the above features. Eukaryotes represent a tiny minority of all living things; even in a human body there are 10 times more microbes than human cells.

Eukaryotic cells are typically much larger than those of prokaryotes. They have a variety of internal membranes and structures, called organelles, and a cytoskeleton composed of microtubules, microfilaments, and intermediate filaments, which play an important role in defining the cell's organization and shape. Eukaryotic DNA is divided into several linear bundles called chromosomes, which are separated by a microtubular spindle during nuclear division.

Eukaryotic cells include a variety of membrane-bound structures, collectively referred to as the endomembrane system. Simple compartments, called vesicles or vacuoles, can form by budding off other membranes. Many cells ingest food and other materials through a process of endocytosis, where the outer membrane invaginates and then pinches off to form a vesicle. It is probable that most other membrane-bound organelles are ultimately derived from such vesicles.

The nucleus is surrounded by a double membrane (commonly referred to as a nuclear envelope), with pores that allow material to move in and out. Various tube-and sheet-like extensions of the nuclear membrane form what is called the endoplasmic reticulum or ER, which is involved in protein transport and maturation. It includes the rough ER where ribosomes are attached to synthesize proteins, which enter the interior space or lumen. Subsequently, they generally enter vesicles, which bud off from the smooth ER. In most eukaryotes, these protein-carrying vesicles are released and further modified in stacks of flattened vesicles, called Golgi bodies or dictyosomes.

Vesicles may be specialized for various purposes. For instance, lysosomes contain enzymes that break down the contents of food vacuoles, and peroxisomes are used to break down peroxide, which is toxic otherwise. Many protozoa have contractile vacuoles, which collect and expel excess water, and extrusomes, which expel material used to deflect predators or capture prey. In multicellular organisms, hormones are often produced in vesicles. In higher plants, most of a cell's volume is taken up by a central vacuole, which primarily maintains its osmotic pressure.

Mitochondria are organelles found in nearly all eukaryotes. They are surrounded by two membranes (each a phospholipid bi-layer), the inner of which is folded into invaginations called cristae, where aerobic respiration takes place. Mitochondria contain their own DNA. They are now generally held to have developed from endosymbiotic prokaryotes, probably proteobacteria. The few protozoa that lack mitochondria have been found to contain mitochondrion-derived organelles, such as hydrogenosomes and mitosomes.

Plants and various groups of algae also have plastids. Again, these have their own DNA and developed from endosymbiotes, in this case cyanobacteria. They usually take the form of chloroplasts, which like cyanobacteria contain chlorophyll and produce organic compounds (such as glucose) through photosynthesis. Others are involved in storing food. Although plastids likely had a single origin, not all plastid-containing groups are closely related. Instead, some eukaryotes have obtained them from others through secondary endosymbiosis or ingestion.

Endosymbiotic origins have also been proposed for the nucleus, for which see below, and for eukaryotic flagella, supposed to have developed from spirochaetes. This is not generally accepted, both from a lack of cytological evidence and difficulty in reconciling this with cellular reproduction.

Many eukaryotes have long slender motile cytoplasmic projections, called flagella, or similar structures called cilia. Flagella and cilia are sometimes referred to as undulipodia, and are variously involved in movement, feeding, and sensation. They are composed mainly of tubulin. These are entirely distinct from prokaryotic flagella. They are supported by a bundle of microtubules arising from a basal body, also called a kinetosome or centriole, characteristically arranged as nine doublets surrounding two singlets. Flagella also may have hairs, or mastigonemes, and scales connecting membranes and internal rods. Their interior is continuous with the cell's cytoplasm.

Microfilamental structures composed by actin and actin binding proteins, *e.g.*, a-actinin, fimbrin, filamin are present in submembraneous cortical layers and bundles, as well. Motor proteins of microtubules, *e.g.*, dynein or kinesin and actin, e.g., myosins provide dynamic character of the network.

Centrioles are often present even in cells and groups that do not have flagella. They generally occur in groups of one or two, called kinetids, that give rise to various microtubular roots. These form a primary component of the cytoskeletal structure, and are often assembled over the course of several cell divisions, with one flagellum retained from the parent and the other derived from it. Centrioles may also be associated in the formation of a spindle during nuclear division.

Significance of cytoskeletal structures is underlined in determination of shape of the cells, as well as their being essential components of migratory responses like chemotaxis and chemokinesis. Some protists have various other microtubule-supported organelles. These include the radiolaria and heliozoa, which produce axopodia used in flotation or to capture prey, and the haptophytes, which have a peculiar flagellum-like organelle called the haptonema. An animal cell is a form of Eukaryotic cell that makes up many tissues in animals.

Plant cells have a cell wall, a fairly rigid layer outside the cell membrane, providing the cell with structural support, protection, and a filtering mechanism. The cell wall also prevents over-expansion when water enters the cell. The major carbohydrates making up the primary cell wall of land plants are cellulose, hemicellulose, and pectin. The cellulose microfibrils are linked via hemicellulosic tethers to form the cellulose-hemicellulose network, which is embedded in the pectin matrix. The most common hemicellulose in the primary cell wall is xyloglucan.

## Differences Among Eukaryotic Cells

There are many different types of eukaryotic cells, though animals and plants are the most familiar eukaryotes, and thus provide an excellent starting point for understanding eukaryotic structure. Fungi and many protists have some substantial differences, however.

## Animal Cell

An animal cell is a form of eukaryotic cell that makes up many tissues in animals. The animal cell is distinct from other eukaryotes, most notably plant cells, as they lack cell walls and chloroplasts, and they have smaller vacuoles. Due to the lack of a rigid cell wall, animal cells can adopt a variety of shapes, and a phagocytic cell can even engulf other structures.

There are many different cell types. For instance, there are approximately 210 distinct cell types in the adult human body.

Plant cells are quite different from the cells of the other eukaryotic organisms. Their distinctive features are:

- A large central vacuole (enclosed by a membrane, the tonoplast), which maintains the cell's turgor and controls movement of molecules between the cytosol and sap.
- A primary cell wall containing cellulose, hemicellulose and pectin, deposited by the protoplast on the outside of the cell membrane; this contrasts with the cell walls of fungi, which contain chitin, and the cell envelopes of prokaryotes, in which peptidoglycans are the main structural molecules.
- The plasmodesmata, linking pores in the cell wall that allow each plant cell to communicate with other adjacent cells; this is different from the functionally analogous system of gap junctions between animal cells.
- Plastids, especially chloroplasts that contain chlorophyll, the pigment that gives plants their green colour and allows them to perform photosynthesis.
- Higher plants, including conifers and flowering plants (Angiospermae) lack the flagellae and centrioles that are present in animal cells.

Fungal cells are most similar to animal cells, with the following exceptions:

- A cell wall that contains chitin.
- Less definition between cells; the hyphae of higher fungi have porous partitions called septa, which allow the passage of cytoplasm, organelles, and, sometimes, nuclei. Primitive fungi have few or no septa, so each organism is essentially a giant multinucleate supercell; these fungi are described as coenocytic.

## Other Eukaryotic Cells

Eukaryotes are a very diverse group, and their cell structures are equally diverse. Many have cell walls; many do not. Many have chloroplasts, derived from primary, secondary, or even tertiary endosymbiosis; and many do not. Some groups have unique structures, such as the cyanelles of the glaucophytes, the haptonema of the haptophytes, or the ejectisomes of the cryptomonads. Other structures, such as pseudopods, are found in various eukaryote groups in different forms, such as the lobose amoebozoans or the reticulose foraminiferans.

## Reproduction

Nuclear division is often coordinated with cell division. This generally takes place by mitosis, a process that allows each daughter nucleus to receive one copy of each chromosome. In most eukaryotes, there is also a process of sexual reproduction, typically involving an alternation between haploid generations, wherein only one copy of each chromosome is present, and diploid generations, wherein two are present, occurring through nuclear fusion (syngamy) and meiosis. There is considerable variation in this pattern, however.

Eukaryotes have a smaller surface area to volume ratio than prokaryotes, and thus have lower metabolic rates and longer generation times. In some multicellular organisms, cells specialized for metabolism will have enlarged surface areas, such as intestinal vili.

The origin of the eukaryotic cell was a milestone in the evolution of life, since they include all complex cells and almost all multi-cellular organisms. The timing of this series of events is hard to determine; Knoll (2006) suggests they developed approximately 1.6-2.1 billion years ago. Some acritarchs are known from at least 1650 million years ago, and the possible alga *Grypania* has been found as far back as 2100 million years ago.

Fossils that are clearly related to modern groups start appearing around 1.2 billion years ago, in the form of a red alga, though recent work suggests the existence of fossilized filamentous algae in the Vindhya basin dating back to 1.6 to 1.7 billion years ago.

Biomarkers suggest that at least stem eukaryotes arose even earlier. The presence of steranes in Australian shales indicates that eukaryotes were present 2.7 billion years ago.

## Phylogeny

rRNA trees constructed during the 1980s and 1990s left most eukaryotes in an unresolved 'crown' group (not technically a true crown), which was usually divided by the form of the mitochondrial cristae. The few groups that lack mitochondria branched separately, and so the absence was believed to be primitive; but this is now considered an artifact of long-branch attraction, and they are known to have lost them secondarily.

## Six Supergroup/Kingdom Model

A classification produced in 2005 for the International Society of Protistologists, which reflected the consensus of the time, divided the eukaryotes into six supposedly monophyletic 'supergroups'. Although the published classification deliberately did not use formal taxonomic ranks, other sources have treated each of the six as a separate Kingdom.

However, in the same year (2005), doubts were expressed as to whether some of these supergroups were monophyletic, particularly the Chromalveolata, and a review in 2006 noted the lack of evidence for several of the supposed six supergroups.

As of 2010[update], there is widespread agreement that the Rhizaria belong with the Stramenopiles and the Alveolata, in a clade dubbed the SAR supergroup, so that Rhizara is not one of the main eukaryote groups; also that the Amoeboza and Opisthokonta are each monophyletic and form a clade, often called the unikonts. Beyond this, there does not appear to be a consensus.

Eukaryotes are more closely related to Archaea than Bacteria, at least in terms of nuclear DNA and genetic machinery, and one controversial idea is to place them with Archaea in the clade Neomura. However, in other respects, such as membrane composition, eukaryotes are similar to Bacteria. Three main explanations for this have been proposed:

1. Eukaryotes resulted from the complete fusion of two or more cells, wherein the cytoplasm formed from a eubacterium, and the nucleus from an archaeon, from a virus, or from a pre-cell.
2. Eukaryotes developed from Archaea, and acquired their eubacterial characteristics from the proto-mitochondrion.
3. Eukaryotes and Archaea developed separately from a modified eubacterium.

There is also the Kronocyte theory for the origin of the Eukaryotic cell. This postulates that a primitive Eukaryotic cell emerged from the pre-DNA world but retained the earlier RNA based chemistry from which all modern life emerged. This primitive cell is called the Kronocyte. According to this hypothesis an RNA based Kronocyte coexisted with the DNA based Archaea (and probably eubacteria) and became the modern eukaryotic cell after a number of major endosymbioses—the first was the incorporation of an Archaea that introduced DNA metabolism and the nucleus, then the incorporation of an alphaproteobacter that became the mitochondria (and photosynthetic bacteria found in today's plants as chloroplasts). The Kronocyte hypothesis explains the large number of genes that are today only found in Eukaryotes but not in Archaea or Bacteria.

## Endomembrane System and Mitochondria

The origins of the endomembrane system and mitochondria are also unclear. The phagotrophic hypothesis proposes that eukaryotic-type membranes lacking a cell wall originated first, with the development of endocytosis, whereas mitochondria were acquired by ingestion as endosymbionts. The syntrophic hypothesis proposes that the proto-eukaryote relied on the proto-mitochondrion for food, and so ultimately grew to surround it. Here the membranes originated after the engulfment of the mitochondrion, in part thanks to mitochondrial genes (the hydrogen hypothesis is one particular version).

In a study using genomes to construct supertrees, Pisani *et al.* (2007) suggest that, along with evidence that there was never a mitochondrion-less eukaryote, eukaryotes evolved from a syntrophy between an archaea closely related to Thermoplasmatales and an a-proteobacterium, likely a symbiosis driven by sulfur or hydrogen. The mitochondrion and its genome is a remnant of the a-proteobacterial endosymbiont.

# 3 Cell Wall

The cell wall is the tough, usually flexible but sometimes fairly rigid layer that surrounds some types of cells. It is located outside the cell membrane and provides these cells with structural support and protection, and also acts as a filtering mechanism. A major function of the cell wall is to act as a pressure vessel, preventing over-expansion when water enters the cell. They are found in plants, bacteria, fungi, algae, and some archaea. Animals and protozoa do not have cell walls.

The materials in a cell wall vary between species, and in plants and fungi also differ between cell types and developmental stages. In plants, the strongest component of the complex cell wall is a carbohydrate called cellulose, which is a polymer of glucose. In bacteria, peptidoglycan forms the cell wall. Archaean cell walls have various compositions, and may be formed of glycoprotein S-layers, pseudopeptidoglycan, or polysaccharides. Fungi possess cell walls made of the glucosamine polymer chitin, and algae typically possess walls made of glycoproteins and polysaccharides. Unusually, diatoms have a cell wall composed of silicic acid. Often, other accessory molecules are found anchored to the cell wall.

The cell wall serves a similar purpose in those organisms that possess them. The wall gives cells rigidity and strength, offering protection against mechanical stress. In multicellular organisms, it permits the organism to build and hold its shape (morphogenesis). The cell wall also limits the entry of large molecules that may be toxic to the cell. It further permits the creation of a stable osmotic environment by preventing osmotic lysis and helping to retain water. The composition, properties, and form of the cell wall may change during the cell cycle and depend on growth conditions.

## Rigidity of Cell Walls

The rigidity of the cell walls is often over-estimated. In most cells, the cell wall is flexible, meaning that it will bend rather than holding a fixed shape, but has considerable tensile strength. The apparent rigidity of primary plant tissues is enabled by cell walls, but not due to the walls' strength. Hydraulic turgor pressure creates this rigidity, along with the wall structure. The flexibility of the cell walls is seen when plants wilt, so that the stems and leaves begin to droop, or in seaweeds that bend in water currents.

As John Howland states it:

> "Think of the cell wall as a wicker basket in which a balloon has been inflated so that it exerts pressure from the inside. Such a basket is very rigid and resistant to mechanical damage. Thus does the prokaryote cell (and eukaryotic cell that possesses a cell wall) gain strength from a flexible plasma membrane pressing against a rigid cell wall".

The rigidity of the cell wall thus results in part from inflation of the cell contained. This inflation is a result of the passive uptake of water.

In plants, a secondary cell wall is a thicker additional layer of cellulose which increases wall rigidity. Additional layers may be formed containing lignin in xylem cell walls, or containing suberin in cork cell walls. These compounds are rigid and waterproof, making the secondary wall stiff. Both wood and bark cells of trees have secondary walls. Other parts of plants such as the leaf stalk may acquire similar reinforcement to resist the strain of physical forces.

Certain single-cell protists and algae also produce a rigid wall. Diatoms build a frustule from silica extracted from the surrounding water; radiolarians also produce a test from minerals. Many green algae, such as the Dasycladales encase their cells in a secreted skeleton of calcium carbonate. In each case, the wall is rigid and essentially inorganic. The primary cell wall of most plant cells is semi-permeable and permit the passage of small molecules and small proteins, with size exclusion estimated to be 30-60 kDa. Key nutrients, especially water and carbon dioxide, are distributed throughout the plant from cell wall to cell wall in apoplastic flow. The pH is an important factor governing the transport of molecules through cell walls.

## Plant Cell Walls

Many plant cells have walls that are strong enough to withstand the osmotic pressure from the difference in solute concentration between the cell interior and distilled water.

### Layers

Up to three strata or layers may be found in plant cell walls:

1. The *middle lamella,* a layer rich in pectins. This outermost layer forming the interface between adjacent plant cells and glues them together.
2. The primary cell wall, generally a thin, flexible and extensible layer formed while the cell is growing.
3. The *secondary cell wall,* a thick layer formed inside the primary cell wall after the cell is fully grown. It is not found in all cell types. In some cells, such as found xylem, the secondary wall contains lignin, which strengthens and waterproofs the wall.

### Composition

In the primary (growing) plant cell wall, the major carbohydrates are cellulose, hemicellulose and pectin. The cellulose microfibrils are linked via hemicellulosic tethers to form the cellulose-hemicellulose network, which is embedded in the pectin matrix. The most common hemicellulose in the primary cell wall is xyloglucan. In grass cell walls, xyloglucan and pectin are reduced in abundance and partially replaced by glucuronarabinoxylan, a hemicellulose. Primary cell walls characteristically extend (grow) by a mechanism called acid growth, which involves turgor-driven movement of the strong cellulose microfibrils within the weaker hemicellulose/pectin matrix, catalyzed by expansin proteins. The outer part of the primary cell wall of the plant epidermis is usually impregnated with cutin and wax, forming a permeability barrier known as the plant cuticle.

Secondary cell walls contain a wide range of additional compounds that modify their mechanical properties and permeability. The major polymers that make up wood (largely secondary cell walls) include:

- cellulose, 35-50 per cent;
- xylan, 20-35 per cent, a type of hemicellulose; and
- lignin, 10-25 per cent, a complex phenolic polymer that penetrates the spaces in the cell wall between cellulose, hemicellulose and pectin components, driving out water and strengthening the wall.

Additionally, structural proteins (1-5%) are found in most plant cell walls; they are classified as hydroxyproline-rich glycoproteins (HRGP), arabinogalactan proteins (AGP), glycine-rich proteins (GRPs), and proline-rich proteins (PRPs). Each class of glycoprotein is defined by a characteristic, highly repetitive protein sequence. Most are glycosylated, contain hydroxyproline (Hyp) and become cross-linked in the cell wall. These proteins are often concentrated in specialized cells and in cell corners. Cell walls of the epidermis and endodermis may also contain suberin or cutin, two polyester-like polymers that protect the cell from herbivores. The relative composition of carbohydrates, secondary compounds and protein varies between plants and between the cell type and age.

Plant cells walls also contain numerous enzymes, such as hydrolases, esterases, peroxidases, and transglycosylases, that cut, trim and cross-link wall polymers.

The walls of cork cells in the bark of trees are impregnated with suberin, and suberin also forms the permeability barrier in primary roots known as the Casparian strip. Secondary walls — especially in grasses - may also contain microscopic silica crystals, which may strengthen the wall and protect it from herbivores.

Cell walls in some plant tissues also function as storage depots for carbohydrates that can be broken down and resorbed to supply the metabolic and growth needs of the plant. For example, endosperm cell walls in the seeds of cereal grasses, nasturtium, and other species, are rich in glucans and other polysaccharides that are readily digested by enzymes during seed germination to form simple sugars that nourish the growing embryo. Cellulose microfibrils are not readily digested by plants, however.

## Formation

The middle lamella is laid down first, formed from the cell plate during cytokinesis, and the primary cell wall is then deposited inside the middle lamella. The actual structure of the cell wall is not clearly defined and several models exist - the covalently linked cross model, the tether model, the diffuse layer model and the stratified layer model. However, the primary cell wall, can be defined as composed of cellulose microfibrils aligned at all angles. Microfibrils are held together by hydrogen bonds to provide a high tensile strength. The cells are held together and share the gelatinous membrane called the *middle lamella,* which contains magnesium and calcium pectates (salts of pectic acid). Cells interact though plasmodesma(ta), which are inter-connecting channels of cytoplasm that connect to the protoplasts of adjacent cells across the cell wall.

In some plants and cell types, after a maximum size or point in development has been reached, a *secondary wall* is constructed between the plant cell and primary wall. Unlike the primary wall, the microfibrils are aligned mostly in the same direction, and with each additional layer the orientation changes slightly. Cells with secondary cell walls are rigid. Cell to cell communication is possible through *pits* in the secondary cell wall that allow plasmodesma to connect cells through the secondary cell walls.

Like plants, algae have cell walls. Algal cell walls contain either polysaccharides (such as cellulose (a glucan)) or a variety of glycoproteins (Volvocales) or both. The inclusion of additional polysaccharides in algal cells walls is used as a feature for algal taxonomy.

## Mannans

They form microfibrils in the cell walls of a number of marine green algae including those from the genera, *Codium*, *Dasycladus*, and *Acetabularia* as well as in the walls of some red algae, like *Porphyra* and *Bangia*.

## Xylans

- *Alginic acid:* It is a common polysaccharide in the cell walls of brown algae.
- *Sulfonated polysaccharides:* They occur in the cell walls of most algae; those common in red algae include agarose, carrageenan, porphyran, furcelleran and funoran.

Other compounds that may accumulate in algal cell walls include sporopollenin and calcium ions.

The group of algae known as the diatoms synthesize their cell walls (also known as frustules or valves) from silicic acid (specifically orthosilicic acid, $H_4SiO_4$). The acid is polymerised intra-cellularly, then the wall is extruded to protect the cell. Significantly, relative to the organic cell walls produced by other groups, silica frustules require less energy to synthesize (approximately 8%), potentially a major saving on the overall cell energy budget and possibly an explanation for higher growth rates in diatoms.

### Fungal Cell Walls

There are several groups of organisms that may be called 'fungi'. Some of these groups have been transferred out of the Kingdom Fungi, in part because of fundamental biochemical differences in the composition of the cell wall. Most true fungi have a cell wall consisting largely of chitin and other polysaccharides. True fungi do not have cellulose in their cell walls, but some fungus-like organisms do.

### True Fungi

Not all species of fungi have cell walls but in those that do, the plasma membrane is followed by three layers of cell wall material. From inside out these are:

- a chitin layer ( polymer consisting mainly of unbranched chains of N-acetyl-D-glucosamine);
- a layer of ß-1,3- glucan ( zymosan); and
- a layer of mannoproteins ( mannose-containing glycoproteins) which are heavily glycosylated at the outside of the cell.

### Fungus-like Protists

The group Oomycetes, also known as water molds, are saprotrophic plant pathogens like fungi. Until recently they were widely believed to be fungi, but structural and molecular evidence has led to their reclassification as heterokonts, related to autotrophic brown algae and diatoms. Unlike fungi, oomycetes typically possess cell walls of cellulose and glucans rather than chitin, although some genera (such as *Achlya* and *Saprolegnia*) do have chitin in their walls. The fraction of cellulose in the walls is no more than 4 to 20 per cent, far less than the fraction comprised by glucans. Oomycete cell walls also contain the amino acid hydroxyproline, which is not found in fungal cell walls.

The dictyostelids are another group formerly classified among the fungi. They are slime molds that feed as unicellular amoebae, but aggregate into a reproductive stalk and sporangium under certain conditions. Cells of the reproductive stalk, as well as the spores formed at the apex, possess a cellulose wall. The spore wall has been shown to possess three layers, the middle of which is composed primarily of cellulose, and the innermost is sensitive to cellulase and pronase.

## Bacterial Cell Walls

Around the outside of the cell membrane is the bacterial cell wall. Bacterial cell walls are made of peptidoglycan (also called murein), which is made from polysaccharide chains cross-linked by unusual peptides containing D-amino acids. Bacterial cell walls are different from the cell walls of plants and fungi which are made of cellulose and chitin, respectively. The cell wall of bacteria is also distinct from that of Archaea, which do not contain peptidoglycan. The cell wall is essential to the survival of many bacteria, although L-form bacteria can be produced in the laboratory that lack a cell wall. The antibiotic penicillin is able to kill bacteria by preventing the cross-linking of peptidoglycan and this causes the cell wall to weaken and lyse. The lysozyme enzyme can also damage bacterial cell walls.

There are broadly speaking two different types of cell wall in bacteria, called Gram-positive and Gram-negative. The names originate from the reaction of cells to the Gram stain, a test long-employed for the classification of bacterial species.

Gram-positive bacteria possess a thick cell wall containing many layers of peptidoglycan and teichoic acids. In contrast, Gram-negative bacteria have a relatively thin cell wall consisting of a few layers of peptidoglycan surrounded by a second lipid membrane containing lipopolysaccharides and lipoproteins. Most bacteria have the Gram-negative cell wall and only the Firmicutes and Actinobacteria (previously known as the low G+C and high G+C Gram-positive bacteria, respectively) have the alternative Gram-positive arrangement. These differences in structure can produce differences in antibiotic susceptibility, for instance vancomycin can kill only Gram-positive bacteria and is ineffective against Gram-negative pathogens, such as *Haemophilus influenzae* or *Pseudomonas aeruginosa*.

### Archaeal Cell Walls

Although not truly unique, the cell walls of Archaea are unusual. Whereas peptidoglycan is a standard component of all bacterial cell walls, all archaeal cell walls lack peptidoglycan, with the exception of one group of methanogens. In that group, the peptidoglycan is a modified form very different from the kind found in bacteria. There are four types of cell wall currently known among the Archaea.

One type of archaeal cell wall is that composed of pseudopeptidoglycan (also called pseudomurein). This type of wall is found in some methanogens, such as *Methanobacterium* and *Methanothermus*. While the overall structure of archaeal *pseudo*peptidoglycan superficially resembles that of bacterial peptidoglycan, there are a number of significant chemical differences. Like the peptidoglycan found in bacterial cell walls, pseudopeptidoglycan consists of polymer chains of glycan cross-linked by short peptide connections. However, unlike peptidoglycan, the sugar N-acetylmuramic acid is replaced by N-acetyltalosaminuronic acid, and the two sugars are bonded with a *ß*,1-3 glycosidic linkage instead of *ß*,1-4. Additionally, the cross-linking peptides are L-amino acids rather than D-amino acids as they are in bacteria.

A second type of archaeal cell wall is found in *Methanosarcina* and *Halococcus*. This type of cell wall is composed entirely of a thick layer of polysaccharides, which may be sulfated in the case of *Halococcus*. Structure in this type of wall is complex and as yet is not fully investigated.

A third type of wall among the Archaea consists of glycoprotein, and occurs in the hyperthermophiles, *Halobacterium*, and some methanogens. In *Halobacterium*, the proteins in the wall have a high content of acidic amino acids, giving the wall an overall negative charge. The result is an unstable structure that is stabilized by the presence of large quantities of positive sodium ions that neutralize the charge. Consequently, *Halobacterium* thrives only under conditions with high salinity.

In other Archaea, such as *Methanomicrobium* and *Desulfurococcus*, the wall may be composed only of surface-layer proteins, known as an *S-layer*. S-layers are common in bacteria, where they serve as either the sole cell-wall component or an outer layer in conjunction with polysaccharides. Most Archaea are Gram-negative, though at least one Gram-positive member is known.

# Cell Membrane

The cell membrane is a biological membrane that separates the interior of all cells from the outside environment. The cell membrane is selectively-permeable to ions and organic molecules and controls the movement of substances in and out of cells. It consists of the phospholipid bilayer with embedded proteins. Cell membranes are involved in a variety of cellular processes such as cell adhesion, ion conductivity and cell signalling and serve as the attachment surface for the extracellular glycocalyx and cell wall and intracellular cytoskeleton.

The cell membrane surrounds the protoplasm of a cell and, in animal cells, physically separates the intracellular components from the extracellular environment. Fungi, bacteria and plants also have the cell wall which provides a mechanical support for the cell and precludes passage of the larger molecules. The cell membrane also plays a role in anchoring the cytoskeleton to provide shape to the cell, and in attaching to the extracellular matrix and other cells to help group cells together to form tissues.

The barrier is differentially permeable and able to regulate what enters and exits the cell, thus facilitating the transport of materials needed for survival. The movement of substances across the membrane can be either *passive*, occurring without the input of cellular energy, or active, requiring the cell to expend energy in moving it. The membrane also maintains the cell potential.

## Prokaryotes

Gram-negative bacteria have plasma membrane and outer membrane separated by the periplasmic space. Other prokaryotic species have only plasma membrane. Prokaryotic cells are also surrounded by a cell wall.

## Fluid Mosaic Model

According to the fluid mosaic model of S.J. Singer and Garth Nicolson 1972, the biological membranes can be considered as a two-dimensional liquid where all lipid and protein molecules diffuse more or less easily. This picture may be valid in the space scale of 10 nm. However, the plasma membranes contain different structures or domains that can be classified as:

*(a)* protein-protein complexes;

*(b)* lipid rafts; and

*(c)* pickets and fences formed by the actin-based cytoskeleton.

## Lipid Bilayer

Diagram of the arrangement of amphipathic lipid molecules to form a lipid bilayer. The yellow polar head groups separate the grey hydrophobic tails from the aqueous cytosolic and extracellular environments.

Lipid bilayers go through a self assembly process in the formation of membranes. The cell membrane consists primarily of a thin layer of amphipathic phospholipids which spontaneously arrange so that the hydrophobic 'tail' regions are shielded from the surrounding polar fluid, causing the more hydrophilic 'head' regions to associate with the cytosolic and extracellular faces of the resulting bilayer. This forms a continuous, spherical lipid bilayer. Forces such as Van der Waal, electrostatic, hyrdogen bonds, and non-covalent interactions, are all forces that contribute to the formation of the lipid bilayer. Overall, hydrophobic interactions are the major driving force in the formation of lipid bilayers.

Lipid bilayers have very low permeability for ions and most polar molecules.The arrangement of hydrophilic heads and hydrophobic tails of the lipid bilayer prevent polar solutes (*e.g.* amino acids, nucleic acids, carbohydrates, proteins, and ions) from diffusing across the membrane, but generally allows for the passive diffusion of hydrophobic molecules. This affords the cell the ability to control the movement of these substances via transmembrane protein complexes such as pores and gates.

Flippases and Scramblases concentrate phosphatidyl serine, which carries a negative charge, on the inner membrane. Along with NANA, this creates an extra barrier to charged moieties moving through the membrane.

Membranes serve diverse functions in eukaryotic and prokaryotic cells. One important role is to regulate the movement of materials into and out of cells. The phospholipid bilayer structure (fluid mosaic model) with specific membrane proteins accounts for the selective permeability of the membrane and passive and active transport mechanisms. In addition, membranes in prokaryotes and in the mitochondria and chloroplasts of eukaryotes facilitate the synthesis of ATP through chemiosmosis.

The apical membrane of a polarized cell is the surface of the plasma membrane that faces the lumen. This is particularly evident in epithelial and endothelial cells, but also describes other polarized cells, such as neurons.

The basolateral membrane of a polarized cell is the surface of the plasma membrane that forms its basal and lateral surfaces. It faces towards the interstitium, and away from the lumen.

'Basolateral membrane' is a compound phrase referring to the terms *basal (base) membrane* and *lateral (side) membrane,* which, especially in epithelial cells, are identical in composition and activity. Proteins (such as ion channels and pumps) are free to move from the basal to the lateral surface of the cell or *vice versa* in accordance with the fluid mosaic model.

Tight junctions that join epithelial cells near their apical surface prevent the migration of proteins from the basolateral membrane to the apical membrane. The basal and lateral surfaces thus remain roughly equivalent to one another, yet distinct from the apical surface.

### Integral Membrane Proteins

The cell membrane contains many integral membrane proteins, which pepper the entire surface. These structures, which can be visualized by electron microscopy or fluorescence microscopy, can be found on the inside of the membrane, the outside, or membrane spanning. These may include integrins, cadherins, desmosomes, clathrin-coated pits, caveolaes, and different structures involved in cell adhesion. Integral proteins are the most abundant type of protein to span the lipid bilayer. They interact widely with hydrocarbon chains of membrane lipids and can be released by agents that compete for the same non-polar interactions.

### Peripheral Membrane Proteins

Peripheral proteins are proteins that are bounded to the membrane by electrostatic interactions and hydrogen bonding with the hydrophilic phospholipid heads. Many of these proteins can be found bounded to the surfaces of integral proteins on either the cytoplasimic side of the cell or the extracellular side of the membrane. Some are anchored to the bilayer through covalent bond with a fatty acid.

### Membrane Skeleton

The cytoskeleton is found underlying the cell membrane in the cytoplasm and provides a scaffolding for membrane proteins to anchor to, as well as forming organelles that extend from the cell. Indeed, cytoskeletal elements interact extensively and intimately with the cell membrane. Anchoring proteins restricts them to a particular cell surface—for example, the *apical surface* of epithelial cells that line the vertebrate gut—and limits how far they may diffuse within the bilayer. The cytoskeleton is able to form appendage-like organelles, such as cilia, which are microtubule-based extensions covered by the cell membrane, and filopodia, which are actin-based extensions. These extensions are ensheathed in membrane and project from the surface of the cell in order to sense the external environment and/or make contact with the substrate or other cells. The apical surfaces of epithelial cells are dense with actin-based finger-like projections known as microvilli, which increase cell surface area and thereby increase the absorption rate of nutrients. Localized decoupling of the cytoskeleton and cell membrane results in formation of a bleb.

## Composition

Cell membranes contain a variety of biological molecules, notably lipids and proteins. Material is incorporated into the membrane, or deleted from it, by a variety of mechanisms:

- Fusion of intracellular vesicles with the membrane (exocytosis) not only excretes the contents of the vesicle but also incorporates the vesicle membrane's components into the cell membrane. The membrane may form blebs around extracellular material that pinch off to become vesicles (endocytosis).
- If a membrane is continuous with a tubular structure made of membrane material, then material from the tube can be drawn into the membrane continuously.
- Although the concentration of membrane components in the aqueous phase is low (stable membrane components have low solubility in water), there is an exchange of molecules between the lipid and aqueous phases.

The cell membrane consists of three classes of amphipathic lipids: phospholipids, glycolipids, and cholesterols. The amount of each depends upon the type of cell, but in the majority of cases phospholipids are the most abundant. In RBC studies, 30 per cent of the plasma membrane is lipid.

The fatty chains in phospholipids and glycolipids usually contain an even number of carbon atoms, typically between 16 and 20. The 16-and 18-carbon fatty acids are the most common. Fatty acids may be saturated or unsaturated, with the configuration of the double bonds nearly always *cis*. The length and the degree of unsaturation of fatty acid chains have a profound effect on membrane fluidity as unsaturated lipids create a kink, preventing the fatty acids from packing together as tightly, thus decreasing the melting temperature (increasing the fluidity) of the membrane. The ability of some organisms to regulate the fluidity of their cell membranes by altering lipid composition is called homeoviscous adaptation.

The entire membrane is held together via non-covalent interaction of hydrophobic tails, however the structure is quite fluid and not fixed rigidly in place. Under physiological conditions phospholipid molecules in the cell membrane are in the liquid crystalline state. It means the lipid molecules are free to diffuse and exhibit rapid lateral diffusion along the layer in which they are present. However, the exchange of phospholipid molecules between intracellular and extracellular leaflets of the bilayer is a very slow process. Lipid rafts and caveolae are examples of cholesterol-enriched microdomains in the cell membrane.

In animal cells cholesterol is normally found dispersed in varying degrees throughout cell membranes, in the irregular spaces between the hydrophobic tails of the membrane lipids, where it confers a stiffening and strengthening effect on the membrane.

Lipid vesicles or liposomes are circular pockets that are enclosed by a lipid bilayer. These structures are used in laboratories to study the effects of chemicals in cells by delivering these chemicals directly to the cell, as well as getting more insight into cell membrane permeability. Lipid vesicles and liposomes are formed by first suspending a lipid in an aqueous solution then agitating the mixture through sonication, resulting in a uniformly circular vesicle. By measuring the rate of efflux from that of the insideof the vesicle to the ambient solution, allows researcher to better understand membrane permeability. Vesicles can be formed with molecules and ions inside the vesicle by forming the vesicle with the desired molecule or ion present in the solution. Proteins can also be embedded into the membrane through solubilizing the desired proteins in the presence of detergents and attaching them to the phospholipids in which the liposome is formed. These provide researchers with a tool to examine various membrane protein functions.

## Carbohydrates

Plasma membranes also contain carbohydrates, predominantly glycoproteins, but with some glycolipids (cerebrosides and gangliosides). For the most part, no glycosylation occurs on membranes within the cell; rather generally glycosylation occurs on the extracellular surface of the plasma membrane.

The glycocalyx is an important feature in all cells, especially epithelia with microvilli. Recent data suggest the glycocalyx participates in cell adhesion, lymphocyte homing, and many others.

The penultimate sugar is galactose and the terminal sugar is sialic acid, as the sugar backbone is modified in the golgi apparatus. Sialic acid carries a negative charge, providing an external barrier to charged particles.

The cell membrane plays host to a large amount of protein that is responsible for its various activities. The amount of protein differs between species and according to function, however the typical amount in a cell membrane is 50 per cent. These proteins are undoubtedly important to a cell: Approximately a third of the genes in yeast code specifically for them, and this number is even higher in multicellular organisms.

The cell membrane, being exposed to the outside environment, is an important site of cell-cell communication. As such, a large variety of protein receptors and identification proteins, such as antigens, are present on the surface of the membrane. Functions of membrane proteins can also include cell-cell contact, surface recognition, cytoskeleton contact, signaling, enzymatic activity, or transporting substances across the membrane.

Most membrane proteins must be inserted in some way into the membrane. For this to occur, an N-terminus 'signal sequence' of amino acids directs proteins to the endoplasmic reticulum, which inserts the proteins into a lipid bilayer. Once inserted, the proteins are then transported to their final destination in vesicles, where the vesicle fuses with the target membrane.

### Variation

The cell membrane has different lipid and protein compositions in distinct types of cells and may have therefore specific names for certain cell types:

- Sarcolemma in myocytes;
- Oolemma in oocytes; and
- Historically, the plasma membrane was also referred to as the plasmalemma.

### Permeability

The permeability of a membrane is the ease of molecules to pass through it. Permeability depends mainly on the electric charge of the molecule and to a lesser extent the molar mass of the molecule. Electrically neutral and small molecules pass the membrane easier than charged, large ones.

The inability of charged molecules to pass through the cell membrane results in pH parturition of substances throughout the fluid compartments of the body.

# 5 Plastid

Plastids are major organelles found in the cells of plants and algae. Plastids are the site of manufacture and storage of important chemical compounds used by the cell. Plastids often contain pigments used in photosynthesis, and the types of pigments present can change or determine the cell's colour.

Plastids are responsible for photosynthesis, storage of products like starch and for the synthesis have the ability to differentiate, or redifferentiate, between these and other forms. All plastids are derived from proplastids (formerly 'eoplasts', *eo*: dawn, early), which are present in the meristematic regions of the plant. Proplastids and young chloroplasts commonly divide, but more mature chloroplasts also have this capacity.

In plants, plastids may differentiate into several forms, depending upon which function they need to play in the cell. Undifferentiated plastids (*proplastids*) may develop into any of the following plastids:

- *Chloroplasts:* for photosynthesis; *etioplasts, the predecessors of chloroplasts.*
- *Chromoplasts:* for pigment synthesis and storage.
- *Gerontoplasts:* control the dismantling of the photosynthetic apparatus during senescence.

- *Leucoplasts:* for monoterpene synthesis; *leucoplasts sometimes differentiate into more specialized plastids.*
- *Amyloplasts:* for starch storage and detecting gravity.
- *Elaioplasts:* for storing fat.
- *Proteinoplasts:* for storing and modifying protein.

Each plastid creates multiple copies of the circular 75-250 kilobase plastome. The number of genome copies per plastid is flexible, ranging from more than 1000 in rapidly dividing cells, which generally contain few plastids, to 100 or fewer in mature cells, where plastid divisions has given rise to a large number of plastids. The plastome contains about 100 genes encoding ribosomal and transfer ribonucleic acids (rRNAs and tRNAs) as well as proteins involved in photosynthesis and plastid gene transcription and translation. However, these proteins only represent a small fraction of the total protein set-up necessary to build and maintain the structure and function of a particular type of plastid. Nuclear genes encode the vast majority of plastid proteins, and the expression of plastid genes and nuclear genes is tightly co-regulated to allow proper development of plastids in relation to cell differentiation.

Plastid DNA exists as large protein-DNA complexes associated with the inner envelope membrane and called 'plastid nucleoids'. Each nucleoid particle may contain more than 10 copies of the plastid DNA. The proplastid contains a single nucleoid located in the centre of the plastid. The developing plastid has many nucleoids, localized at the periphery of the plastid, bound to the inner envelope membrane. During the development of proplastids to chloroplasts, and when plastids convert from one type to another, nucleoids change in morphology, size and location within the organelle. The remodelling of nucleoids is believed to occur by modifications to the composition and abundance of nucleoid proteins.

Many plastids, particularly those responsible for photosynthesis, possess numerous internal membrane layers.

In plant cells, long thin protuberances called stromules sometimes form and extend from the main plastid body into the cytosol and interconnect several plastids. Proteins, and presumably smaller molecules, can move within stromules. Most cultured cells that are relatively large compared to other plant cells have very long and abundant stromules that extend to the cell periphery.

## Plastids in Algae

In algae, the term leucoplast is used for all unpigmented plastids and their function differs from the leucoplasts of plants. Etioplasts, amyloplasts and chromoplasts are plant-specific and do not occur in algae. Plastids in algae and hornworts may also differ from plant plastids in that they contain pyrenoids.

Glaucocystophytic algae contain muroplasts which are similar to chloroplasts except that they have a cell wall that is similar to that of prokaryotes. Rhydophytic algae contain rhydoplasts which are red chloroplasts which allow the algae to photosynthesise to a depth of up to 268m.

## Inheritance of Plastids

Most plants inherit the plastids from only one parent. Angiosperms generally inherit plastids from the female gamete, while many gymnosperms inherit plastids from the male pollen. Algae also inherit plastids from only one parent. The plastid DNA of the other parent is thus completely lost.

In normal intraspecific crossings (resulting in normal hybrids of one species), the inheritance of plastid DNA appears to be quite strictly 100 per cent uniparental. In interspecific hybridisations, however, the inheritance of plastids appears to be more erratic. Although plastids inherit mainly maternally in interspecific hybridisations, there are many reports of hybrids of flowering plants that contain plastids of the father. Approximately ~20 per cent of angiosperms, including alfalfa (Medicago), normally show biparental inheritance of plastids.

## Origin of Plastids

Plastids are thought to have originated from endosymbiotic cyanobacteria. They developed around 1500 million years ago and allowed eukaryotes to carry out oxygenic photosynthesis. Due to a split-up into three evolutionary lineages, the plastids are named differently: chloroplasts in green algae and plants, rhodoplasts in red algae and cyanelles in the glaucophytes. The plastids differ by their pigmentation, but also in ultrastructure. The chloroplasts *e.g.* have lost all phycobilisomes, the light harvesting complexes found in cyanobacteria, red algae and glaucophytes, but—only in plants and in closely related green algae—contain stroma and grana thylakoids. The glaucocystophycean plastid—in contrast to the chloroplasts and the rhodoplasts—is still surrounded by the remains of the cyanobacterial cell wall. All these primary plastids are surrounded by two membranes.

Complex plastids start by secondary endosymbiosis, when a eukaryote engulfs a red or green alga and retains the algal plastid, which is typically surrounded by more than two membranes. In some cases these plastids may be reduced in their metabolic and/or photosynthetic capacity. Algae with complex plastids derived by secondary endosymbiosis of a red alga include the heterokonts, haptophytes, cryptomonads, and most dinoflagellates (= rhodoplasts). Those that endosymbiosed a green alga include the euglenids and chlorarachniophytes (= chloroplasts). The Apicomplexa, a phylum of obligate parasitic protozoa including the causative agents of malaria (*Plasmodium* spp.), toxoplasmosis (*Toxoplasma gondii*), and many other human or animal diseases also harbour a complex plastid (although this organelle has been lost in some apicomplexans, such as *Cryptosporidium parvum*, which causes cryptosporidiosis). The 'apicoplast' is no longer capable of photosynthesis, but is an essential organelle, and a promising target for antiparasitic drug development.

Some dinoflagellates and sea slugs, particularly of the genus Elysia, take up algae as food and keep the plastid of the digested alga to profit from the photosynthesis; after a while the plastids are also digested. These captured plastids are known as kleptoplastids.

## Chloroplast

Chloroplasts (English pronunciation: are organelles found in plant cells and other eukaryotic organisms that conduct photosynthesis. Chloroplasts capture light energy to conserve free energy in the form of ATP and reduce NADP to NADPH through a complex set of processes called photosynthesis.

The word chloroplast is derived from the Greek words *chloros* , which means green, and *plastis* , which means 'the one who forms'. Chloroplasts are members of a class of organelles known as plastids.

Chloroplasts are one of the many different types of organelles in the plant cell. In general, they are considered to have originated from cyanobacteria through endosymbiosis. This was first suggested by Mereschkowsky in 1905 after an observation by Schimper in 1883 that chloroplasts closely resemble cyanobacteria. All chloroplasts are thought to derive directly or indirectly from a single endosymbiotic event (in the Archaeplastida), except for *Paulinella chromatophora,* which has recently acquired a photosynthetic cyanobacterial endosymbiont which is not closely related to chloroplasts of other eukaryotes.

In that they derive from an endosymbiotic event, chloroplasts are similar to mitochondria, but chloroplasts are found only in plants and protista. The chloroplast is surrounded by a double-layered composite membrane with an intermembrane space; further, it has reticulations, or many infoldings, filling the inner spaces. The chloroplast has its own DNA, which codes for redox proteins involved in electron transport in photosynthesis; this is termed the plastome.

In green plants, chloroplasts are surrounded by two lipid-bilayer membranes. They are believed to correspond to the outer and inner membranes of the ancestral cyanobacterium. Chloroplasts have their own genome, which is considerably reduced compared to that of free-living cyanobacteria, but the parts that are still present show clear similarities with the cyanobacterial genome. Plastids may contain 60-100 genes whereas cyanobacteria often contain more than 1500 genes. Many of the missing genes are encoded in the nuclear genome of the host. The transfer of nuclear information has been estimated in tobacco plants at one gene for every 16000 pollen grains.

In some algae (such as the heterokonts and other protists such as Euglenozoa and Cercozoa), chloroplasts seem to have evolved through a secondary event of endosymbiosis, in which a eukaryotic cell engulfed a second eukaryotic cell containing chloroplasts, forming chloroplasts with three or four membrane layers. In some cases, such secondary endosymbionts may have themselves been engulfed by still other eukaryotes, thus forming tertiary endosymbionts. In the alga *Chlorella*, there is only one chloroplast, which is bell-shaped.

In some groups of mixotrophic protists such as the dinoflagellates, chloroplasts are separated from a captured alga or diatom and used temporarily. These klepto chloroplasts may only have a lifetime of a few days and are then replaced.

Chloroplasts are observable as flat discs usually 2 to 10 micrometers in diameter and 1 micrometer thick. In land plants, they are, in general, 5 μm in diameter and 2.3 μm thick. The chloroplast is contained by an envelope that consists of an inner and an outer phospholipid membrane. Between these two layers is the intermembrane space. A typical parenchyma cell contains about 10 to 100 chloroplasts.

The material within the chloroplast is called the stroma, corresponding to the cytosol of the original bacterium, and contains one or more molecules of small circular DNA. It also contains ribosomes; however most of its proteins are encoded by genes contained in the host cell nucleus, with the protein products transported to the chloroplast.

Within the stroma are stacks of thylakoids, the sub-organelles, which are the site of photosynthesis. The thylakoids are arranged in stacks called grana (singular: granum).

A thylakoid has a flattened disk shape. Inside it is an empty area called the thylakoid space or lumen. Photosynthesis takes place on the thylakoid membrane; as in mitochondrial oxidative phosphorylation, it involves the coupling of cross-membrane fluxes with biosynthesis via the dissipation of a proton electrochemical gradient.

In the electron microscope, thylakoid membranes appear as alternating light-and-dark bands, each 0.01 μm thick. Embedded in the thylakoid membrane are antenna complexes, each of which consists of the light-absorbing pigments, including chlorophyll and carotenoids, as well as proteins that bind the pigments.

This complex both increases the surface area for light capture, and allows capture of photons with a wider range of wavelengths. The energy of the incident photons is absorbed by the pigments and funneled to the reaction centre of this complex through resonance energy transfer. Two chlorophyll molecules are then ionised, producing an excited electron, which then passes onto the photochemical reaction centre.

Recent studies have shown that chloroplasts can be interconnected by tubular bridges called stromules, formed as extensions of their outer membranes. Chloroplasts appear to be able to exchange proteins via stromules, and thus function as a network.

Recently, chloroplasts have caught attention by developers of genetically modified plants. In most flowering plants, chloroplasts are not inherited from the male parent, although in plants such as pines, chloroplasts are inherited from males. Where chloroplasts are inherited only from the female, transgenes in these plastids cannot be disseminated by pollen. This makes plastid transformation a valuable tool for the creation and cultivation of genetically modified plants that are biologically contained, thus posing significantly lower environmental risks.

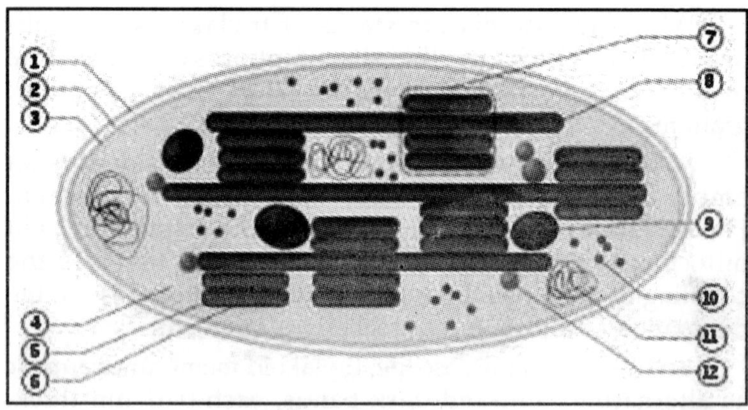


**Chloroplast Ultrastructure**

1. *Outer Membrane;* 2. *Intermembrane Space;* 3. *Inner Membrane (1+2+3: Envelope);* 4. *Stroma (Aqueous Fluid);* 5. *Thylakoid Lumen (Inside of Thylakoid);* 6. *Thylakoid Membrane;* 7. *Granum (Stack of Thylakoids);* 8. *Thylakoid (Lamella);* 9. *Starch;* 10. *Ribosome;* 11. *Plastidial DNA;* 12. *Plastoglobule (Drop of Lipids)*

This biological containment strategy is therefore suitable for establishing the coexistence of conventional and organic agriculture. While the reliability of this mechanism has not yet been studied for all relevant crop species, recent results in tobacco plants are promising, showing a failed containment rate of transplastomic plants at 3 in 1,000,000.

# 6 Nitrogen Cycle and Plants

The nitrogen cycle is the process by which nitrogen is converted between its various chemical forms. This transformation can be carried out via both biological and non-biological processes. Important processes in the nitrogen cycle include fixation, mineralization, nitrification, and denitrification. The majority of Earth's atmosphere (approximately 78%) is nitrogen, making it the largest pool of nitrogen. However, atmospheric nitrogen is unavailable for biological use, leading to a scarcity of usable nitrogen in many types of ecosystems. The nitrogen cycle is of particular interest to ecologists because nitrogen availability can affect the rate of key ecosystem processes, including primary production and decomposition. Human activities such as fossil fuel combustion, use of artificial nitrogen fertilizers, and release of nitrogen in wastewater have dramatically altered the global nitrogen cycle.

Nitrogen is essential for many processes; it is crucial for any life on Earth. It is a component in all amino acids, is incorporated into proteins, and is present in the bases that make up nucleic acids, such as DNA and RNA. In plants, much of the nitrogen is used in chlorophyll molecules, which are essential for photosynthesis and further growth. Although earth's atmosphere is an abundant source of nitrogen, most is relatively unusable by plants. Chemical processing, or natural fixation (through processes such as bacterial conversion—see rhizobium), are necessary to convert gaseous nitrogen into forms usable by living organisms. This makes nitrogen a crucial part of food production. The abundance or scarcity of this 'fixed' form of nitrogen, (also known as reactive nitrogen), dictates how much food can be grown on a piece of land.

## The Processes of the Nitrogen Cycle

Nitrogen is present in the environment in a wide variety of chemical forms including organic nitrogen, ammonium ($NH_4^+$), nitrite ($NO_2^-$), nitrate ($NO_3^-$), and nitrogen gas ($N_2$). The organic nitrogen may be in the form of any living organism, or humus, and in the intermediate products of organic matter decomposition or humus built up. The processes of the nitrogen cycle transform nitrogen from one chemical form to another. Many of the processes are carried out by microbes either to produce energy or to accumulate nitrogen in the form needed for growth.

## Nitrogen Fixation

Atmospheric nitrogen must be processed, or 'fixed' to be used by plants. Some fixation occurs in lightning strikes, but most fixation is done by free-living or symbiotic bacteria. These bacteria have the nitrogenase enzyme that combines gaseous nitrogen with hydrogen to produce ammonia, which is then further converted by the bacteria to make their own organic compounds. Most biological nitrogen fixation occurs by the activity of Mo-nitrogenase, found in a wide variety of bacteria and some Archaea. Mo-nitrogenase is a complex two component enzyme that contains multiple metal-containing prosthetic groups. Some nitrogen fixing bacteria, such as *Rhizobium,* live in the root nodules of legumes (such as peas or beans). Here they form a mutualistic relationship with the plant, producing ammonia in exchange for carbohydrates. Nutrient-poor soils can be planted with legumes to enrich them with nitrogen. A few other plants can form such symbioses. Today, about 30 per cent of the total fixed nitrogen is manufactured in ammonia chemical plants.

## Conversion of $N_2$

The conversion of nitrogen ($N_2$) from the atmosphere into a form readily available to plants and hence to animals and humans is an important step in the nitrogen cycle, which distributes the supply of this essential nutrient. There are four ways to convert $N_2$ (atmospheric nitrogen gas) into more chemically reactive forms:

- *Biological fixation:* Some symbiotic bacteria (most often associated with leguminous plants) and some free-living bacteria are able to fix nitrogen as organic nitrogen. An example of mutualistic nitrogen fixing bacteria are the *Rhizobium* bacteria, which live in legume root nodules. These species are diazotrophs. An example of the free-living bacteria is *Azotobacter*.
- *Industrial N-fixation:* Under great pressure, at a temperature of 600 C, and with the use of an iron catalyst, atmospheric nitrogen and hydrogen (usually derived from natural gas or petroleum) can be combined to form ammonia ($NH_3$). In the Haber-Bosch process, $N_2$ is converted together with hydrogen gas ($H_2$) into ammonia ($NH_3$), which is used to make fertilizer and explosives.
- *Combustion of fossil fuels:* Automobile engines and thermal power plants, which release various nitrogen oxides ($NO_x$).
- *Other processes:* In addition, the formation of NO from $N_2$ and $O_2$ due to photons and especially lightning, can fix nitrogen.

## Assimilation

Plants get nitrogen from the soil, by absorption of their roots in the form of either nitrate ions or ammonium ions. All nitrogen obtained by animals can be traced back to the eating of plants at some stage of the food chain.

Plants can absorb nitrate or ammonium ions from the soil via their root hairs. If nitrate is absorbed, it is first reduced to nitrite ions and then ammonium ions for incorporation into amino acids, nucleic acids, and chlorophyll. In plants that have a mutualistic relationship with rhizobia, some nitrogen is assimilated in the form of ammonium ions directly from the nodules. Animals, fungi, and other heterotrophic organisms obtain nitrogen as amino acids, nucleotides and other small organic molecules.

## Ammonification

When a plant dies, an animal dies, or an animal expels waste, the initial form of nitrogen is organic. Bacteria, or in some cases, fungi, convert the organic nitrogen within the remains back into ammonium ($NH_4^+$), a process called ammonification or mineralization. Enzymes Involved:

- *GS:* Gln Synthetase (Cytosolic & PLastid)
- *GOGAT:* Glu 2-oxoglutarate aminotransferase (Ferredoxin & NADH dependent)
- *GDH:* Glu Dehydrogenase.
- Minor Role in ammonium assimilation.
- Important in amino acid catabolism.

## Nitrification

The conversion of ammonium to nitrate is performed primarily by soil-living bacteria and other nitrifying bacteria. The primary stage of nitrification, the oxidation of ammonium ($NH_4^+$) is performed by bacteria such as the *Nitrosomonas* species, which converts ammonia to nitrites ($NO_2^-$). Other bacterial species, such as the *Nitrobacter*, are responsible for the oxidation of the nitrites into nitrates ($NO_3^-$). It is important for the nitrites to be converted to nitrates because accumulated nitrites are toxic to plant life.

Due to their very high solubility, nitrates can enter groundwater. Elevated nitrate in groundwater is a concern for drinking water use because nitrate can interfere with blood-oxygen levels in infants and cause methemoglobinemia or blue-baby syndrome. Where groundwater recharges stream flow, nitrate-enriched groundwater can contribute to eutrophication, a process leading to high algal, especially blue-green algal populations and the death of aquatic life due to excessive demand for oxygen. While not directly toxic to fish life like ammonia, nitrate can have indirect effects on fish if it contributes to this eutrophication. Nitrogen has contributed to severe eutrophication problems in some water bodies. As of 2006, the application of nitrogen fertilizer is being increasingly controlled in Britain and the United States. This is occurring along the same lines as control of phosphorus fertilizer, restriction of which is normally considered essential to the recovery of eutrophied waterbodies.

## Denitrification

Denitrification is the reduction of nitrates back into the largely inert nitrogen gas ($N_2$), completing the nitrogen cycle. This process is performed by bacterial species such as *Pseudomonas* and *Clostridium* in anaerobic conditions. They use the nitrate as an electron acceptor in the place of oxygen during respiration. These facultatively anaerobic bacteria can also live in aerobic conditions.

## Anaerobic Ammonium Oxidation

In this biological process, nitrite and ammonium are converted directly into dinitrogen gas. This process makes up a major proportion of dinitrogen conversion in the oceans.

## Human Influences on the Nitrogen Cycle

As a result of extensive cultivation of legumes (particularly soy, alfalfa, and clover), growing use of the Haber-Bosch process in the creation of chemical fertilizers, and pollution emitted by vehicles and industrial plants, human beings have more than doubled the annual transfer of nitrogen into biologically-available forms. In addition, humans have significantly contributed to the transfer of nitrogen trace gases from Earth to the atmosphere, and from the land to aquatic systems. Human alterations to the global nitrogen cycle are most intense in developed countries and in Asia, where vehicle emissions and industrial agriculture are highest.

$N_2O$ (nitrous oxide) has risen in the atmosphere as a result of agricultural fertilization, biomass burning, cattle and feedlots, and other industrial sources. $N_2O$ has deleterious effects in the stratosphere, where it breaks down and acts as a catalyst in the destruction of atmospheric ozone.

$N_2O$ in the atmosphere is a greenhouse gas, currently the third largest contributor to global warming, after carbon dioxide and methane. While not as abundant in the atmosphere as carbon dioxide, for an equivalent mass, nitrous oxide is nearly 300 times more potent in its ability to warm the planet.

$NH_3$ (ammonia) in the atmosphere has tripled as the result of human activities. It is a reactant in the atmosphere, where it acts as an aerosol, decreasing air quality and clinging on to water droplets, eventually resulting in nitric acid ($HNO_3$) acid rain. Atmospheric $NH_3$ and $HNO_3$ damage respiratory systems.

All forms of high-temperature combustion have contributed to a 6 or 7 fold increase in $NO_x$ flux to the atmosphere. It is a function of combustion temperature — the higher the temperature, the more $NO_x$ is produced. Fossil fuel combustion is a primary contributor, but so are biofuels and even burning hydrogen. The higher combustion temperature of hydrogen produces more $NO_x$ than natural gas combustion. The very-high temperature of lightning produces small amounts of $NO_x$, $NH_3$, and $HNO_3$.

$NH_3$ and $NO_x$ actively alter atmospheric chemistry. They are precursors of tropospheric (lower atmosphere) ozone production, which contributes to smog, acid rain, damages plants and increases nitrogen inputs to ecosystems. Ecosystem processes can increase with nitrogen fertilization, but anthropogenic input can also result in nitrogen saturation, which weakens productivity and can damage the health of plants, animals, fish, and humans.

Decreases in biodiversity can also result if higher nitrogen availability increases nitrogen-demanding grasses, causing a degradation of nitrogen-poor, species diverse heathlands.

## Wastewater Treatment

Onsite sewage facilities such as septic tanks and holding tanks release large amounts of nitrogen into the environment by discharging through a drainfield into the ground. Microbial activity consumes the nitrogen and other contaminants in the wastewater.

However, in certain areas, the soil is unsuitable to handle some or all of the wastewater, and, as a result, the wastewater with the contaminants enters the aquifers. These contaminants accumulate and eventually end up in drinking water. One of the contaminants concerned about the most is nitrogen in the form of nitrates. A nitrate concentration of 10 ppm (parts per million) or 10 milligrams per liter is the current EPA limit for drinking water and typical household wastewater can produce a range of 20-85 ppm.

The health risk associated with drinking water (with >10 ppm nitrate) is the development of methemoglobinemia and has been found to cause blue baby syndrome. Several states have now started programmes to introduce advanced wastewater treatment systems to the typical onsite sewage facilities. The result of these systems is an overall reduction of nitrogen, as well as other contaminants in the wastewater.

## Environmental Impacts

Additional risks posed by increased availability of inorganic nitrogen in aquatic ecosystems include water acidification; eutrophication of fresh and saltwater systems; and toxicity issues for animals, including humans. Eutrophication often leads to lower dissolved oxygen levels in the water column, including hypoxic and anoxic conditions, which can cause cause death of aquatic fauna. Relatively sessile benthos, or bottom-dwelling creatures, are particularly vulnerable because of their lack of mobility, though large fish kills are not uncommon. Oceanic dead zones near the mouth of the Mississippi in the Gulf of Mexico are a well-known examples of algal bloom-induced hypoxia.

The New York Adirondack Lakes, Catskills, Hudson Highlands, Rensselaer Plateau and parts of Long Island are examples of the impact of nitric acid raid deposition, killing fish and many other aquatic species.

Ammonia ($NH_3$) is highly toxic to fish and the water discharge level of ammonia from wastewater treatment facilities must often be closely monitored. To prevent fish deaths, nitrification prior to discharge is often desirable. Land application can be an attractive alternative to the mechanical aeration needed for nitrification.

## Nitrogen Fixation

Nitrogen fixation is the natural process, either biological or abiotic, by which nitrogen ($N_2$) in the atmosphere is converted into ammonia ($NH_3$). This process is essential for life because fixed nitrogen is required to biosynthesize the basic building blocks of life, e.g., nucleotides for DNA and RNA and amino acids for proteins. Nitrogen fixation also refers to other biological conversions of nitrogen, such as its conversion to nitrogen dioxide.

Microorganisms that fix nitrogen are bacteria called diazotrophs. Some higher plants, and some animals (termites), have formed associations (symbioses) with diazotrophs. Nitrogen fixation also occurs as a result of non-biological processes. These include lightning, industrially through the Haber-Bosch Process, and combustion. Biological nitrogen fixation was discovered by the Dutch microbiologist Martinus Beijerinck.

Biological nitrogen fixation (BNF) occurs when atmospheric nitrogen is converted to ammonia by an enzyme called nitrogenase. The reaction for BNF is:

$$N_2 + 8\,H^+ + 8\,e^- = 2\,NH_3 + H_2$$

The process is coupled to the hydrolysis of 16 equivalents of ATP and is accompanied by the co-formation of one molecule of $H_2$. In free-living diazotrophs, the nitrogenase-generated ammonium is assimilated into glutamate through the glutamine synthetase/glutamate synthase pathway.

Enzymes responsible for nitrogenase action are very susceptible to destruction by oxygen. (In fact, many bacteria cease production of the enzyme in the presence of oxygen). Many nitrogen-fixing organisms exist only in anaerobic conditions, respiring to draw down oxygen levels, or binding the oxygen with a protein such as Leghemoglobin.

Microorganisms that fix nitrogen (Diazotrophs)

- Cyanobacteria
- *Azotobacteraceae*
- *Rhizobia*
- *Frankia*

## Nitrogen Fixation by Rhizobia

Rhizobia are soil, Gram-negative bacteria with the unique ability to establish a $N_2$-fixing symbiosis on legume roots and on the stems of some aquatic legumes. During this interaction bacteroids, as rhizobia are called in the symbiotic state, are contained in intracellular compartments within a specialized organ, the nodule, where they fix $N_2$.

## Nitrogen Fixation by Cyanobacteria

Cyanobacteria inhabit nearly all illuminated environments on Earth and play key roles in the carbon and nitrogen cycle of the biosphere. In general, cyanobacteria are able to utilize a variety of inorganic and organic sources of combined nitrogen, like nitrate, nitrite, ammonium, urea, or some amino acids. Several cyanobacterial strains are also capable of diazotrophic growth. Genome sequencing has provided a large amount of information on the genetic basis of nitrogen metabolism and its control in different cyanobacteria. Comparative genomics, together with functional studies, has led to a significant advance in this field over the past years.

2-Oxoglutarate has turned out to be the central signalling molecule reflecting the carbon/nitrogen balance of cyanobacteria. Central players of nitrogen control are the global transcriptional factor NtcA, which controls the expression of many genes involved in nitrogen metabolism, as well as the $P_{II}$ signalling protein, which fine-tunes cellular activities in response to changing C/N conditions. These two proteins are sensors of the cellular 2-oxoglutarate level and have been conserved in all cyanobacteria. In contrast, the adaptation to nitrogen starvation involves heterogeneous responses in different strains. Nitrogen fixation by cyanobacteria in coral reefs can fix twice the amount of nitrogen than on land–around 1.8 kg of nitrogen is fixed per hectare per day.

## Symbiotic Nitrogen Fixing Plants

### *Legume Family*

Plants that contribute to nitrogen fixation include the legume family – Fabaceae – with taxa such as clover, soybeans, alfalfa, lupines, peanuts, and rooibos. They contain symbiotic bacteria called *Rhizobia* within nodules in their root systems, producing nitrogen compounds that help the plant to grow and compete with other plants. When the plant dies, the fixed nitrogen is released, making it available to other plants and this helps to fertilize the soil The great majority of legumes have this association, but a few genera (*e.g.*, *Styphnolobium*) do not. In many traditional and organic farming practices, fields are rotated through various types of crops, which usually includes one consisting mainly or entirely of clover or buckwheat (family *Polygonaceae*), which were often referred to as 'green manure'.

Although by far the majority of nitrogen-fixing plants are in the legume family Fabaceae, there are a few non-leguminous plants, such as alder and bayberry, that can also fix nitrogen, thanks to a symbiotic associatioin with Frankia bacteria. These plants, referred to as 'actinorhizal plants', consist of 24 genera of woody shrubs or trees distributed among 8 plant families. The ability to fix nitrogen is far from universally present in these families. For instance, of 122 genera in the Rosaceae, only 4 genera are capable of fixing nitrogen. All these families belong to the orders Cucurbitales, Fagales, and Rosales, which together with the Fabales form a clade of eurosids. In this clade, Fabales were the first lineage to branch off; thus, the ability to fix nitrogen may be plesiomorphic and subsequently lost in most descendants of the original nitrogen-fixing plant; however, it may be that the basic genetic and physiological requirements were present in an incipient state in the last common ancestors of all these plants, but only evolved to full function in some of them.

## Haber Process

Nitrogen can also be artificially fixed as ammonia for use in fertilizers, explosives, or in other products. The most common method is the Haber process. Artificial fertilizer production is now the largest source of human-produced fixed nitrogen in the Earth's ecosystem.

The Haber process requires high pressures (around 200 atm) and high temperatures (at least 400 °C), routine conditions for industrial catalysis. This highly efficient process uses natural gas as a hydrogen source and air as a nitrogen source.

## Dinitrogen Complexes

Much research has been conducted on the discovery of catalysts for nitrogen fixation, often with the goal of reducing the energy required for this conversion. However, such research has thus far failed to even approach the efficiency and ease of the Haber process. Many compounds react with atmospheric nitrogen under ambient conditions. For example, lithium metal converts to lithium nitride under an atmosphere of nitrogen. Treatment of the resulting nitride gives ammonia.

The first dinitrogen complex was reported in 1965 based on ammonia coordinated to ruthenium ($[Ru(NH_3)_5(N_2)]^{2+}$). Research in chemical fixation from then on focussed on transition metal complexes. Since then, a large number of transition metal compounds that contain dinitrogen as a ligand have been discovered. The dinitrogen ligand can either be bound to a single metal or bridge two (or more) metals. The coordination chemistry of dinitrogen is complex and currently under intense investigation. This research may lead to new ways of using dinitrogen in synthesis and on an industrial scale.

## Ambient Nitrogen Reduction

Catalytic chemical nitrogen fixation at temperatures considerably lower than the Haber process is an ongoing scientific endeavour. Nitrogen was successfully converted to ammonia and hydrazine by Alexander E. Shilov in 1970 The first example of homolytic cleavage of dinitrogen under mild conditions was published in 1995. Two equivalents of a molybdenum complex reacted with one equivalent of dinitrogen, creating a triple bonded MoN complex. Since then, this triple bounded complex has been used to make nitriles.

The first catalytic system converting nitrogen to ammonia at room temperature and pressure was discovered in 2003 and is based on another molybdenum compound, a proton source, and a strong reducing agent. However, this catalytic reduction fixates only a few nitrogen molecules.

## Human Impact on the Nitrogen Cycle

Human impact on the nitrogen cycle is diverse. Agricultural and industrial nitrogen (N) inputs to the environment currently exceed inputs from natural N fixation. As a consequence of anthropogenic inputs, the global nitrogen cycle has been significantly altered over the past century. Global atmospheric nitrous oxide ($N_2O$) mole fractions have increased from a pre-industrial value of ~270 nmol/mol to ~319 nmol/mol in 2005. Human activities account for over one-third of $N_2O$ emissions, most of which are due to the agricultural sector. This article is intended to give a brief review of the history of anthropogenic N inputs, and reported impacts of nitrogen inputs on selected terrestrial and aquatic ecosystems.

Approximately 78 per cent of earth's atmosphere is N gas ($N_2$), which is an inert compound and biologically unavailable to most organisms. In order to be utilized in most biological processes, $N_2$ must be converted to reactive N (Nr), which includes inorganic reduced forms ($NH_3$ and $NH_4^+$), inorganic oxidized forms (NO, $NO_2$, $HNO_3$, $N_2O$, and $NO_3^-$), and organic compounds (urea, amines, and proteins). $N_2$ has a strong triple bond, and so a significant amount of energy (226 kcal mol-1) is required to convert $N_2$ to Nr. Prior to industrial processes, the only sources of such energy were solar radiation and electrical discharges. Utilizing a large amount of metabolic energy and the enzyme nitrogenase, some bacteria and cyanobacteria convert atmospheric $N_2$ to $NH_3$, a process known as biological nitrogen fixation (BNF). The anthropogenic analogue to BNF is the Haber-Bosch process, in which fossil fuel $H_2$ is reacted with atmospheric $N_2$ at high temperatures and pressures to produce $NH_3$. Lastly, $N_2$ is converted to NO by energy from lightning, which is negligible in current temperate ecosystems, or by fossil fuel combustion.

Until 1850, natural BNF, cultivation-induced BNF (*e.g.*, planting of leguminous crops), and incorporated organic matter were the only sources of N for agricultural production. Near the turn of the century, Nr from guano and sodium nitrate deposits was harvested and exported from the arid Pacific islands and South American deserts. By the late 1920s, early industrial processes, albeit inefficient, were commonly used to produce NH3. Due to the efforts of Fritz Haber and Carl Bosch, the Haber-Bosch process became the largest source of nitrogenous fertilizer after the 1950s, and replaced BNF as the dominant source of NH3 production. From 1890 to 1990, anthropogenically created Nr increased almost ninefold. During this time, global population more than tripled, partly due to increased food production.

Since the industrial revolution, an additional source of anthropogenic N input has been fossil fuel combustion, which is used to generate energy (*e.g.*, to power automobiles).

During combustion of fossil fuels, high temperatures and pressures provide energy to produce NO from $N_2$ oxidation. Additionally, when fossil fuel is extracted and burned, fossil N may become reactive (*i.e.*, $NO_x$ emissions). During the 1970s, scientists began to recognize that N inputs were accumulating in the environment and affecting ecosystem functioning.

### Impacts of Anthropogenic Inputs on the Nitrogen Cycle

Between 1890 and 1990, global reactive nitrogen (Nr) creation had increased nearly 50 per cent. During this period, atmospheric emissions of Nr species reportedly increased 250 per cent and deposition to marine and terrestrial ecosystems increased over 200 per cent. Additionally, there was a reported fourfold increase in riverine dissolved inorganic N fluxes to coasts. N is a critical limiting nutrient in many systems, including forests, wetlands, and coastal and marine ecosystems; therefore, this change in emissions and distribution of Nr has resulted in substantial consequences for aquatic and terrestrial ecosystems.

### Atmosphere

Atmospheric Nr inputs mainly include oxides of N ($NO_x$), ammonia ($NH_3$), and nitrous oxide ($N_2O$) from aquatic and terrestrial ecosystems, and $NO_x$ from fossil fuel and biomass combustion.

In agroecosystems, fertilizer application has increased microbial nitrification (aerobic process in which microorganisms oxidize ammonium [$NH_4$+] to nitrate [$NO_3$-]) and denitrification (anaerobic process in which microorganisms reduce $NO_3^-$ to atmospheric nitrogen gas [N2]). Both processes naturally leak nitric oxide (NO) and nitrous oxide ($N_2O$) to the atmosphere. Of particular concern is $N_2O$, which has an average atmospheric lifetime of 114-120 years, and is 300 times more effective than $CO_2$ as a greenhouse gas. $NO_x$ produced by industrial processes, automobiles and agricultural fertilization and $NH_3$ emitted from soils (*i.e.*, as an additional byproduct of nitrification) and livestock operations are transported to downwind ecosystems, influencing N cycling and nutrient losses. Six major effects of $NO_x$ and $NH_3$ emissions have been cited):

1. decreased atmospheric visibility due to ammonium aerosols (fine particulate matter [PM]);
2. elevated ozone concentrations;
3. ozone and PM affects human health (*e.g.* respiratory diseases, cancer);
4. increases in relative forcing and global climate change;
5. decreased agricultural productivity due to ozone deposition; and
6. ecosystem acidification and eutrophication.

## Biosphere

Terrestrial and aquatic ecosystems receive Nr inputs from the atmosphere through wet and dry deposition. Atmospheric Nr species can be deposited to ecosystems in precipitation (*e.g.*, $NO_3^-$, $NH_4^+$, organic N compounds), as gases (*e.g.*, $NH_3$ and gaseous nitric acid [$HNO_3$]), or as aerosols (*e.g.*, ammonium nitrate [$NH_4NO_3$]). Aquatic ecosystems receive additional nitrogen from surface runoff and riverine inputs.

Increased N deposition can acidify soils, streams, and lakes and alter forest and grassland productivity. In forest and grassland ecosystems, Nr inputs have produced initial increases in productivity followed by declines as critical thresholds are exceeded. Nr effects on biodiversity, carbon cycling, and changes in species composition have also been demonstrated. In highly developed areas of near shore coastal ocean and estuarine systems, rivers deliver direct (*e.g.*, surface runoff) and indirect (*e.g.*, groundwater contamination) N inputs from agroecosystems. Increased N inputs can result in freshwater acidification and eutrophication of marine waters.

## Terrestrial Ecosystems

### *Impacts on Productivity and Nutrient Cycling*

Much of terrestrial growth in temperate systems is limited by N; therefore, N inputs (*i.e.*, through deposition and fertilization) can increase N availability, which temporarily increases N uptake, plant and microbial growth, and N accumulation in plant biomass and soil organic matter. Incorporation of greater amounts of N in organic matter decreases C:N ratios, increasing mineral N release ($NH_4^+$) during organic matter decomposition by heterotrophic microbes (*i.e.* ammonification). As ammonification increases, so does nitrification of the mineralized N. Because microbial nitrification and denitrification are 'leaky', N deposition is expected to increase trace gas emissions. Additionally, with increasing $NH_4^+$ accumulation in the soil, nitrification processes release hydrogen ions, which acidify the soil. $NO_3^-$, the product of nitrification, is highly mobile and can be leached from the soil, along with positively charged alkaline minerals such as calcium and magnesium. In acid soils, mobilized aluminum ions can reach toxic concentrations, negatively affecting both terrestrial and adjacent aquatic ecosystems.

Anthropogenic sources of N generally reach upland forests through deposition. A potential concern of increased N deposition due to human activities is altered nutrient cycling in forest ecosystems. Numerous studies have demonstrated both positive and negative impacts of atmospheric N deposition on forest productivity and carbon storage. Added N is often rapidly immobilized by microbes, and the effect of the remaining available N depends on the plant community's capacity for N uptake. In systems with high uptake, N is assimilated into the plant biomass, leading to enhanced net primary productivity (NPP) and possibly increased carbon sequestration through greater photosynthetic capacity. However, ecosystem responses to N additions are contingent upon many site-specific factors including climate, land-use history, and amount of N additions. For example, in the Northeastern United States, hardwood stands receiving chronic N inputs have demonstrated greater capacity to retain N and increase annual net primary productivity (ANPP) than conifer stands. Once N input exceeds system demand, N may be lost via leaching and gas fluxes. When available N exceeds the ecosystem's (*i.e.*, vegetation, soil, and microbes, etc.) uptake capacity, N saturation occurs and excess N is lost to surface waters, groundwater, and the atmosphere. N saturation can result in nutrient imbalances (*e.g.*, loss of calcium due to nitrate leaching) and possible forest decline.

A 15-year study of chronic N additions at the Harvard Forest Long Term Ecological Research (LTER) programme has elucidated many impacts of increased nitrogen deposition on nutrient cycling in temperate forests. It found that chronic N additions resulted in greater leaching losses, increased pine mortality, and cessation of biomass accumulation. Another study reported that chronic N additions resulted in accumulation of non-photosynthetic N and subsequently reduced photosynthetic capacity, supposedly leading to severe carbon stress and mortality. These findings negate previous hypotheses that increased N inputs would increase NPP and carbon sequestration.

### Impacts on Plant Species Diversity

Many plant communities have evolved under low nutrient conditions; therefore, increased N inputs can alter biotic and abiotic interactions, leading to changes in community composition. Several nutrient addition studies have shown that increased N inputs lead to dominance of fast-growing plant species, with associated declines in species richness. Other studies have found that secondary responses of the system to N enrichment, including soil acidification and changes in mycorrhizal communities have allowed stress-tolerant species to out-compete sensitive species. Two other studies found evidence that increased N availability has resulted in declines in species-diverse heathlands. Heathlands are characterized by N-poor soils, which exclude N-demanding grasses; however, with increasing N deposition and soil acidification, invading grasslands replace lowland heath.

In a more recent experimental study of N fertilization and disturbance (*i.e.*, tillage) in old field succession, it was found that species richness decreased with increasing N, regardless of disturbance level. Competition experiments showed that competitive dominants excluded competitively inferior species between disturbance events. With increased N inputs, competition shifted from belowground to aboveground (*i.e.*, to competition for light), and patch colonization rates significantly decreased. These internal changes can dramatically affect the community by shifting the balance of competition-colonization tradeoffs between species. In patch-based systems, regional coexistence can occur through tradeoffs in competitive and colonizing abilities given sufficiently high disturbance rates. That is, with inverse ranking of competitive and colonizing abilities, plants can coexist in space and time as disturbance removes superior competitors from patches, allowing for establishment of superior colonizers. However, as demonstrated by Wilson and Tilman, increased nutrient inputs can negate tradeoffs, resulting in competitive exclusion of these superior colonizers/poor competitors.

## Aquatic Ecosystems

Aquatic ecosystems also exhibit varied responses to nitrogen enrichment. $NO_3^-$ loading from N saturated, terrestrial ecosystems can lead to acidification of downstream freshwater systems and eutrophication of downstream marine systems. Freshwater acidification can cause aluminum toxicity and mortality of pH-sensitive fish species. Because marine systems are generally nitrogen-limited, excessive N inputs can result in water quality degradation due to toxic algal blooms, oxygen deficiency, habitat loss, decreases in biodiversity, and fishery losses.

## Acidification of Freshwaters

Atmospheric N deposition in terrestrial landscapes can be transformed through soil microbial processes to biologically available nitrogen, which can result in surface-water acidification, and loss of biodiversity. $NO_3^-$ and $NH_4^+$ inputs from terrestrial systems and the atmosphere can acidify freshwater systems when there is little buffering capacity due to soil acidification. N pollution in Europe, the Northeastern United States, and Asia is a current concern for freshwater acidification. Lake acidification studies in the Experimental Lake Area (ELA) in northwestern Ontario clearly demonstrated the negative effects of increased acidity on a native fish species: lake trout (Salvelinus namaycush) recruitment and growth dramatically decreased due to extirpation of its key prey species during acidification.

### Eutrophication of Marine Systems

Urbanization, deforestation, and agricultural activities largely contribute sediment and nutrient inputs to coastal waters via rivers. Increased nutrient inputs to marine systems have shown both short-term increases in productivity and fishery yields, and long-term detrimental effects of eutrophication. Tripling of $NO_3^-$ loads in the Mississippi River in the last half of the 20th century have been correlated with increased fishery yields in waters surrounding the Mississippi delta; however, these nutrient inputs have produced seasonal hypoxia (oxygen concentrations less than 2-3 mg $L^{-1}$, 'dead zones') in the Gulf of Mexico. In estuarine and coastal systems, high nutrient inputs increase primary production (*e.g.*, phytoplankton, sea grasses, macroalgae), which increase turbidity with resulting decreases in light penetration throughout the water column. Consequently, submerged vegetation growth declines, which reduces habitat complexity and oxygen production. The increased primary (*i.e.*, phytoplankton, macroalgae, etc.) production leads to a flux of carbon to bottom waters when decaying organic matter (i.e., senescent primary production) sinks and is consumed by aerobic bacteria lower in the water column. As a result, oxygen consumption in bottom waters is greater than diffusion of oxygen from surface waters.

# 7 Photosynthesis

Photosynthesis (English pronunciation: is a process that converts carbon dioxide into organic compounds, especially sugars, using the energy from sunlight. Photosynthesis occurs in plants, algae, and many species of bacteria, but not in archaea. Photosynthetic organisms are called *photoautotrophs,* since they can create their own food. In plants, algae, and cyanobacteria, photosynthesis uses carbon dioxide and water, releasing oxygen as a waste product. Photosynthesis is vital for all aerobic life on Earth. As well as maintaining the normal level of oxygen in the atmosphere, nearly all life either depends on it directly as a source of energy, or indirectly as the ultimate source of the energy in their food (the exceptions are chemoautotrophs that live in rocks or around deep sea hydrothermal vents). The rate of energy capture by photosynthesis is immense, approximately 100 terawatts, which is about six times larger than the power consumption of human civilization. As well as energy, photosynthesis is also the source of the carbon in all the organic compounds within organisms' bodies. In all, photosynthetic organisms convert around 100-115 teragrams of carbon into biomass per year.

Although photosynthesis can happen in different ways in different species, some features are always the same. For example, the process always begins when energy from light is absorbed by proteins called photosynthetic reaction centres that contain chlorophylls. In plants, these proteins are held inside organelles called chloroplasts, while in bacteria they are embedded in the plasma membrane. Some of the light energy gathered by chlorophylls is stored in the form of adenosine triphosphate (ATP). The rest of the energy is used to remove electrons from a substance such as water. These electrons are then used in the reactions that turn carbon dioxide into organic compounds. In plants, algae and cyanobacteria, this is done by a sequence of reactions called the Calvin cycle, but different sets of reactions are found in some bacteria, such as the reverse Krebs cycle in *Chlorobium*. Many photosynthetic organisms have adaptations that concentrate or store carbon dioxide. This helps reduce a wasteful process called photorespiration that can consume part of the sugar produced during photosynthesis.

Overview of cycle between autotrophs and heterotrophs. Photosynthesis is the main means by which plants, algae and many bacteria produce organic compounds and oxygen from carbon dioxide and water.

The first photosynthetic organisms probably evolved about 3,500 million years ago, early in the evolutionary history of life, when all forms of life on Earth were microorganisms and the atmosphere had much more carbon dioxide. They most likely used hydrogen or hydrogen sulfide as sources of electrons, rather than water. Cyanobacteria appeared later, around 3,000 million years ago, and drastically changed the Earth when they began to oxygenate the atmosphere, beginning about 2,400 million years ago. This new atmosphere allowed the evolution of complex life such as protists. Eventually, no later than a billion years ago, one of these protists formed a symbiotic relationship with a cyanobacterium, producing the ancestor of many plants and algae. The chloroplasts in modern plants are the descendants of these ancient symbiotic cyanobacteria.

Photosynthetic organisms are photoautotrophs, which means that they are able to synthesize food directly from carbon dioxide using energy from light. However, not all organisms that use light as a source of energy carry out photosynthesis, since *photoheterotrophs* use organic compounds, rather than carbon dioxide, as a source of carbon. In plants, algae and cyanobacteria, photosynthesis releases oxygen. This is called *oxygenic photosynthesis*. Although there are some differences between oxygenic photosynthesis in plants, algae and cyanobacteria, the overall process is quite similar in these organisms. However, there are some types of bacteria that carry out anoxygenic photosynthesis, which consumes carbon dioxide but does not release oxygen.

Carbon dioxide is converted into sugars in a process called carbon fixation. Carbon fixation is a redox reaction, so photosynthesis needs to supply both a source of energy to drive this process, and the electrons needed to convert carbon dioxide into carbohydrate, which is a reduction reaction. In general outline, photosynthesis is the opposite of cellular respiration, where glucose and other compounds are oxidized to produce carbon dioxide, water, and release chemical energy. However, the two processes take place through a different sequence of chemical reactions and in different cellular compartments.

The general equation for photosynthesis is therefore:

$2n\ CO_2 + 2n\ H_2O + \text{photons} \text{->} 2(CH_2O)_n + n\ O_2 + 2n\ A$

Carbon dioxide + electron donor + light energy ? carbohydrate + oxygen + oxidized electron donor.

Since water is used as the electron donor in oxygenic photosynthesis, the equation for this process is:

$2n\ CO_2 + 2n\ H_2O + \text{photons} \text{->} 2(CH_2O)_n + 2n\ O_2$

carbon dioxide + water + light energy -> carbohydrate + oxygen

Other processes substitute other compounds (such as arsenite) for water in the electron-supply role; the microbes use sunlight to oxidize arsenite to arsenate: The equation for this reaction is:

$(AsO_3^{3-}) + CO_2$ + photons -> $CO + (AsO_4^{3-})$

carbon dioxide + arsenite + light energy ->arsenate + carbon monoxide (used to build other compounds in subsequent reactions)

Photosynthesis occurs in two stages. In the first stage, *light-dependent reactions* or *light reactions* capture the energy of light and use it to make the energy-storage molecules ATP and NADPH. During the second stage, the *light-independent reactions* use these products to capture and reduce carbon dioxide.

Most organisms that utilize photosynthesis to produce oxygen use visible light to do so, although at least three use infrared radiation.

The proteins that gather light for photosynthesis are embedded within cell membranes. The simplest way these are arranged is in photosynthetic bacteria, where these proteins are held within the plasma membrane. However, this membrane may be tightly folded into cylindrical sheets called thylakoids, or bunched up into round vesicles called *intracytoplasmic membranes*. These structures can fill most of the interior of a cell, giving the membrane a very large surface area and therefore increasing the amount of light that the bacteria can absorb.

In plants and algae, photosynthesis takes place in organelles called chloroplasts. A typical plant cell contains about 10 to 100 chloroplasts. The chloroplast is enclosed by a membrane. This membrane is composed of a phospholipid inner membrane, a phospholipid outer membrane, and an intermembrane space between them. Within the membrane is an aqueous fluid called the stroma. The stroma contains stacks (grana) of thylakoids, which are the site of photosynthesis. The thylakoids are flattened disks, bounded by a membrane with a lumen or thylakoid space within it. The site of photosynthesis is the thylakoid membrane, which contains integral and peripheral membrane protein complexes, including the pigments that absorb light energy, which form the photosystems.

Plants absorb light primarily using the pigment chlorophyll, which is the reason that most plants have a green color. Besides chlorophyll, plants also use pigments such as carotenes and xanthophylls. Algae also use chlorophyll, but various other pigments are present as phycocyanin, carotenes, and xanthophylls in green algae, phycoerythrin in red algae (rhodophytes) and fucoxanthin in brown algae and diatoms resulting in a wide variety of colours.

These pigments are embedded in plants and algae in special antenna-proteins. In such proteins all the pigments are ordered to work well together. Such a protein is also called a light-harvesting complex.

Although all cells in the green parts of a plant have chloroplasts, most of the energy is captured in the leaves. The cells in the interior tissues of a leaf, called the mesophyll, can contain between 450,000 and 800,000 chloroplasts for every square millimeter of leaf. The surface of the leaf is uniformly coated with a water-resistant waxy cuticle that protects the leaf from excessive evaporation of water and decreases the absorption of ultraviolet or blue light to reduce heating. The transparent epidermis layer allows light to pass through to the palisade mesophyll cells where most of the photosynthesis takes place.

In the light reactions, one molecule of the pigment chlorophyll absorbs one photon and loses one electron. This electron is passed to a modified form of chlorophyll called pheophytin, which passes the electron to a quinone molecule, allowing the start of a flow of electrons down an electron transport chain that leads to the ultimate reduction of NADP to NADPH. In addition, this creates a proton gradient across the chloroplast membrane; its dissipation is used by ATP synthase for the concomitant synthesis of ATP. The chlorophyll molecule regains the lost electron from a water molecule through a process called photolysis, which releases a dioxygen ($O_2$) molecule. The overall equation for the light-dependent reactions under the conditions of non-cyclic electron flow in green plants is:

$2\ H_2O + 2\ NADP^+ + 3\ ADP + 3\ P_i$ + light ->2 NADPH + 2 $H^+ + 3\ ATP + O_2$

Not all wavelengths of light can support photosynthesis. The photosynthetic action spectrum depends on the type of accessory pigments present. For example, in green plants, the action spectrum resembles the absorption spectrum for chlorophylls and carotenoids with peaks for violet-blue and red light. In red algae, the action spectrum overlaps with the absorption spectrum of phycobilins for blue-green light, which allows these algae to grow in deeper waters that filter out the longer wavelengths used by green plants. The non-absorbed part of the light spectrum is what gives photosynthetic organisms their color (*e.g.*, green plants, red algae, purple bacteria) and is the least effective for photosynthesis in the respective organisms.

In plants, light-dependent reactions occur in the thylakoid membranes of the chloroplasts and use light energy to synthesize ATP and NADPH. The light-dependent reaction has two forms: cyclic and non-cyclic. In the non-cyclic reaction, the photons are captured in the light-harvesting antenna complexes of photosystem II by chlorophyll and other accessory pigments. When a chlorophyll molecule at the core of the photosystem II reaction center obtains sufficient excitation energy from the adjacent antenna pigments, an electron is transferred to the primary electron-acceptor molecule, pheophytin, through a process called photoinduced charge separation. These electrons are shuttled through an electron transport chain, the so called *Z-scheme* that initially functions to generate a chemiosmotic potential across the membrane. An ATP synthase enzyme uses the chemiosmotic potential to make ATP during photophosphorylation, whereas NADPH is a product of the terminal redox reaction in the *Z-scheme*. The electron enters a chlorophyll molecule in Photosystem I. The electron is excited due to the light absorbed by the photosystem. A second electron carrier accepts the electron, which again is passed down lowering energies of electron acceptors. The energy created by the electron acceptors is used to move hydrogen ions across the thylakoid membrane into the lumen. The electron is used to reduce the co-enzyme NADP, which has functions in the light-independent reaction. The cyclic reaction is similar to that of the non-cyclic, but differs in the form that it generates only ATP, and no reduced NADP (NADPH) is created. The cyclic reaction takes place only at photosystem I. Once the electron is displaced from the photosystem, the electron is passed down the electron acceptor molecules and returns back to photosystem I, from where it was emitted, hence the name *cyclic reaction*.

### Water Photolysis

The NADPH is the main reducing agent in chloroplasts, providing a source of energetic electrons to other reactions. Its production leaves chlorophyll with a deficit of electrons (oxidized), which must be obtained from some other reducing agent. The excited electrons lost from chlorophyll in photosystem I are replaced from the electron transport chain by plastocyanin. However, since photosystem II includes the first steps of the *Z-scheme*, an external source of electrons is required to reduce its oxidized chlorophyll *a* molecules. The source of electrons in green-plant and cyanobacterial photosynthesis is water. Two water molecules are oxidized by four successive charge-separation reactions by photosystem II to yield a molecule of diatomic oxygen and four hydrogen ions; the electron yielded in each step is transferred to a redox-active tyrosine residue that then reduces the photoxidized paired-chlorophyll *a* species called P680 that serves as the primary (light-driven) electron donor in the photosystem II reaction center. The oxidation of water is catalyzed in photosystem II by a redox-active structure that contains four manganese ions and a calcium ion; this oxygen-evolving complex binds two water molecules and stores the four oxidizing equivalents that are required to drive the water-oxidizing reaction. Photosystem II is the only known biological enzyme that carries out this oxidation of water. The hydrogen ions contribute to the transmembrane chemiosmotic potential that leads to ATP synthesis. Oxygen is a waste product of light-dependent reactions, but the majority of organisms on Earth use oxygen for cellular respiration, including photosynthetic organisms.

## Light-independent Reactions

### *The Calvin Cycle*

In the Light-independent or dark reactions the enzyme RuBisCO captures $CO_2$ from the atmosphere and in a process that requires the newly formed NADPH, called the Calvin-Benson Cycle, releases three-carbon sugars, which are later combined to form sucrose and starch. The overall equation for the light-independent reactions in green plants is:

$$3\,CO_2 + 9\,ATP + 6\,NADPH + 6\,H^+ \rightarrow C_3H_6O_3\text{-phosphate} + 9\,ADP + 8\,P_i + 6\,NADP^+ + 3\,H_2O$$

Carbon fixation produces an intermediate product, which is then converted to the final carbohydrate products. The carbon skeletons produced by photosynthesis are then variously used to form other organic compounds, such as the building material cellulose, as precursors for lipid and amino acid biosynthesis, or as a fuel in cellular respiration. The latter occurs not only in plants but also in animals when the energy from plants gets passed through a food chain.

The fixation or reduction of carbon dioxide is a process in which carbon dioxide combines with a five-carbon sugar, ribulose 1,5-bisphosphate (RuBP), to yield two molecules of a three-carbon compound, glycerate 3-phosphate (GP), also known as 3-phosphoglycerate (PGA). GP, in the presence of ATP and NADPH from the light-dependent stages, is reduced to glyceraldehyde 3-phosphate (G3P). This product is also referred to as 3-phosphoglyceraldehyde (PGAL) or even as triose phosphate. Triose is a 3-carbon sugar (see carbohydrates). Most (5 out of 6 molecules) of the G3P produced is used to regenerate RuBP so the process can continue (see Calvin-Benson cycle). The 1 out of 6 molecules of the triose phosphates not 'recycled' often condense to form hexose phosphates, which ultimately yield sucrose, starch and cellulose. The sugars produced during carbon metabolism yield carbon skeletons that can be used for other metabolic reactions like the production of amino acids and lipids.

In hot and dry conditions, plants close their stomata to prevent the loss of water. Under these conditions, $CO_2$ will decrease, and oxygen gas, produced by the light reactions of photosynthesis, will decrease in the stem, not leaves, causing an increase of photorespiration by the oxygenase activity of ribulose-1,5-bisphosphate carboxylase/oxygenase and decrease in carbon fixation. Some plants have evolved mechanisms to increase the $CO_2$ concentration in the leaves under these conditions.

$C_4$ plants chemically fix carbon dioxide in the cells of the mesophyll by adding it to the three-carbon molecule phosphoenolpyruvate (PEP), a reaction catalyzed by an enzyme called PEP carboxylase, creating the four-carbon organic acid oxaloacetic acid. Oxaloacetic acid or malate synthesized by this process is then translocated to specialized bundle sheath cells where the enzyme RuBisCO and other Calvin cycle enzymes are located, and where $CO_2$ released by decarboxylation of the four-carbon acids is then fixed by RuBisCO activity to the three-carbon sugar 3-phosphoglyceric acids. The physical separation of RuBisCO from the oxygen-generating light reactions reduces photorespiration and increases $CO_2$ fixation and, thus, photosynthetic capacity of the leaf. $C_4$ plants can produce more sugar than $C_3$ plants in conditions of high light and temperature. Many important crop plants are $C_4$ plants, including maize, sorghum, sugarcane, and millet. Plants that do not use PEP-carboxylase in carbon fixation are called $C_3$ plants because the primary carboxylation reaction, catalyzed by RuBisCO, produces the three-carbon sugar 3-phosphoglyceric acids directly in the Calvin-Benson cycle. Over 90 per cent of plants use $C_3$ carbon fixation, compared to 3 per cent that use $C_4$ carbon fixation.

Xerophytes, such as cacti and most succulents, also use PEP carboxylase to capture carbon dioxide in a process called Crassulacean acid metabolism (CAM). In contrast to $C_4$

metabolism, which *physically* separates the $CO_2$ fixation to PEP from the Calvin cycle, CAM *temporally* separates these two processes. CAM plants have a different leaf anatomy from $C_3$ plants, and fix the $CO_2$ at night, when their stomata are open. CAM plants store the $CO_2$ mostly in the form of malic acid via carboxylation of phosphoenolpyruvate to oxaloacetate, which is then reduced to malate. Decarboxylation of malate during the day releases $CO_2$ inside the leaves, thus allowing carbon fixation to 3-phosphoglycerate by RuBisCO. Sixteen thousand species of plants use CAM.

## In Water

Cyanobacteria possess carboxysomes, which increase the concentration of $CO_2$ around RuBisCO to increase the rate of photosynthesis. This operates by carbonic anhydrase, producing hydrocarbonate ions ($HCO_3^-$), which are then pumped into the carboxysome, before being processed by a different carbonic anhydrase to produce $CO_2$. Pyrenoids in algae and hornworts also act to concentrate $CO_2$ around rubisco.

Plants usually convert light into chemical energy with a photosynthetic efficiency of 3-6 per cent. Actual plants' photosynthetic efficiency varies with the frequency of the light being converted, light intensity, temperature and proportion of carbon dioxide in the atmosphere, and can vary from 0.1 per cent to 8 per cent. By comparison, solar panels convert light into electric energy at an efficiency of approximately 6-20 per cent for mass-produced panels, and up to 41 per cent in a research laboratory.

## Evolution

Early photosynthetic systems, such as those from green and purple sulfur and green and purple non-sulfur bacteria, are thought to have been anoxygenic, using various molecules as electron donors. Green and purple sulfur bacteria are thought to have used hydrogen and sulfur as an electron donor. Green non-sulfur bacteria used various amino and other organic acids. Purple non-sulfur bacteria used a variety of non-specific organic molecules. The use of these molecules is consistent with the geological evidence that the atmosphere was highly reduced at that time.

Fossils of what are thought to be filamentous photosynthetic organisms have been dated at 3.4 billion years old.

The main source of oxygen in the atmosphere is oxygenic photosynthesis, and its first appearance is sometimes referred to as the oxygen catastrophe. Geological evidence suggests that oxygenic photosynthesis, such as that in cyanobacteria, became important during the Paleoproterozoic era around 2 billion years ago. Modern photosynthesis in plants and most photosynthetic prokaryotes is oxygenic. Oxygenic photosynthesis uses water as an electron donor, which is oxidized to molecular oxygen ($O_2$) in the photosynthetic reaction centre.

## Symbiosis and the Origin of Chloroplasts

Several groups of animals have formed symbiotic relationships with photosynthetic algae. These are most common in corals, sponges and sea anemones. It is presumed that this is due to the particularly simple body plans and large surface areas of these animals compared to their volumes. In addition, a few marine mollusks *Elysia viridis* and *Elysia chlorotica* also maintain a symbiotic relationship with chloroplasts they capture from the algae in their diet and then store in their bodies. This allows the molluscs to survive solely by photosynthesis for several months at a time. Some of the genes from the plant cell nucleus have even been transferred to the slugs, so that the chloroplasts can be supplied with proteins that they need to survive.

An even closer form of symbiosis may explain the origin of chloroplasts. Chloroplasts have many similarities with photosynthetic bacteria, including a circular chromosome, prokaryotic-type ribosomes, and similar proteins in the photosynthetic reaction center. The endosymbiotic theory suggests that photosynthetic bacteria were acquired (by endocytosis) by early eukaryotic cells to form the first plant cells. Therefore, chloroplasts may be photosynthetic bacteria that adapted to life inside plant cells. Like mitochondria, chloroplasts still possess their own DNA, separate from the nuclear DNA of their plant host cells and the genes in this chloroplast DNA resemble those in cyanobacteria. DNA in chloroplasts codes for redox proteins such as photosynthetic reaction centers. The CoRR Hypothesis proposes that this Co-location is required for Redox Regulation.

## Cyanobacteria and the Evolution of Photosynthesis

The biochemical capacity to use water as the source for electrons in photosynthesis evolved once, in a common ancestor of extant cyanobacteria. The geological record indicates that this transforming event took place early in Earth's history, at least 2450-2320 million years ago (Ma), and, it is speculated, much earlier. Available evidence from geobiological studies of Archean (>2500 Ma) sedimentary rocks indicates that life existed 3500 Ma, but the question of when oxygenic photosynthesis evolved is still unanswered. A clear paleontological window on cyanobacterial evolution opened about 2000 Ma, revealing an already-diverse biota of blue-greens. Cyanobacteria remained principal primary producers throughout the Proterozoic Eon (2500-543 Ma), in part because the redox structure of the oceans favored photoautotrophs capable of nitrogen fixation. Green algae joined blue-greens as major primary producers on continental shelves near the end of the Proterozoic, but only with the Mesozoic (251-65 Ma) radiations of dinoflagellates, coccolithophorids, and diatoms did primary production in marine shelf waters take modern form. Cyanobacteria remain critical to marine ecosystems as primary producers in oceanic gyres, as agents of biological nitrogen fixation, and, in modified form, as the plastids of marine algae.

A 2010 study by researchers at Tel Aviv University discovered that the Oriental hornet (*Vespa orientalis*) converts sunlight into electric power using a pigment called xanthopterin. This is the first scientific evidence of a member of the animal kingdom engaging in photosynthesis.

## Discovery

Although some of the steps in photosynthesis are still not completely understood, the overall photosynthetic equation has been known since the 19th century.

Jan van Helmont began the research of the process in the mid-17th century when he carefully measured the mass of the soil used by a plant and the mass of the plant as it grew. After noticing that the soil mass changed very little, he hypothesized that the mass of the growing plant must come from the water, the only substance he added to the potted plant. His hypothesis was partially accurate—much of the gained mass also comes from carbon dioxide as well as water. However, this was a signaling point to the idea that the bulk of a plant's biomass comes from the inputs of photosynthesis, not the soil itself.

Joseph Priestley, a chemist and minister, discovered that, when he isolated a volume of air under an inverted jar, and burned a candle in it, the candle would burn out very quickly, much before it ran out of wax. He further discovered that a mouse could similarly 'injure' air. He then showed that the air that had been 'injured' by the candle and the mouse could be restored by a plant.

In 1778, Jan Ingenhousz, court physician to the Austrian Empress, repeated Priestley's experiments. He discovered that it was the influence of sunlight on the plant that could cause it to revive a mouse in a matter of hours.

In 1796, Jean Senebier, a Swiss pastor, botanist, and naturalist, demonstrated that green plants consume carbon dioxide and release oxygen under the influence of light. Soon afterward, Nicolas-Théodore de Saussure showed that the increase in mass of the plant as it grows could not be due only to uptake of $CO_2$ but also to the incorporation of water. Thus, the basic reaction by which photosynthesis is used to produce food (such as glucose) was outlined.

Cornelis Van Niel made key discoveries explaining the chemistry of photosynthesis. By studying purple sulfur bacteria and green bacteria he was the first scientist to demonstrate that photosynthesis is a light-dependent redox reaction, in which hydrogen reduces carbon dioxide.

Robert Emerson discovered two light reactions by testing plant productivity using different wavelengths of light. With the red alone, the light reactions were suppressed. When blue and red were combined, the output was much more substantial. Thus, there were two photosystems, one aborbing up to 600 nm wavelengths, the other up to 700. The former is known as PSII, the latter is PSI. PSI contains only chlorophyll a, PSII contains primarily chlorophyll a with most of the available chlorophyll b, among other pigments.

Further experiments to prove that the oxygen developed during the photosynthesis of green plants came from water, were performed by Robert Hill in 1937 and 1939. He showed that isolated chloroplasts give off oxygen in the presence of unnatural reducing agents like iron oxalate, ferricyanide or benzoquinone after exposure to light. The Hill reaction is as follows:

$2\ H_2O + 2\ A + (\text{light, chloroplasts}) \rightarrow 2\ AH_2 + O_2$

where A is the electron acceptor. Therefore, in light, the electron acceptor is reduced and oxygen is evolved. Cyt $b_6$, now known as a plastoquinone, is one electron acceptor.

Samuel Ruben and Martin Kamen used radioactive isotopes to determine that the oxygen liberated in photosynthesis came from the water.

Melvin Calvin and Andrew Benson, along with James Bassham, elucidated the path of carbon assimilation (the photosynthetic carbon reduction cycle) in plants. The carbon reduction cycle is known as the Calvin cycle, which ignores the contribution of Bassham and Benson. Many scientists refer to the cycle as the Calvin-Benson Cycle, Benson-Calvin, and some even call it the Calvin-Benson-Bassham (or CBB) Cycle.

Nobel Prize-winning scientist Rudolph A. Marcus was able to discover the function and significance of the electron transport chain.

Otto Heinrich Warburg and Dean Burk discovered the I-quantum photosynthesis reaction that splits the $CO_2$, activated by the respiration.

## Factors

There are three main factors affecting photosynthesis and several corollary factors. The three main are:

- Light irradiance and wavelength
- Carbon dioxide concentration
- Temperature.

## Light Intensity (Irradiance), Wavelength and Temperature

In the early 20th century, Frederick Frost Blackman along with Albert Einstein investigated the effects of light intensity (irradiance) and temperature on the rate of carbon assimilation.

At constant temperature, the rate of carbon assimilation varies with irradiance, initially increasing as the irradiance increases. However, at higher irradiance, this relationship no longer holds and the rate of carbon assimilation reaches a plateau.

At constant irradiance, the rate of carbon assimilation increases as the temperature is increased over a limited range. This effect is seen only at high irradiance levels. At low irradiance, increasing the temperature has little influence on the rate of carbon assimilation.

These two experiments illustrate vital points: First, from research it is known that, in general, photochemical reactions are not affected by temperature. However, these experiments clearly show that temperature affects the rate of carbon assimilation, so there must be two sets of reactions in the full process of carbon assimilation. These are, of course, the light-dependent 'photochemical' stage and the light-independent, temperature-dependent stage. Second, Blackman's experiments illustrate the concept of limiting factors. Another limiting factor is the wavelength of light. Cyanobacteria, which reside several meters underwater, cannot receive the correct wavelengths required to cause photoinduced charge separation in conventional photosynthetic pigments. To combat this problem, a series of proteins with different pigments surround the reaction centre.This unit is called a phycobilisome.

## Carbon Dioxide Levels and Photorespiration

As carbon dioxide concentrations rise, the rate at which sugars are made by the light-independent reactions increases until limited by other factors. RuBisCO, the enzyme that captures carbon dioxide in the light-independent reactions, has a binding affinity for both carbon dioxide and oxygen. When the concentration of carbon dioxide is high, RuBisCO will fix carbon dioxide. However, if the carbon dioxide concentration is low, RuBisCO will bind oxygen instead of carbon dioxide. This process, called photorespiration, uses energy, but does not produce sugars.

RuBisCO oxygenase activity is disadvantageous to plants for several reasons:

- One product of oxygenase activity is phosphoglycolate (2 carbon) instead of 3-phosphoglycerate (3 carbon). Phosphoglycolate cannot be metabolized by the Calvin-Benson cycle and represents carbon lost from the cycle. A high oxygenase activity, therefore, drains the sugars that are required to recycle ribulose 5-bisphosphate and for the continuation of the Calvin-Benson cycle.
- Phosphoglycolate is quickly metabolized to glycolate that is toxic to a plant at a high concentration; it inhibits photosynthesis.
- Salvaging glycolate is an energetically expensive process that uses the glycolate pathway, and only 75 per cent of the carbon is returned to the Calvin-Benson cycle as 3-phosphoglycerate. The reactions also produce ammonia ($NH_3$), which is able to diffuse out of the plant, leading to a loss of nitrogen.

A highly simplified summary is:

2 glycolate + ATP->3-phosphoglycerate + carbon dioxide + ADP +$NH_3$

The salvaging pathway for the products of RuBisCO oxygenase activity is more commonly known as photorespiration, since it is characterized by light-dependent oxygen consumption and the release of carbon dioxide.

## Oxygen Evolution

Oxygen evolution is the process of generating molecular oxygen through chemical reaction. Mechanisms of oxygen evolution include the oxidation of water during oxygenic photosynthesis, electrolysis of water into oxygen and hydrogen, and electrocatalytic oxygen evolution from oxides and oxoacids.

## Oxygen Evolution in Nature

Photosynthetic oxygen evolution is the fundamental process by which breathable oxygen is generated in earth's biosphere. The reaction is part of the light-dependent reactions of photosynthesis in cyanobacteria and the chloroplasts of green algae and plants. It utilizes the energy of light to split a water molecule into its protons and electrons for photosynthesis. Free oxygen is generated as a by-product of this reaction, and is released into the atmosphere.

## Biochemical Reaction

Photosynthetic oxygen evolution occurs via the light-dependent oxidation of water to molecular oxygen and can be written as the following simplified chemical reaction:

$2H_2O$ $4e^-$ + $4H^+$ + $O_2$

The reaction requires the energy of four photons. The electrons from the oxidized water molecules replace electrons in the $P_{680}$ component of photosystem II which have been removed into an electron transport chain via light-dependent excitation and resonance energy transfer onto plastoquinone. Photosytem II therefore has also been referred to as water-plastoquinone oxido-reductase. The protons are released into the thylakoid lumen, thus contributing to the generation of a proton gradient across the thylakoid membrane. This proton gradient is the driving force for ATP synthesis via photophosphorylation and coupling the absorption of light energy and oxidation of water to the creation of chemical energy during photosynthesis.

## Oxygen-evolving Complex

Water oxidation is catalyzed by a manganese-containing cofactor contained in photosystem II known as the oxygen evolving complex (OEC) or water-splitting complex. Manganese is an important cofactor, and calcium and chloride are also required for the reaction to occur.

X-ray crystallography studies have recently provided detailed models of the structure of the oxygen-evolving complex and its manganese cluster. Based on structural and spectroscopic experiments, oxygen evolution involves a core three-plus-one cluster of three manganese ions and one calcium ion, with one additional manganese, which are oxidized via intermediate states called *S-states*. The O-O bond of molecular oxygen is formed between manganese-ligated oxygen atoms at the most oxidized, or S4, state.

## Evolution of Oxygen Evolution

Oxygen production during photosynthesis evolved on earth around 3.5 billion years ago. Oxygen was not only a waste product of this reaction, but was also toxic to many metabolic processes such as nitrogen fixation. Consequently, it was released into the atmosphere as a means of detoxification. This contributed to the conversion of earth's atmosphere from anaerobic to its current aerobic composition, triggering the oxygen catastrophe and the evolution of aerobic metabolism utilizing the oxygen that was released by photosynthetic organisms as part of the oxygen cycle.

## History of Discovery

It wasn't until the end of the 18th century that Joseph Priestley discovered by accident the ability of plants to 'restore' air that had been 'injured' by the burning of a candle. He followed up on the experiment by showing that air 'restored' by vegetation was *"not at all inconvenient to a mouse."* He was later awarded a medal for his discoveries that: *"...no vegetable grows in vain... but cleanses and purifies our atmosphere."* Priestley's experiments were followed up by Jan Ingenhousz, a Dutch physician, who showed that 'restoration' of air only worked in the presence of light and green plant parts.

Ingenhousz suggested in 1796 that $CO_2$ (carbon dioxide) is split during photosynthesis to release oxygen, while the carbon combined with water to form carbohydrates. While this hypothesis was attractive and reasonable and thus widely accepted for a long time, it was later proven incorrect. Graduate student C.B. Van Niel at Stanford University found that purple sulfur bacteria reduce carbon to carbohydrates, but accumulate sulfur instead of releasing oxygen. He boldly proposed that in analogy to the sulfur bacteria forming elemental sulfur from $H_2S$ (hydrogen sulfide), plants would form oxygen from $H_2O$ (water). In 1937, this hypothesis was corroborated by the discovery that plants are capable of producing oxygen in the absence of $CO_2$. This discovery was made by Robin Hill, and subsequently the light-driven release of oxygen in the absence of $CO_2$ was called the *Hill reaction*. Our current knowledge of the mechanism of oxygen evolution during photosynthesis was further established in experiments tracing isotopes of oxygen from water to oxygen gas.

## Technological Oxygen Evolution

Oxygen evolution occurs as a byproduct of hydrogen production via electrolysis of water. While oxygen production is not the main focus of industrial applications of water electrolysis, it becomes essential for life support systems in situations that require the generation of oxygen for air revitalization. Human exploration of regions that lack breathable oxygen, such as the deep sea or outer space, requires means of reliably generating oxygen apart from earth's atmosphere. Submarines and spacecraft utilize either an electrolytic mechanism (water or solid oxide electrolysis) or chemical oxygen generators as part of their life support equipment.

# Carbohydrates

A carbohydrate is an organic compound with the empirical formula $C_m(H_2O)_n$; that is, consists only of carbon, hydrogen, and oxygen, with a hydrogen:oxygen atom ratio of 2:1 (as in water). Carbohydrates can be viewed as hydrates of carbon, hence their name. Structurally however, it is more accurate to view them as polyhydroxy aldehydes and ketones.

The term is most common in biochemistry, where it is a synonym of saccharide. The carbohydrates (saccharides) are divided into four chemical groupings: monosaccharides, disaccharides, oligosaccharides, and polysaccharides. In general, the monosaccharides and disaccharides, which are smaller (lower molecular weight) carbohydrates, are commonly referred to as sugars. The word *saccharide* comes from the Greek word (*sákkharon*), meaning 'sugar'. While the scientific nomenclature of carbohydrates is complex, the names of the monosaccharides and disaccharides very often end in the suffix -ose. For example, blood sugar is the monosaccharide glucose, table sugar is the disaccharide sucrose, and milk sugar is the disaccharide lactose.

Carbohydrates perform numerous roles in living things. Polysaccharides serve for the storage of energy (*e.g.*, starch and glycogen), and as structural components (*e.g.*, cellulose in plants and chitin in arthropods). The 5-carbon monosaccharide ribose is an important component of coenzymes (e.g., ATP, FAD, and NAD) and the backbone of the genetic molecule known as RNA. The related deoxyribose is a component of DNA. Saccharides and their derivatives include many other important biomolecules that play key roles in the immune system, fertilization, preventing pathogenesis, blood clotting, and development. nce and in many informal contexts, the term carbohydrate often means any food that is particularly rich in the complex carbohydrate starch (such as cereals, bread, and pasta) or simple carbohydrates, such as sugar (found in candy, jams, and desserts).

Formerly the name 'carbohydrate' was used in chemistry for any compound with the formula $C_m(H_2O)_n$. Following this definition, some chemists considered formaldehyde $CH_2O$ to be the simplest carbohydrate, while others claimed that title for glycolaldehyde. Today the term is generally understood in the biochemistry sense, which excludes compounds with only one or two carbons.

Natural saccharides are generally built of simple carbohydrates called monosaccharides with general formula $(CH_2O)_n$ where *n* is three or more. A typical monosaccharide has the structure H-$(CHOH)_x$(C=O)-$(CHOH)_y$-H, that is, an aldehyde or ketone with many hydroxyl groups added, usually one on each carbon atom that is not part of the aldehyde or ketone functional group. Examples of monosaccharides are glucose, fructose, and glyceraldehyde. However, some biological substances commonly called 'monosaccharides' do not conform to this formula (*e.g.*, uronic acids and deoxy-sugars such as fucose), and there are many chemicals that do conform to this formula but are not considered to be monosaccharides (*e.g.*, formaldehyde $CH_2O$ and inositol $(CH_2O)_6$).

The open-chain form of a monosaccharide often coexists with a closed ring form where the aldehyde/ketone carbonyl group carbon (C=O) and hydroxyl group (-OH) react forming a hemiacetal with a new C-O-C bridge.

Monosaccharides can be linked together into what are called polysaccharides (or oligosaccharides) in a large variety of ways. Many carbohydrates contain one or more modified monosaccharide units that have had one or more groups replaced or removed. For example, deoxyribose, a component of DNA, is a modified version of ribose; chitin is composed of repeating units of N-acetylglucosamine, a nitrogen-containing form of glucose.

Monosaccharides are classified according to three different characteristics: the placement of its carbonyl group, the number of carbon atoms it contains, and its chiral handedness. If the carbonyl group is an aldehyde, the monosaccharide is an aldose; if the carbonyl group is a ketone, the monosaccharide is a ketose. Monosaccharides with three carbon atoms are called trioses, those with four are called tetroses, five are called pentoses, six are hexoses, and so on. These two systems of classification are often combined. For example, glucose is an aldohexose (a six-carbon aldehyde), ribose is an aldopentose (a five-carbon aldehyde), and fructose is a ketohexose (a six-carbon ketone).

Each carbon atom bearing a hydroxyl group (-OH), with the exception of the first and last carbons, are asymmetric, making them stereocenters with two possible configurations each (R or S). Because of this asymmetry, a number of isomers may exist for any given monosaccharide formula. The aldohexose D-glucose, for example, has the formula $(C{\cdot}H_2O)_6$, of which all but two of its six carbons atoms are stereogenic, making D-glucose one of $2^4 = 16$ possible stereoisomers. In the case of glyceraldehyde, an aldotriose, there is one pair of possible stereoisomers, which are enantiomers and epimers. 1,3-dihydroxyacetone, the ketose corresponding to the aldose glyceraldehyde, is a symmetric molecule with no stereocenters). The assignment of D or L is made according to the orientation of the asymmetric carbon furthest from the carbonyl group: in a standard Fischer projection if the hydroxyl group is on the right the molecule is a D sugar, otherwise it is an L sugar. The 'D-' and 'L-' prefixes should not be confused with 'd-' or 'l-', which indicate the direction that the sugar rotates plane polarized light. This usage of 'd-' and 'l-' is no longer followed in carbohydrate chemistry.

The aldehyde or ketone group of a straight-chain monosaccharide will react reversibly with a hydroxyl group on a different carbon atom to form a hemiacetal or hemiketal, forming a heterocyclic ring with an oxygen bridge between two carbon atoms. Rings with five and six atoms are called furanose and pyranose forms, respectively, and exist in equilibrium with the straight-chain form.

During the conversion from straight-chain form to the cyclic form, the carbon atom containing the carbonyl oxygen, called the anomeric carbon, becomes a stereogenic center with two possible configurations: The oxygen atom may take a position either above or below the plane of the ring. The resulting possible pair of stereoisomers are called anomers. In the *a anomer*, the -OH substituent on the anomeric carbon rests on the opposite side (trans) of the ring from the $CH_2OH$ side branch. The alternative form, in which the $CH_2OH$ substituent and the anomeric hydroxyl are on the same side (cis) of the plane of the ring, is called the *ß anomer*. You can remember that the ß anomer is cis by the mnemonic, "It's always better to ße up". Because the ring and straight-chain forms readily interconvert, both anomers exist in equilibrium.[8] In a Fischer Projection, the a anomer is represented with the anomeric hydroxyl group *trans* to the $CH_2OH$ and *cis* in the ß anomer.

## Use in Living Organisms

Monosaccharides are the major source of fuel for metabolism, being used both as an energy source (glucose being the most important in nature) and in biosynthesis. When monosaccharides are not immediately needed by many cells they are often converted to more space efficient forms, often polysaccharides. In many animals, including humans, this storage form is glycogen, especially in liver and muscle cells. In plants, starch is used for the same purpose.

Two joined monosaccharides are called a disaccharide and these are the simplest polysaccharides. Examples include sucrose and lactose. They are composed of two monosaccharide units bound together by a covalent bond known as a glycosidic linkage formed via a dehydration reaction, resulting in the loss of a hydrogen atom from one monosaccharide and a hydroxyl group from the other. The formula of unmodified disaccharides is $C_{12}H_{22}O_{11}$. Although there are numerous kinds of disaccharides, a handful of disaccharides are particularly notable.

Sucrose, pictured to the right, is the most abundant disaccharide, and the main form in which carbohydrates are transported in plants. It is composed of one D-glucose molecule and one D-fructose molecule. The systematic name for sucrose, *O*-a-D-glucopyranosyl-(1?2)-D-fructofuranoside, indicates four things:

1. *Its monosaccharides:* glucose and fructose.
2. *Their ring types:* glucose is a pyranose, and fructose is a furanose.
3. *How they are linked together:* the oxygen on carbon number 1 (C1) of a-D-glucose is linked to the C2 of D-fructose.
4. The *-oside* suffix indicates that the anomeric carbon of both monosaccharides participates in the glycosidic bond.

Lactose, a disaccharide composed of one D-galactose molecule and one D-glucose molecule, occurs naturally in mammalian milk. The systematic name for lactose is *O*-ß-D-galactopyranosyl-(1?4)-D-glucopyranose. Other notable disaccharides include maltose (two D-glucoses linked a-1,4) and cellulobiose (two D-glucoses linked ß-1,4). disaccharides can be classified into two types.They are reducing and non-reducing disaccahrides if the functional group is present in bonding with another sugar unit it is called as reducing disaccharide.

## Oligosaccharides and Polysaccharides

Amylose is a linear polymer of glucose mainly linked with a(1-4) bonds. It can be made of several thousands of glucose units. It is one of the two components of starch, the other being amylopectin.

Oligosaccharides and polysaccharides are composed of longer chains of monosaccharide units bound together by glycosidic bonds. The distinction between the two is based upon the number of monosaccharide units present in the chain. Oligosaccharides typically contain between three and ten monosaccharide units, and polysaccharides contain greater than ten monosaccharide units. Definitions of how large a carbohydrate must be to fall into each category vary according to personal opinion. Examples of oligosaccharides include the disaccharides mentioned above, the trisaccharide raffinose and the tetrasaccharide stachyose.

Oligosaccharides are found as a common form of protein posttranslational modification. Such posttranslational modifications include the Lewis and ABO oligosaccharides responsible for blood group classifications and so of tissue incompatibilities, the alpha-Gal epitope responsible for hyperacute rejection in xenotransplantation, and O-GlcNAc modifications.

Polysaccharides represent an important class of biological polymers. Their function in living organisms is usually either structure-or storage-related. Starch (a polymer of glucose) is used as a storage polysaccharide in plants, being found in the form of both amylose and the branched amylopectin. In animals, the structurally similar glucose polymer is the more densely branched glycogen, sometimes called 'animal starch'. Glycogen's properties allow it to be metabolized more quickly, which suits the active lives of moving animals.

Cellulose and chitin are examples of structural polysaccharides. Cellulose is used in the cell walls of plants and other organisms, and is claimed to be the most abundant organic molecule on earth. It has many uses such as a significant role in the paper and textile industries, and is used as a feedstock for the production of rayon (via the viscose process), cellulose acetate, celluloid, and nitrocellulose. Chitin has a similar structure, but has nitrogen-containing side branches, increasing its strength. It is found in arthropod exoskeletons and in the cell walls of some fungi. It also has multiple uses, including surgical threads.

Other polysaccharides include callose or laminarin, chrysolaminarin, xylan, arabinoxylan, mannan, fucoidan and galactomannan.

## Nutrition

Foods high in carbohydrate include fruits, sweets, soft drinks, breads, pastas, beans, potatoes, bran, rice, and cereals. Carbohydrates are a common source of energy in living organisms, however, no carbohydrate is an essential nutrient in humans.

Carbohydrates are not necessary building blocks of other molecules, and the body can obtain all its energy from protein and fats. The brain and neurons generally cannot burn fat for energy, but use glucose or ketones. Humans can synthesize some glucose (in a set of processes known as gluconeogenesis) from specific amino acids, from the glycerol backbone in triglycerides and in some cases from fatty acids. Carbohydrate contains 15.8 kilojoules (3.75 kilocalories) and proteins 16.8 kilojoules (4 kilocalories) per gram, while fats contain 37.8 kilojoules (9 kilocalories) per gram. In the case of protein, this is somewhat misleading as only some amino acids are usable for fuel.

Organisms typically cannot metabolize all types of carbohydrate to yield energy. Glucose is a nearly universal and accessible source of calories. Many organisms also have the ability to metabolize other monosaccharides and Disaccharides, though glucose is preferred. In *Escherichia coli*, for example, the *lac* operon will express enzymes for the digestion of lactose when it is present, but if both lactose and glucose are present the *lac* operon is repressed, resulting in the glucose being used first. Polysaccharides are also common sources of energy. Many organisms can easily break down starches into glucose, however, most organisms cannot metabolize cellulose or other polysaccharides like chitin and arabinoxylans. These carbohydrates types can be metabolized by some bacteria and protists. Ruminants and termites, for example, use microorganisms to process cellulose. Even though these complex carbohydrates are not very digestible, they may comprise important dietary elements for humans. Called dietary fiber, these carbohydrates enhance digestion among other benefits.

Based on the effects on risk of heart disease and obesity, the Institute of Medicine recommends that American and Canadian adults get between 45-65 per cent of dietary energy from carbohydrates. The Food and Agriculture Organization and World Health Organization jointly recommend that national dietary guidelines set a goal of 55-75 per cent of total energy from carbohydrates, but only 10 per cent directly from sugars (their term for simple carbohydrates).

## Classification

Historically nutritionists have classified carbohydrates as either simple or complex, however, the exact delineation of these categories is ambiguous. Today, simple carbohydrate typically refers to monosaccharides and disaccharides and complex carbohydrate means polysaccharides (and oligosaccharides). However, the term *complex carbohydrate* was first used in slightly different context in the U.S. Senate Select Committee on Nutrition and Human Needs publication *Dietary Goals for the United States* (1977). In this work, complex carbohydrate were defined as "fruit, vegetables and whole-grains". Some nutritionists use complex carbohydrate to refer to any sort of digestible saccharide present in a whole food, where fiber, vitamins and minerals are also found (as opposed to processed carbohydrates, which provide calories but few other nutrients).

A commonly held belief, even among nutritionists, is that complex carbohydrates (polysaccharides, *e.g.* starches) are digested more slowly than simple carbohydrates (sugars) and thus are healthier.

However, there appears to be no significant difference between simple and complex carbs in terms of their effect on blood sugar Some simple carbohydrates (*e*.g. fructose) are digested very slowly, while some complex carbohydrates (starches), especially if processed, raise blood sugar rapidly. The speed of digestion is determined by a variety of factors including which other nutrients are consumed with the carbohydrate, how the food is prepared, individual differences in metabolism, and the chemistry of the carbohydrate.

Dietary guidelines generally recommend that complex carbohydrates (starches) and nutrient-rich simple carbohydrates such as fruits and vegetables, and dairy products make up the bulk of carbohydrate consumption. Highly processed sources of carbohydrate such as corn or potato chips, candy, sugary drinks, pastries and white rice are generally considered unhealthy in excess.

The USDA's *Dietary Guidelines for Americans 2005* dispensed with the simple/complex distinction, instead recommending fiber-rich foods and whole grains.

The glycemic index and glycemic load concepts have been developed to characterize food behaviour during human digestion. They rank carbohydrate-rich foods based on the rapidity and magnitude of their effect on blood glucose levels. Glycemic index is a measure of how quickly food glucose is absorbed, while glycemic load is a measure of the total absorbable glucose in foods. The insulin index is a similar, more recent classification method that ranks foods based on their effects on blood insulin levels, which are caused by glucose (or starch) and some amino acids in food.

Catabolism is the metabolic reaction cells undergo to extract energy. There are two major metabolic pathways of monosaccharide catabolism: glycolysis and the citric acid cycle.

In glycolysis, oligo/polysaccharides are cleaved first to smaller monosaccharides by enzymes called glycoside hydrolases. The monosaccharide units can then enter into monosaccharide catabolism. In some cases, as with humans, not all carbohydrate types are usable as the digestive and metabolic enzymes necessary are not present.

## Carbohydrate Metabolism

Carbohydrate metabolism denotes the various biochemical processes responsible for the formation, breakdown and interconversion of carbohydrates in living organisms.

The most important carbohydrate is glucose, a simple sugar (monosaccharide) that is metabolized by nearly all known organisms. Glucose and other carbohydrates are part of a wide variety of metabolic pathways across species: plants synthesize carbohydrates from atmospheric gases by photosynthesis storing the absorbed energy internally, often in the form of starch or lipids. Plant components are eaten by animals and fungi, and used as fuel for cellular respiration. Oxidation of one gram of carbohydrate yields approximately 4 kcal of energy and from lipids about 9 kcal. Energy obtained from metabolism (*e.g*. oxidation of glucose) is usually stored temporarily within cells in the form of ATP. Organisms capable of aerobic respiration metabolize glucose and oxygen to release energy with carbon dioxide and water as byproducts.

Carbohydrates are a superior short-term fuel for organisms because they are simpler to metabolize than fats or those amino acid portions of proteins that are used for fuel. In animals, the most important carbohydrate is glucose; so much so, that the level of glucose is used as the main control for the central metabolic hormone, insulin. Starch, and cellulose in a few organisms (*e.g*., termites, ruminants, and some bacteria), both being glucose polymers, are disassembled during digestion and absorbed as glucose. Some simple carbohydrates have their own enzymatic oxidation pathways, as do only a few of the more complex carbohydrates. The disaccharide lactose, for instance, requires the enzyme lactase to be broken into its monosaccharides components; many animals lack this enzyme in adulthood.

Carbohydrates are typically stored as long polymers of glucose molecules with glycosidic bonds for structural support (*e.g.* chitin, cellulose) or for energy storage (*e.g.* glycogen, starch). However, the strong affinity of most carbohydrates for water makes storage of large quantities of carbohydrates inefficient due to the large molecular weight of the solvated water-carbohydrate complex. In most organisms, excess carbohydrates are regularly catabolised to form acetyl-CoA, which is a feed stock for the fatty acid synthesis pathway; fatty acids, triglycerides, and other lipids are commonly used for long-term energy storage. The hydrophobic character of lipids makes them a much more compact form of energy storage than hydrophilic carbohydrates. However, animals, including humans, lack the necessary enzymatic machinery and so do not synthesize glucose from lipids.

All carbohydrates share a general formula of approximately $C_nH_{2n}O_n$; glucose is $C_6H_{12}O_6$. Monosaccharides may be chemically bonded together to form disaccharides such as sucrose and longer polysaccharides such as starch and cellulose.

Oligo/polysaccharides are typically cleaved into smaller monosaccharides by enzymes called glycoside hydrolases. The monosaccharide units then enter monosaccharide catabolism. Organisms vary in the range of monosaccharides they can absorb and use, and also in the range of more complex carbohydrates they are capable of disassembling.

## Metabolic Pathways

- Carbon fixation, or photosynthesis, in which $CO_2$ is reduced to carbohydrate.
- Glycolysis — the oxidation metabolism of glucose molecules to obtain ATP and pyruvate.

- Pyruvate from glycolysis enters the Krebs cycle, also known as the citric acid cycle, in aerobic organisms after moving through pyruvate dehydrogenase complex.
- The pentose phosphate pathway, which acts in the conversion of hexoses into pentoses and in NADPH regeneration.
- Glycogenesis — the conversion of excess glucose into glycogen as a cellular storage mechanism; this prevents excessive osmotic pressure buildup inside the cell.
- Glycogenolysis — the breakdown of glycogen into glucose, which provides a glucose supply for glucose-dependent tissues.
- Gluconeogenesis — *de novo* synthesis of glucose molecules from simple organic compounds. an example in humans is the conversion of a few amino acids in cellular protein to glucose.

Metabolic use of glucose is highly important as an energy source for muscle cells and in the brain, and red blood cells.

## Glucoregulation

Glucoregulation is the maintenance of steady levels of glucose in the body; it is part of homeostasis, and so keeps a constant internal environment around cells in the body.

The hormone insulin is the primary regulatory signal in animals, suggesting that the basic mechanism is very old and very central to animal life. When present, it causes many tissue cells to take up glucose from the circulation, causes some cells to store glucose internally in the form of glycogen, causes some cells to take in and hold lipids, and in many cases controls cellular electrolyte balances and amino acid uptake as well. Its absence turns off glucose uptake into cells, reverses electrolyte adjustments, begins glycogen breakdown and glucose release into the circulation by some cells, begins lipid release *from* lipid storage cells, etc. The level of circulatory glucose (known informally as 'blood sugar') is the most important signal to the insulin producing cells. Because the level of circulatory glucose is largely determined by the intake of dietary carbohydrates, diet controls major aspects of metabolism via insulin. In humans, insulin is made by beta cells in the pancreas, fat is stored in adipose tissue cells, and glycogen is both stored and released as needed by liver cells. Regardless of insulin levels, no glucose is released to the blood from internal glycogen stores from muscle cells.

The hormone glucagon, on the other hand, has an effect opposite to that of insulin, forcing the conversion of glycogen in liver cells to glucose, which is then released into the blood. Muscle cells, however, lack the ability to export glucose into the blood. The release of glucagon is precipitated by low levels of blood glucose. Other hormones, notably growth hormone, cortisol, and certain catecholamines (such as epinepherine) have glucoregulatory actions similar to glucagon.

# Plant Hormone

Plant hormones (also known as phytohormones) are chemicals that regulate plant growth, which, in the UK, are termed 'plant growth substances'. Plant hormones are signal molecules produced within the plant, and occur in extremely low concentrations. Hormones regulate cellular processes in targeted cells locally and when moved to other locations, in other locations of the plant. Hormones also determine the formation of flowers, stems, leaves, the shedding of leaves, and the development and ripening of fruit. Plants, unlike animals, lack glands that produce and secrete hormones, instead each cell is capable of producing hormones. Plant hormones shape the plant, affecting seed growth, time of flowering, the sex of flowers, senescence of leaves and fruits. They affect which tissues grow upward and which grow downward, leaf formation and stem growth, fruit development and ripening, plant longevity, and even plant death. Hormones are vital to plant growth and lacking them, plants would be mostly a mass of undifferentiated cells.

The word hormone is derived from Greek, meaning 'set in motion.' Plant hormones affect gene expression and transcription levels, cellular division, and growth. They are naturally produced within plants, though very similar chemicals are produced by fungi and bacteria that can also affect plant growth. A large number of related chemical compounds are synthesized by humans, they are used to regulate the growth of cultivated plants, weeds, and in vitro-grown plants and plant cells; these manmade compounds are called Plant Growth Regulators or PGRs for short. Early in the study of plant hormones, 'phytohormone' was the commonly used term, but its use is less widely applied now.

Plant hormones are not nutrients, but chemicals that in small amounts promote and influence the growth, development, and differentiation of cells and tissues. The biosynthesis of plant hormones within plant tissues is often diffuse and not always localized. Plants lack glands to produce and store hormones, because, unlike animals, which have two circulatory systems (lymphatic and cardiovascular) powered by a heart that moves fluids around the body, plants use more passive means to move chemicals around the plant. Plants utilize simple chemicals as hormones, which move more easily through the plant's tissues. They are often produced and used on a local basis within the plant body, plant cells even produce hormones that affect different regions of the cell producing the hormone.

Hormones are transported within the plant by utilizing four types of movements. For localized movement, cytoplasmic streaming within cells and slow diffusion of ions and molecules between cells are utilized. Vascular tissues are used to move hormones from one part of the plant to another; these include sieve tubes that move sugars from the leaves to the roots and flowers, and xylem that moves water and mineral solutes from the roots to the foliage.

Not all plant cells respond to hormones, but those cells that do are programmed to respond at specific points in their growth cycle. The greatest effects occur at specific stages during the cell's life, with diminished effects occurring before or after this period. Plants need hormones at very specific times during plant growth and at specific locations. They also need to disengage the effects that hormones have when they are no longer needed. The production of hormones occurs very often at sites of active growth within the meristems, before cells have fully differentiated. After production they are sometimes moved to other parts of the plant where they cause an immediate effect or they can be stored in cells to be released later. Plants use different pathways to regulate internal hormone quantities and moderate their effects; they can regulate the amount of chemicals used to biosynthesize hormones. They can store them in cells, inactivate them, or cannibalise already-formed hormones by conjugating them with carbohydrates, amino acids or peptides. Plants can also break down hormones chemically, effectively destroying them. Plant hormones frequently regulate the concentrations of other plant hormones. Plants also move hormones around the plant diluting their concentrations.

The concentration of hormones required for plant responses are very low ($10^{-6}$ to $10^{-5}$ mol/L). Because of these low concentrations, it has been very difficult to study plant hormones, and only since the late 1970s have scientists been able to start piecing together their effects and relationships to plant physiology. Much of the early work on plant hormones involved studying plants that were genetically deficient in one or involved the use of tissue-cultured plants grown *in vitro* that were subjected to differing ratios of hormones, and the resultant growth compared. The earliest scientific observation and study dates to the 1880s; the determination and observation of plant hormones and their identification was spread-out over the next 70 years.

## Classes of Plant Hormones

In general it is accepted that there are five major classes of plant hormones, some of which are made up of many different chemicals that can vary in structure from one plant to the next. The chemicals are each grouped together into one of these classes based on their structural similarities and on their effects on plant physiology. Other plant hormones and growth regulators are not easily grouped into these classes; they exist naturally or are synthesized by humans or other organisms, including chemicals that inhibit plant growth or interrupt the physiological processes within plants. Each class has positive as well as inhibitory functions, and most often work in tandem with each other, with varying ratios of one or more interplaying to affect growth regulation.

## Abscisic Acid

Abscisic acid also called ABA, was discovered and researched under two different names before its chemical properties were fully known, it was called *dormin* and *abscicin II*. Once it was determined that the two latter compounds were the same; it was named abscisic acid. The name 'abscisic acid' was given because it was found in high concentrations in newly abscissed or freshly fallen leaves.

This class of PGR is composed of one chemical compound normally produced in the leaves of plants, originating from chloroplasts, especially when plants are under stress. In general, it acts as an inhibitory chemical compound that affects bud growth, seed and bud dormancy. It mediates changes within the apical meristem causing bud dormancy and the alteration of the last set of leaves into protective bud covers. Since it was found in freshly abscissed leaves, it was thought to play a role in the processes of natural leaf drop but further research has disproven this. In plant species from temperate parts of the world it plays a role in leaf and seed dormancy by inhibiting growth, but, as it is dissipated from seeds or buds, growth begins. In other plants, as ABA levels decrease, growth then commences as gibberellin levels increase. Without ABA, buds and seeds would start to grow during warm periods in winter and be killed when it froze again. Since ABA dissipates slowly from the tissues and its effects take time to be offset by other plant hormones, there is a delay in physiological pathways that provide some protection from premature growth. It accumulates within seeds during fruit maturation, preventing seed germination within the fruit, or seed germination before winter. Abscisic acid's effects are degraded within plant tissues during cold temperatures or by its removal by water washing in out of the tissues, releasing the seeds and buds from dormancy.

In plants under water stress, ABA plays a role in closing the stomata. Soon after plants are water-stressed and the roots are deficient in water, a signal moves up to the leaves, causing the formation of ABA precursors there, which then move to the roots. The roots then release ABA, which is translocated to the foliage through the vascular system and modulates the potassium and sodium uptake within the guard cells, which then lose turgidity, closing the stomata. ABA exists in all parts of the plant and its concentration within any tissue seems to mediate its effects and function as a hormone; its degradation, or more properly catabolism, within the plant affects metabolic reactions and cellular growth and production of other hormones. Plants start life as a seed with high ABA levels, just before the seed germinates ABA levels decrease; during germination and early growth of the seedling, ABA levels decrease even more. As plants begin to produce shoots with fully functional leaves — ABA levels begin to increase, slowing down cellular growth in more 'mature' areas of the plant. Stress from water or predation affects ABA production and catabolism rates, mediating another cascade of effects that trigger specific responses from targeted cells. Scientists are still piecing together the complex interactions and effects of this and other phytohormones.

## Auxins

Auxins are compounds that positively influence cell enlargement, bud formation and root initiation. They also promote the production of other hormones and in conjunction with cytokinins, they control the growth of stems, roots, and fruits, and convert stems into flowers. Auxins were the first class of growth regulators discovered. They affect cell elongation by altering cell wall plasticity. Auxins decrease in light and increase where it is dark. They stimulate cambium, a subtype of meristem cells, to divide and in stems cause secondary xylem to differentiate. Auxins act to inhibit the growth of buds lower down the stems (apical dominance), and also to promote lateral and adventitious root development and growth. Leaf abscission is initiated by the growing point of a plant ceasing to produce auxins. Auxins in seeds regulate specific protein synthesis, as they develop within the flower after pollination, causing the flower to develop a fruit to contain the developing seeds. Auxins are toxic to plants in large concentrations; they are most toxic to dicots and less so to monocots. Because of this property, synthetic auxin herbicides including 2,4-D and 2,4,5-T have been developed and used for weed control. Auxins, especially 1-Naphthaleneacetic acid (NAA) and Indole-3-butyric acid (IBA), are also commonly applied to stimulate root growth when taking cuttings of plants. The most common auxin found in plants is indoleacetic acid or IAA. The correlation of auxins and cytokinins in the plants is a constant (A/C = const.).

### Cytokinins

Cytokinins or CKs are a group of chemicals that influence cell division and shoot formation. They were called kinins in the past when the first cytokinins were isolated from yeast cells. They also help delay senescence or the aging of tissues, are responsible for mediating auxin transport throughout the plant, and affect internodal length and leaf growth. They have a highly synergistic effect in concert with auxins and the ratios of these two groups of plant hormones affect most major growth periods during a plant's lifetime. Cytokinins counter the apical dominance induced by auxins; they in conjunction with ethylene promote abscission of leaves, flower parts and fruits. The correlation of auxins and cytokinins in the plants is a constant (A/C = const.).

### Ethylene

Ethylene is a gas that forms through the Yang Cycle from the breakdown of methionine, which is in all cells. Ethylene has very limited solubility in water and does not accumulate within the cell but diffuses out of the cell and escapes out of the plant. Its effectiveness as a plant hormone is dependent on its rate of production versus its rate of escaping into the atmosphere. Ethylene is produced at a faster rate in rapidly growing and dividing cells, especially in darkness. New growth and newly germinated seedlings produce more ethylene than can escape the plant, which leads to elevated amounts of ethylene, inhibiting leaf expansion. As the new shoot is exposed to light, reactions by phytochrome in the plant's cells produce a signal for ethylene production to decrease, allowing leaf expansion. Ethylene affects cell growth and cell shape; when a growing shoot hits an obstacle while underground, ethylene production greatly increases, preventing cell elongation and causing the stem to swell. The resulting thicker stem can exert more pressure against the object impeding its path to the surface. If the shoot does not reach the surface and the ethylene stimulus becomes prolonged, it affects the stems natural geotropic response, which is to grow upright, allowing it to grow around an object. Studies seem to indicate that ethylene affects stem diameter and height: When stems of trees are subjected to wind, causing lateral stress, greater ethylene production occurs, resulting in thicker, more sturdy tree trunks and branches. Ethylene affects fruit-ripening: Normally, when the seeds are mature, ethylene production increases and builds-up within the fruit, resulting in a climacteric event just before seed dispersal. The nuclear protein Ethylene Insensitive (EIN2) is regulated by ethylene production, and, in turn, regulates other hormones including ABA and stress hormones.

### Gibberellins

Gibberellins, or GAs, include a large range of chemicals that are produced naturally within plants and by fungi. They were first discovered when Japanese researchers, including Eiichi Kurosawa, noticed a chemical produced by a fungus called *Gibberella fujikuroi* that produced abnormal growth in rice plants. Gibberellins are important in seed germination, affecting enzyme production that mobilizes food production used for growth of new cells. This is done by modulating chromosomal transcription. In grain (rice, wheat, corn, etc.) seeds, a layer of cells called the aleurone layer wraps around the endosperm tissue. Absoption of water by the seed causes production of GA. The GA is transported to the aleurone layer, which responds by producing enzymes that break down stored food reserves within the endosperm, which are utilized by the growing seedling. GAs produce bolting of rosette-forming plants, increasing internodal length. They promote flowering, cellular division, and in seeds growth after germination. Gibberellins also reverse the inhibition of shoot growth and dormancy induced by ABA.

### Other Known Hormones

Other identified plant growth regulators include:

- Brassinosteroids, are a class of polyhydroxysteroids, a group of plant growth regulators. Brassinosteroids have been recognized as a sixth class of plant hormones which stimulate cell elongation and division, gravitropism, resistance to stress and xylem differentiation. They inhibit root growth and leaf abscission. Brassinolide was the first identified brassinosteroid and was isolated from organic extracts of rapeseed (*Brassica napus*) pollen in 1970.
- Salicylic acid — activates genes in some plants that produce chemicals that aid in the defense against pathogenic invaders.
- Jasmonates — are produced from fatty acids and seem to promote the production of defense proteins that are used to fend off invading organisms. They are believed to also have a role in seed germination, and affect the storage of protein in seeds, and seem to affect root growth.
- Plant peptide hormones — encompasses all small secreted peptides that are involved in cell-to-cell signaling. These small peptide hormones play crucial roles in plant growth and development, including defense mechanisms, the control of cell division and expansion, and pollen self-incompatibility.

- Polyamines — are strongly basic molecules with low molecular weight that have been found in all organisms studied thus far. They are essential for plant growth and development and affect the process of mitosis and meiosis.
- Nitric oxide (NO) — serves as signal in hormonal and defense responses.
- Strigolactones, implicated in the inhibition of shoot branching.
- Karrikins, a group of plant growth regulators found in the smoke of burning plant material that have the ability to stimulate the germination of seeds.

## Potential Medical Applications

Plant stress hormones activate cellular responses, including cell death, to diverse stress situations in plants. Researchers have found that some plant stress hormones share the ability to adversely affect human cancer cells . For example, sodium salicylate has been found to suppress proliferation of lymphoblastic leukemia, prostate, breast, and melanoma human cancer cells. Jasmonic acid, a plant stress hormone that belongs to the jasmonate family, induced death in lymphoblastic leukemia cells. Methyl jasmonate has been found to induce cell death in a number of cancer cell lines.

## Hormones and Plant Propagation

Synthetic plant hormones or PGRs are commonly used in a number of different techniques involving plant propagation from cuttings, grafting, micropropagation, and tissue culture.

The propagation of plants by cuttings of fully developed leaves, stems, or roots is performed by gardeners utilizing auxin as a rooting compound applied to the cut surface; the auxins are taken into the plant and promote root initiation. In grafting, auxin promotes callus tissue formation, which joins the surfaces of the graft together. In micropropagation, different PGRs are used to promote multiplication and then rooting of new plantlets. In the tissue-culturing of plant cells, PGRs are used to produce callus growth, multiplication, and rooting.

Plant hormones affect seed germinations and dormancy by affecting different parts of the seed.

Embryo dormancy is characterized by a high ABA/GA ratio, whereas the seed has a high ABA sensitivity and low GA sensitivity. To release the seed from this type of dormancy and initiate seed germination, an alteration in hormone biosynthesis and degradation towards a low ABA/GA ratio, along with a decrease in ABA sensitivity and an increase in GA sensitivity needs to occur.

ABA controls embryo dormancy, and GA embryo germination. Seed coat dormancy involves the mechanical restriction of the seed coat, this along with a low embryo growth potential, effectively produces seed dormancy. GA releases this dormancy by increasing the embryo growth potential, and/or weakening the seed coat so the radical of the seedling can break through the seed coat. Different types of seed coats can be made up of living or dead cells and both types can be influenced by hormones; those composed of living cells are acted upon after seed formation while the seed coats composed of dead cells can be influenced by hormones during the formation of the seed coat.

ABA affects testa or seed coat growth characteristics, including thickness, and effects the GA-mediated embryo growth potential. These conditions and effects occur during the formation of the seed, often in response to environmental conditions. Hormones also mediate endosperm dormancy: Endosperm in most seeds is composed of living tissue that can actively respond to hormones generated by the embryo. The endosperm often acts as a barrier to seed germination, playing a part in seed coat dormancy or in the germination process. Living cells respond to and also affect the ABA/GA ratio, and mediate cellular sensitivity; GA thus increases the embryo growth potential and can promote endosperm weakening. GA also affects both ABA-independent and ABA-inhibiting processes within the endosperm.

# Flowering Plant

The flowering plants (angiosperms), also known as Angiospermae or Magnoliophyta, are the most diverse group of land plants. Angiosperms are seed-producing plants like the gymnosperms and can be distinguished from the gymnosperms by a series of synapomorphies (derived characteristics). These characteristics include flowers, endosperm within the seeds, and the production of fruits that contain the seeds.

The ancestors of flowering plants diverged from gymnosperms around 245-202 million years ago, and the first flowering plants known to exist are from 140 million years ago. They diversified enormously during the Lower Cretaceous and became widespread around 100 million years ago, but replaced conifers as the dominant trees only around 60-100 million years ago.

## Angiosperm Derived Characteristics

The flowers, which are the reproductive organs of flowering plants, are the most remarkable feature distinguishing them from other seed plants. Flowers aid angiosperms by enabling a wider range of adaptability and broadening the ecological niches open to them. This has allowed flowering plants to largely dominate terrestrial ecosystems.

Stamens are much lighter than the corresponding organs of gymnosperms and have contributed to the diversification of angiosperms through time with adaptations to specialized pollination syndromes, such as particular pollinators. Stamens have also become modified through time to prevent self-fertilization, which has permitted further diversification, allowing angiosperms eventually to fill more niches.

The male gametophyte in angiosperms is significantly reduced in size compared to those of gymnosperm seed plants. The smaller pollen decreases the time from pollination—the pollen grain reaching the female plant—to fertilization of the ovary; in gymnosperms fertilization can occur up to a year after pollination, while in angiosperms the fertilization begins very soon after pollination. The shorter time leads to angiosperm plants setting seeds sooner and faster than gymnosperms, which is a distinct evolutionary advantage.

The closed carpel of angiosperms also allows adaptations to specialized pollination syndromes and controls. This helps to prevent self-fertilization, thereby maintaining increased diversity. Once the ovary is fertilized, the carpel and some surrounding tissues develop into a fruit. This fruit often serves as an attractant to seed-dispersing animals. The resulting cooperative relationship presents another advantage to angiosperms in the process of dispersal.

The reduced female gametophyte, like the reduced male gametophyte, may be an adaptation allowing for more rapid seed set, eventually leading to such flowering plant adaptations as annual herbaceous life cycles, allowing the flowering plants to fill even more niches.

Endosperm formation generally begins after fertilization and before the first division of the zygote. Endosperm is a highly nutritive tissue that can provide food for the developing embryo, the cotyledons, and sometimes for the seedling when it first appears.

These distinguishing characteristics taken together have made the angiosperms the most diverse and numerous land plants and the most commercially important group to humans. The major exception to the dominance of terrestrial ecosystems by flowering plants is the coniferous forest.

Land plants have existed for about 425 million years. Early land plants reproduced sexually with flagellated, swimming sperm, like the green algae from which they evolved. An adaptation to terrestrialization was the development of upright meiosporangia for dispersal by spores to new habitats. This feature is lacking in the descendants of their nearest algal relatives, the Charophycean green algae. A later terrestrial adaptation took place with retention of the delicate, avascular sexual stage, the gametophyte, within the tissues of the vascular sporophyte. This occurred by spore germination within sporangia rather than spore release, as in non-seed plants. A current example of how this might have happened can be seen in the precocious spore germination in *Sellaginella*, the spike-moss. The result for the ancestors of angiosperms was enclosing them in a case, the seed. The first seed bearing plants, like the ginkgo, and conifers (such as pines and firs), did not produce flowers. Interestingly, the pollen grains (males) of *Ginkgo* and cycads produce a pair of flagellated, mobile sperm cells that 'swim' down the developing pollen tube to the female and her eggs.

The apparently sudden appearance of relatively modern flowers in the fossil record initially posed such a problem for the theory of evolution that it was called an *'abominable mystery'* by Charles Darwin. However, the fossil record has considerably grown since the time of Darwin, and recently discovered angiosperm fossils such as *Archaefructus*, along with further discoveries of fossil gymnosperms, suggest how angiosperm characteristics may have been acquired in a series of steps. Several groups of extinct gymnosperms, particularly seed ferns, have been proposed as the ancestors of flowering plants but there is no continuous fossil evidence showing exactly how flowers evolved. Some older fossils, such as the upper Triassic *Sanmiguelia*, have been suggested. Based on current evidence, some propose that the ancestors of the angiosperms diverged from an unknown group of gymnosperms during the late Triassic (245-202 million years ago). A close relationship between angiosperms and gnetophytes, proposed on the basis of morphological evidence, has more recently been disputed on the basis of molecular evidence that suggest gnetophytes are instead more closely related to other gymnosperms.

The evolution of seed plants and later angisperms appear to be the result of two distinct rounds of whole genome duplication events. These occurred in 319 million years ago and 192 million years ago respectively.

The earliest known macrofossil confidently identified as an angiosperm, *Archaefructus liaoningensis*, is dated to about 125 million years BP (the Cretaceous period), while pollen considered to be of angiosperm origin takes the fossil record back to about 130 million years BP. However, one study has suggested that the early-middle Jurassic plant *Schmeissneria*, traditionally considered a type of ginkgo, may be the earliest known angiosperm, or at least a close relative. Additionally, circumstantial chemical evidence has been found for the existence of angiosperms as early as 250 million years ago. Oleanane, a secondary metabolite produced by many flowering plants, has been found in Permian deposits of that age together with fossils of gigantopterids. Gigantopterids are a group of extinct seed plants that share many morphological traits with flowering plants, although they are not known to have been flowering plants themselves.

Recent DNA analysis based on molecular systematics showed that *Amborella trichopoda*, found on the Pacific island of New Caledonia, belongs to a sister group of the other flowering plants, and morphological studies suggest that it has features that may have been characteristic of the earliest flowering plants.

The orders Amborellales, Nymphaeales and Austrobaileyales diverged as separate lineages from the remaining angiosperm clade at a very early stage in flowering plant evolution.

The great angiosperm radiation, when a great diversity of angiosperms appears in the fossil record, occurred in the mid-Cretaceous (approximately 100 million years ago). However, a study in 2007 estimated that the division of the five most recent (the genus *Ceratophyllum*, the family Chloranthaceae, the eudicots, the magnoliids, and the monocots) of the eight main groups occurred around 140 million years ago. By the late Cretaceous, angiosperms appear to have dominated environments formerly occupied by ferns and cycadophytes, but large canopy-forming trees replaced conifers as the dominant trees only close to the end of the Cretaceous 65 millions years ago or even later, at the beginning of the Tertiary. The radiation of herbaceous angiosperm occurred much later. Yet, many fossil plants recognizable as belonging to modern families (including beech, oak, maple, and magnolia) appeared already at late Cretaceous.

It is generally assumed that the function of flowers, from the start, was to involve mobile animals in their reproduction processes. That is, pollen can be scattered even if the flower is not brightly coloured or oddly shaped in a way that attracts animals; however, by expending the energy required to create such traits, angiosperms can enlist the aid of animals and thus reproduce more efficiently.

Island genetics provides one proposed explanation for the sudden, fully developed appearance of flowering plants. Island genetics is believed to be a common source of speciation in general, especially when it comes to radical adaptations that seem to have required inferior transitional forms. Flowering plants may have evolved in an isolated setting like an island or island chain, where the plants bearing them were able to develop a highly specialized relationship with some specific animal (a wasp, for example). Such a relationship, with a hypothetical wasp carrying pollen from one plant to another much the way fig wasps do today, could result in both the plant(s) and their partners developing a high degree of specialization. Note that the wasp example is not incidental; bees, which apparently evolved specifically due to mutualistic plant relationships, are descended from wasps.

Animals are also involved in the distribution of seeds. Fruit, which is formed by the enlargement of flower parts, is frequently a seed-dispersal tool that attracts animals to eat or otherwise disturb it, incidentally scattering the seeds it contains (see frugivory). While many such mutualistic relationships remain too fragile to survive competition and to spread widely, flowering proved to be an unusually effective means of reproduction, spreading (whatever its origin) to become the dominant form of land plant life.

Flower ontogeny uses a combination of genes normally responsible for forming new shoots. The most primitive flowers are thought to have had a variable number of flower parts, often separate from (but in contact with) each other. The flowers would have tended to grow in a spiral pattern, to be bisexual (in plants, this means both male and female parts on the same flower), and to be dominated by the ovary (female part). As flowers grew more advanced, some variations developed parts fused together, with a much more specific number and design, and with either specific sexes per flower or plant, or at least 'ovary inferior'.

Flower evolution continues to the present day; modern flowers have been so profoundly influenced by humans that some of them cannot be pollinated in nature. Many modern, domesticated flowers used to be simple weeds, which only sprouted when the ground was disturbed. Some of them tended to grow with human crops, perhaps already having symbiotic companion plant relationships with them, and the prettiest did not get plucked because of their beauty, developing a dependence upon and special adaptation to human affection.

A few palaeontologists have also come up with a theory that flowering plants, or angiosperms, might possibly have evolved because of dinosaurs; in other words, they believe that dinosaurs 'created' flowers. One of the theory's biggest proponents is Robert T. Bakker. He theorizes that herbivorous dinosaurs, with their eating habits, forced plants to find new ways to develop new adaptations, in order to avoid predation by herbivores.

There are eight groups of living angiosperms:

1. *Amborella* — a single species of shrub from New Caledonia.
2. *Nymphaeales* — about 80 species—Water Lilies and Hydatellaceae.
3. *Austrobaileyales* — about 100 species of woody plants from various parts of the world.
4. *Chloranthales* — several dozen species of aromatic plants with toothed leaves.
5. *Magnoliidae* — about 9,000 species, characterized by trimerous flowers, pollen with one pore, and usually branching-veined leaves—for example magnolias, bay laurel, and black pepper.
6. *Monocotyledonae* — about 70,000 species, characterized by trimerous flowers, a single cotyledon, pollen with one pore, and usually parallel-veined leaves—for example grasses, orchids, and palms.
7. *Ceratophyllum* — about 6 species of aquatic plants, perhaps most familiar as aquarium plants.
8. *Eudicotyledonae* — about 175,000 species, characterized by 4-or 5-merous flowers, pollen with three pores, and usually branching-veined leaves—for example sunflowers, petunia, buttercup, apples and oaks.

The exact relationship between these eight groups is not yet clear, although there is agreement that the first three groups to diverge from the ancestral angiosperm were Amborellales, Nymphaeales, and Austrobaileyales. The term basal angiosperms refers to these three groups. The five other groups form the clade Mesangiospermae. The relationship between the three largest of these groups (magnoliids, monocots and eudicots) remains unclear. Some analyses make the magnoliids the first to diverge, others the monocots. *Ceratophyllum* seems to group with the eudicots rather than with the monocots.

The botanical term 'Angiosperm', from the Ancient Greek, *angeíon* (receptacle, vessel) and sp, (seed), was coined in the form Angiospermae by Paul Hermann in 1690, as the name of that one of his primary divisions of the plant kingdom. This included flowering plants possessing seeds enclosed in capsules, distinguished from his Gymnospermae, or flowering plants with achenial or schizo-carpic fruits, the whole fruit or each of its pieces being here regarded as a seed and naked. The term and its antonym were maintained by Carolus Linnaeus with the same sense, but with restricted application, in the names of the orders of his class Didynamia. Its use with any approach to its modern scope only became possible after 1827, when Robert Brown established the existence of truly naked ovules in the Cycadeae and Coniferae, and applied to them the name Gymnosperms. From that time onwards, so long as these Gymnosperms were, as was usual, reckoned as dicotyledonous flowering plants, the term Angiosperm was used antithetically by botanical writers, with varying scope, as a group-name for other dicotyledonous plants.

In 1851, Hofmeister discovered the changes occurring in the embryo-sac of flowering plants, and determined the correct relationships of these to the Cryptogamia. This fixed the position of Gymnosperms as a class distinct from Dicotyledons, and the term Angiosperm then gradually came to be accepted as the suitable designation for the whole of the flowering plants other than Gymnosperms, including the classes of Dicotyledons and Monocotyledons. This is the sense in which the term is used today.

In most taxonomies, the flowering plants are treated as a coherent group. The most popular descriptive name has been Angiospermae (Angiosperms), with Anthophyta ("flowering plants") a second choice. These names are not linked to any rank. The Wettstein system and the Engler system use the name Angiospermae, at the assigned rank of subdivision. The Reveal system treated flowering plants as subdivision Magnoliophytina, but later split it to Magnoliopsida, Liliopsida and Rosopsida. The Takhtajan system and Cronquist system treat this group at the rank of division, leading to the name Magnoliophyta (from the family name Magnoliaceae). The

Dahlgren system and Thorne system (1992) treat this group at the rank of class, leading to the name Magnoliopsida. The APG system of 1998, and the later 2003 and 2009 revisions, treat the flowering plants as a clade called angiosperms without a formal botanical name. However, a formal classification was published alongside the 2009 revision in which the flowering plants form the Subclass Magnoliidae.

The internal classification of this group has undergone considerable revision. The Cronquist system, proposed by Arthur Cronquist in 1968 and published in its full form in 1981, is still widely used but is no longer believed to accurately reflect phylogeny. A consensus about how the flowering plants should be arranged has recently begun to emerge through the work of the Angiosperm Phylogeny Group (APG), which published an influential reclassification of the angiosperms in 1998. Updates incorporating more recent research were published as APG II in 2003 and as APG III in 2009.

Traditionally, the flowering plants are divided into two groups, which in the Cronquist system are called *Magnoliopsida* (at the rank of class, formed from the family name *Magnoliacae*) and *Liliopsida* (at the rank of class, formed from the family name *Liliaceae*). Other descriptive names allowed by Article 16 of the ICBN include *Dicotyledones* or *Dicotyledoneae*, and *Monocotyledones* or *Monocotyledoneae*, which have a long history of use. In English a member of either group may be called a *dicotyledon* (plural *dicotyledons*) and *monocotyledon* (plural *monocotyledons*), or abbreviated, as *dicot* (plural *dicots*) and *monocot* (plural *monocots*). These names derive from the observation that the dicots most often have two *cotyledons*, or embryonic leaves, within each seed. The monocots usually have only one, but the rule is not absolute either way. From a diagnostic point of view the number of cotyledons is neither a particularly handy nor reliable character.

Recent studies, as by the APG, show that the monocots form a monophyletic group (clade) but that the dicots do not (they are paraphyletic). Nevertheless, the majority of dicot species do form a monophyletic group, called the *eudicots* or *tricolpates*. Of the remaining dicot species, most belong to a third major clade known as the Magnoliidae, containing about 9,000 species. The rest include a paraphyletic grouping of primitive species known collectively as the basal angiosperms, plus the families Ceratophyllaceae and Chloranthaceae.

## Flowering Plant Diversity

The number of species of flowering plants is estimated to be in the range of 250,000 to 400,000. The number of families in APG (1998) was 462. In APG II 2003) it is not settled; at maximum it is 457, but within this number there are 55 optional segregates, so that the minimum number of families in this system is 402. In APG III (2009) there are 415 families.

The diversity of flowering plants is not evenly distributed. Nearly all species belong to the eudicot (75%), monocot (23%) and magnoliid (2%) clades. The remaining 5 clades contain a little over 250 species in total, *i.e.*, less than 0.1 per cent of flowering plant diversity, divided among 9 families.

The amount and complexity of tissue-formation in flowering plants exceeds that of gymnosperms. The vascular bundles of the stem are arranged such that the xylem and phloem form concentric rings.

In the dicotyledons, the bundles in the very young stem are arranged in an open ring, separating a central pith from an outer cortex. In each bundle, separating the xylem and phloem, is a layer of meristem or active formative tissue known as cambium. By the formation of a layer of cambium between the bundles (interfascicular cambium) a complete ring is formed, and a regular periodical increase in thickness results from the development of xylem on the inside and phloem on the outside. The soft phloem becomes crushed, but the hard wood persists and forms the bulk of the stem and branches of the woody perennial. Owing to differences in the character of the elements produced at the beginning and end of the season, the wood is marked out in transverse section into concentric rings, one for each season of growth, called annual rings.

Among the monocotyledons, the bundles are more numerous in the young stem and are scattered through the ground tissue. They contain no cambium and once formed the stem increases.

The characteristic feature of angiosperms is the flower. Flowers show remarkable variation in form and elaboration, and provide the most trustworthy external characteristics for establishing relationships among angiosperm species. The function of the flower is to ensure fertilization of the ovule and development of fruit containing seeds. The floral apparatus may arise terminally on a shoot or from the axil of a leaf (where the petiole attaches to the stem). Occasionally, as in violets, a flower arises singly in the axil of an ordinary foliage-leaf. More typically, the flower-bearing portion of the plant is sharply distinguished from the foliage-bearing or vegetative portion, and forms a more or less elaborate branch-system called an inflorescence.

The reproductive cells produced by flowers are of two kinds. Microspores, which will divide to become pollen grains, are the 'male' cells and are borne in the stamens (or microsporophylls). The 'female' cells called megaspores, which will divide to become the egg-cell (megagameto-genesis), are contained in the ovule and enclosed in the carpel (or megasporophyll).

The flower may consist only of these parts, as in willow, where each flower comprises only a few stamens or two carpels. Usually other structures are present and serve to protect the sporophylls and to form an envelope attractive to pollinators. The individual members of these surrounding structures are known as sepals and petals (or tepals in flowers such as *Magnolia* where sepals and petals are not distinguishable from each other). The outer series (calyx of sepals) is usually green and leaf-like, and functions to protect the rest of the flower, especially the bud. The inner series (corolla of petals) is generally white or brightly coloured, and is more delicate in structure. It functions to attract insect or bird pollinators. Attraction is effected by colour, scent, and nectar, which may be secreted in some part of the flower. The characteristics that attract pollinators account for the popularity of flowers and flowering plants among humans.

While the majority of flowers are perfect or hermaphrodite (having both male and female parts in the same flower structure), flowering plants have developed numerous morphological and physiological mechanisms to reduce or prevent self-fertilization. Heteromorphic flowers have short carpels and long stamens, or vice versa, so animal pollinators cannot easily transfer pollen to the pistil (receptive part of the carpel). Homomorphic flowers may employ a biochemical (physiological) mechanism called self-incompatibility to discriminate between self- and non-self pollen grains. In other species, the male and female parts are morphologically separated, developing on different flowers.

Double fertilization refers to a process in which two sperm cells fertilize cells in the ovary. This process begins when a pollen grain adheres to the stigma of the pistil (female reproductive structure), germinates, and grows a long pollen tube. While this pollen tube is growing, a haploid generative cell travels down the tube behind the tube nucleus. The generative cell divides by mitosis to produce two haploid (*n*) sperm cells. As the pollen tube grows, it makes its way from the stigma, down the style and into the ovary. Here the pollen tube reaches the micropyle of the ovule and digests its way into one of the synergids, releasing its contents (which include the sperm cells). The synergid that the cells were released into degenerates and one sperm makes its way to fertilize the egg cell, producing a diploid (2*n*) zygote. The second sperm cell fuses with both central cell nuclei, producing a triploid (3*n*) cell. As the zygote develops into an embryo, the triploid cell develops into the endosperm, which serves as the embryo's food supply. The ovary now will develop into fruit and the ovule will develop into seed.

As the development of embryo and endosperm proceeds within the embryo-sac, the sac wall enlarges and combines with the nucellus (which is likewise enlarging) and the integument to form the *seed-coat*. The ovary wall develops to form the fruit or pericarp, whose form is closely associated with the manner of distribution of the seed.

Frequently the influence of fertilization is felt beyond the ovary, and other parts of the flower take part in the formation of the fruit, *e.g.* the floral receptacle in the apple, strawberry and others.

The character of the seed-coat bears a definite relation to that of the fruit. They protect the embryo and aid in dissemination; they may also directly promote germination. Among plants with indehiscent fruits, the fruit generally provides protection for the embryo and secures dissemination. In this case, the seed-coat is only slightly developed. If the fruit is dehiscent and the seed is exposed, the seed-coat is generally well developed, and must discharge the functions otherwise executed by the fruit.

## Economic Importance

Agriculture is almost entirely dependent on angiosperms, either directly or indirectly through livestock feed. Of all the families plants, the Poaceae, or grass family, is by far the most important, providing the bulk of all feedstocks (rice, corn—maize, wheat, barley, rye, oats, pearl millet, sugarcane, sorghum). The Fabaceae, or legume family, comes in second place. Also of high importance are the Solanaceae, or nightshade family (potatoes, tomatoes, and peppers, among others), the Cucurbitaceae, or gourd family (also including pumpkins and melons), the Brassicaceae, or mustard plant family (including rapeseed and the innumerable varieties of the cabbage species *Brassica oleracea*), and the Apiaceae, or parsley family. Many of our fruits come from the Rutaceae, or rue family, and the Rosaceae, or rose family (including apples, pears, cherries, apricots, plums, etc.).

In some parts of the world, certain single species assume paramount importance because of their variety of uses, for example the coconut (*Cocos nucifera*) on Pacific atolls, and the olive (*Olea europaea*) in the Mediterranean region.

Flowering plants also provide economic resources in the form of wood, paper, fiber (cotton, flax, and hemp, among others), medicines (digitalis, camphor), decorative and landscaping plants, and many other uses. The main area in which they are surpassed by other plants is timber production.

## Flower

A flower, sometimes known as a bloom or blossom, is the reproductive structure found in flowering plants (plants of the division Magnoliophyta, also called angiosperms). The biological function of a flower is to effect reproduction, usually by providing a mechanism for the union of sperm with eggs. Flowers may facilitate outcrossing (fusion of sperm and eggs from different individuals in a population) or allow selfing (fusion of sperm and egg from the same flower). Some flowers produce diaspores without fertilization (parthenocarpy). Flowers contain sporangia and are the site where gametophytes develop. Flowers give rise to fruit and seeds. Many flowers have evolved to be attractive to animals, so as to cause them to be vectors for the transfer of pollen.

In addition to facilitating the reproduction of flowering plants, flowers have long been admired and used by humans to beautify their environment but also as objects of romance, ritual, religion, medicine and as a source of food.

A stereotypical flower consists of four kinds of structures attached to the tip of a short stalk. Each of these kinds of parts is arranged in a whorl on the receptacle. The four main whorls (starting from the base of the flower or lowest node and working upwards) are as follows:

- *Calyx*: The outermost whorl consisting of units called *sepals*; these are typically green and enclose the rest of the flower in the bud stage, however, they can be absent or prominent and petal-like in some species.
- *Corolla*: The next whorl toward the apex, composed of units called *petals*, which are typically thin, soft and coloured to attract animals that help the process of pollination.

- *Androecium* (from Greek *andros oikia*: man's house): The next whorl (sometimes multiplied into several whorls), consisting of units called stamens. Stamens consist of two parts: a stalk called a filament, topped by an anther where pollen is produced by meiosis and eventually dispersed.
- *Gynoecium* (from Greek *gynaikos oikia*: woman's house): The innermost whorl of a flower, consisting of one or more units called carpels. The carpel or multiple fused carpels form a hollow structure called an ovary, which produces ovules internally. Ovules are megasporangia and they in turn produce megaspores by meiosis which develop into female gametophytes. These give rise to egg cells. The gynoecium of a flower is also described using an alternative terminology wherein the structure one sees in the innermost whorl (consisting of an ovary, style and stigma) is called a pistil. A pistil may consist of a single carpel or a number of carpels fused together. The sticky tip of the pistil, the stigma, is the receptor of pollen. The supportive stalk, the style, becomes the pathway for pollen tubes to grow from pollen grains adhering to the stigma.

Although the arrangement described above is considered "typical", plant species show a wide variation in floral structure. These modifications have significance in the evolution of flowering plants and are used extensively by botanists to establish relationships among plant species.

The four main parts of a flower are generally defined by their positions on the receptacle and not by their function. Many flowers lack some parts or parts may be modified into other functions and/or look like what is typically another part. In some families, like Ranunculaceae, the petals are greatly reduced and in many species the sepals are colorful and petal-like. Other flowers have modified stamens that are petal-like, the double flowers of Peonies and Roses are mostly petaloid stamens. Flowers show great variation and plant scientists describe this variation in a systematic way to identify and distinguish species.

Specific terminology is used to descried flowers and their parts. Many flower parts are fused together; fused parts originating from the same whorl are connate, while fused parts originating from different whorls are adnate, parts that are not fused are free. When petals are fused into a tube or ring that falls away as a single unit, they are sympetalous (also called gamopetalous.) Petals that are connate may have distinctive regions: the cylindrical base is the tube, the expanding region is the throat and the flaring outer region is the limb. A sympetalous flower, with bilateral symmetry with an upper and lower lip, is bilabiate. Flowers with connate petals or sepals may have various shaped corolla or calyx including: campanulate, funnelform, tubular, urceolate, salverform or rotate.

Many flowers have a symmetry, if the perianth is bisected through the central axis from any point, symmetrical halves are produced—the flower is called regular or actinomorphic, *e.g.* rose or trillium. When flowers are bisected and produce only one line that produces symmetrical halves the flower is said to be irregular or zygomorphic. *e.g.* snapdragon or most orchids.

Flowers may be directly attached to the plant at their base (sessile—the supporting stalk or stem is highly reduced or absent). The stem or stalk subtending a flower is called a peduncle. If a peduncle supports more than one flower, the stems connecting each flower to the main axis are called pedicels. The apex of a flowering stem forms a terminal swelling which is called the *torus* or receptacle.

In those species that have more than one flower on an axis, the collective cluster of flowers is termed an *inflorescence*. Some inflorescences are composed of many small flowers arranged in a formation that resembles a single flower. The common example of this is most members of the very large composite (Asteraceae) group. A single daisy or sunflower, for example, is not a flower but a flower *head*—an inflorescence composed of numerous flowers (or florets).

An inflorescence may include specialized stems and modified leaves known as bracts.

## Development

A flower is a modified stem tip with compressed internodes, bearing structures that are highly modified leaves. In essence, a flower develops on a modified shoot or *axis* from a determinate apical meristem (*determinate* meaning the axis grows to a set size).

## Flowering Transition

The transition to flowering is one of the major phase changes that a plant makes during its life cycle. The transition must take place at a time that is favourable for fertilization and the formation of seeds, hence ensuring maximal reproductive success. To meet these needs a plant is able to interpret important endogenous and environmental cues such as changes in levels of plant hormones and seasonable temperature and photoperiod changes. Many perennial and most biennial plants require vernalization to flower. The molecular interpretation of these signals is through the transmission of a complex signal known as florigen, which involves a variety of genes, including constrans, flowering locus C and flowering locus T. Florigen is produced in the leaves in reproductively favorable conditions and acts in buds and growing tips to induce a number of different physiological and morphological changes. The first step is the transformation of the vegetative stem primordia into floral primordia. This occurs as biochemical changes take place to change cellular differentiation of leaf, bud and stem tissues into tissue that will grow into the reproductive organs. Growth of the central part of the stem tip stops or flattens out and the sides develop protuberances in a whorled or spiral fashion around the outside of the stem end. These protuberances develop into the sepals, petals, stamens, and carpels. Once this process begins, in most plants, it cannot be reversed and the stems develop flowers, even if the initial start of the flower formation event was dependent of some environmental cue. Once the process begins, even if that cue is removed the stem will continue to develop a flower.

## Organ Development

The molecular control of floral organ identity determination is fairly well understood. In a simple model, three gene activities interact in a combinatorial manner to determine the developmental identities of the organ primordia within the floral meristem. These gene functions are called A, B and C-gene functions. In the first floral whorl only A-genes are expressed, leading to the formation of sepals. In the second whorl both A- and B-genes are expressed, leading to the formation of petals. In the third whorl, B and C genes interact to form stamens and in the center of the flower C-genes alone give rise to carpels. The model is based upon studies of homeotic mutants in *Arabidopsis thaliana* and snapdragon, *Antirrhinum majus*. For example, when there is a loss of B-gene function, mutant flowers are produced with sepals in the first whorl as usual, but also in the second whorl instead of the normal petal formation. In the third whorl the lack of B function but presence of C-function mimics the fourth whorl, leading to the formation of carpels also in the third whorl. See also The ABC Model of Flower Development.

Most genes central in this model belong to the MADS-box genes and are transcription factors that regulate the expression of the genes specific for each floral organ.

The principal purpose of a flower is the reproduction of the individual and the species. All flowering plants are *heterosporous*, producing two types of spores. Microspores are produced by meiosis inside anthers while megaspores are produced inside ovules, inside an ovary. In fact, anthers typically consist of four microsporangia and an ovule is an integumented megasporangium. Both types of spores develop into gametophytes inside sporangia. As with all heterosporous plants, the gametophytes also develop inside the spores (are endosporic).

In the majority of species, individual flowers have both functional carpels and stamens. These flowers are described by botanists as being *perfect* or *bisexual*. Some flowers lack one or the other reproductive organ and called *imperfect* or *unisexual* If unisex flowers are found on the same individual plant but in different locations, the species is said to be *monoecious*. If each type of unisex flower is found only on separate individuals, the plant is *dioecious*.

## Flower Specialization and Pollination

Flowering plants usually face selective pressure to optimize the transfer of their pollen, and this is typically reflected in the morphology of the flowers and the behaviour of the plants. Pollen may be transferred between plants via a number of 'vectors'. Some plants make use of abiotic vectors—namely wind (anemophily) or, much less commonly, water (hydrophily). Others use biotic vectors including insects (entomophily), birds (ornithophily), bats (chiropterophily) or other animals. Some plants make use of multiple vectors, but many are highly specialised.

Cleistogamous flowers are self pollinated, after which they may or may not open. Many Viola and some Salvia species are known to have these types of flowers.

The flowers of plants that make use of biotic pollen vectors commonly have glands called nectaries that act as an incentive for animals to visit the flower. Some flowers have patterns, called nectar guides, that show pollinators where to look for nectar. Flowers also attract pollinators by scent and colour. Still other flowers use mimicry to attract pollinators. Some species of orchids, for example, produce flowers resembling female bees in color, shape, and scent. Flowers are also specialized in shape and have an arrangement of the stamens that ensures that pollen grains are transferred to the bodies of the pollinator when it lands in search of its attractant (such as nectar, pollen, or a mate). In pursuing this attractant from many flowers of the same species, the pollinator transfers pollen to the stigmas—arranged with equally pointed precision—of all of the flowers it visits.

Anemophilous flowers use the wind to move pollen from one flower to the next. Examples include grasses, birch trees, ragweed and maples. They have no need to attract pollinators and therefore tend not to be 'showy' flowers. Male and female reproductive organs are generally found in separate flowers, the male flowers having a number of long filaments terminating in exposed stamens, and the female flowers having long, feather-like stigmas. Whereas the pollen of animal-pollinated flowers tends to be large-grained, sticky, and rich in protein (another 'reward' for pollinators), anemophilous flower pollen is usually small-grained, very light, and of little nutritional value to animals.

The primary purpose of a flower is reproduction. Since the flowers are the reproductive organs of plant, they mediate the joining of the sperm, contained within pollen, to the ovules — contained in the ovary. Pollination is the movement of pollen from the anthers to the stigma. The joining of the sperm to the ovules is called fertilization. Normally pollen is moved from one plant to another, but many plants are able to self pollinate. The fertilized ovules produce seeds that are the next generation. Sexual reproduction produces genetically unique offspring, allowing for adaptation. Flowers have specific designs which encourages the transfer of pollen from one plant to another of the same species. Many plants are dependent upon external factors for pollination, including: wind and animals, and especially insects. Even large animals such as birds, bats, and pygmy possums can be employed. The period of time during which this process can take place (the flower is fully expanded and functional) is called *anthesis*.

Plants cannot move from one location to another, thus many flowers have evolved to attract animals to transfer pollen between individuals in dispersed populations. Flowers that are insect-pollinated are called *entomophilous*; literally 'insect-loving' in Greek. They can be highly modified along with the pollinating insects by co-evolution. Flowers commonly have glands called *nectaries* on various parts that attract animals looking for nutritious nectar. Birds and bees have colour vision, enabling them to seek out 'colorful' flowers. Some flowers have patterns, called nectar guides, that show pollinators where to look for nectar; they may be visible only under ultraviolet light, which is visible to bees and some other insects. Flowers also attract pollinators by scent and some of those scents are pleasant to our sense of smell. Not all flower scents are appealing to humans, a number of flowers are pollinated by insects that are attracted to rotten flesh and have flowers that smell like dead animals, often called Carrion flowers including *Rafflesia*, the titan arum, and the North American pawpaw (*Asimina triloba*). Flowers pollinated by night visitors, including bats and moths, are likely to concentrate on scent to attract pollinators and most such flowers are white.

Still other flowers use mimicry to attract pollinators. Some species of orchids, for example, produce flowers resembling female bees in color, shape, and scent. Male bees move from one such flower to another in search of a mate.

Most flowers can be divided between two broad groups of pollination methods:

- *Entomophilous*: flowers attract and use insects, bats, birds or other animals to transfer pollen from one flower to the next. Often they are specialized in shape and have an arrangement of the stamens that ensures that pollen grains are transferred to the bodies of the pollinator when it lands in search of its attractant (such as nectar, pollen, or a mate). In pursuing this attractant from many flowers of the same species, the pollinator transfers pollen to the stigmas—arranged with equally pointed precision—of all of the flowers it visits. Many flowers rely on simple proximity between flower parts to ensure pollination. Others, such as the *Sarracenia* or lady-slipper orchids, have elaborate designs to ensure pollination while preventing self-pollination.
- *Anemophilous*: flowers use the wind to move pollen from one flower to the next, examples include the grasses, Birch trees, Ragweed and Maples. They have no need to attract

pollinators and therefore tend not to be 'showy' flowers. Whereas the pollen of entomophilous flowers tends to be large-grained, sticky, and rich in protein (another 'reward' for pollinators), anemophilous flower pollen is usually small-grained, very light, and of little nutritional value to insects, though it may still be gathered in times of dearth. Honeybees and bumblebees actively gather anemophilous corn (maize) pollen, though it is of little value to them.

Some flowers are self pollinated and use flowers that never open or are self pollinated before the flowers open, these flowers are called cleistogamous. Many Viola species and some Salvia have these types of flowers.

Many flowers have close relationships with one or a few specific pollinating organisms. Many flowers, for example, attract only one specific species of insect, and therefore rely on that insect for successful reproduction. This close relationship is often given as an example of coevolution, as the flower and pollinator are thought to have developed together over a long period of time to match each other's needs.

This close relationship compounds the negative effects of extinction. The extinction of either member in such a relationship would mean almost certain extinction of the other member as well. Some endangered plant species are so because of shrinking pollinator populations.

While land plants have existed for about 425 million years, the first ones reproduced by a simple adaptation of their aquatic counterparts: spores. In the sea, plants—and some animals—can simply scatter out genetic clones of themselves to float away and grow elsewhere. This is how early plants reproduced. But plants soon evolved methods of protecting these copies to deal with drying out and other abuse which is even more likely on land than in the sea. The protection became the seed, though it had not yet evolved the flower. Early seed-bearing plants include the ginkgo and conifers. The earliest fossil of a flowering plant, *Archaefructus liaoningensis*, is dated about 125 million years old.[6] Several groups of extinct gymnosperms, particularly seed ferns, have been proposed as the ancestors of flowering plants but there is no continuous fossil evidence showing exactly how flowers evolved. The apparently sudden appearance of relatively modern flowers in the fossil record posed such a problem for the theory of evolution that it was called an 'abominable mystery' by Charles Darwin. Recently discovered angiosperm fossils such as *Archaefructus*, along with further discoveries of fossil gymnosperms, suggest how angiosperm characteristics may have been acquired in a series of steps.

Recent DNA analysis (molecular systematics) shows that *Amborella trichopoda*, found on the Pacific island of New Caledonia, is the sister group to the rest of the flowering plants, and morphological studies suggest that it has features which may have been characteristic of the earliest flowering plants.

The general assumption is that the function of flowers, from the start, was to involve animals in the reproduction process. Pollen can be scattered without bright colors and obvious shapes, which would therefore be a liability, using the plant's resources, unless they provide some other benefit. One proposed reason for the sudden, fully developed appearance of flowers is that they evolved in an isolated setting like an island, or chain of islands, where the plants bearing them were able to develop a highly specialized relationship with some specific animal (a wasp, for example), the way many island species develop today. This symbiotic relationship, with a hypothetical wasp bearing pollen from one plant to another much the way fig wasps do today, could have eventually resulted in both the plant(s) and their partners developing a high degree of specialization. Island genetics is believed to be a common source of speciation, especially when it comes to radical adaptations which seem to have required inferior transitional forms. Note that the wasp example is not incidental; bees, apparently evolved specifically for symbiotic plant relationships, are descended from wasps.

Likewise, most fruit used in plant reproduction comes from the enlargement of parts of the flower. This fruit is frequently a tool which depends upon animals wishing to eat it, and thus scattering the seeds it contains.

While many such symbiotic relationships remain too fragile to survive competition with mainland organisms, flowers proved to be an unusually effective means of production, spreading (whatever their actual origin) to become the dominant form of land plant life.

While there is only hard proof of such flowers existing about 130 million years ago, there is some circumstantial evidence that they did exist up to 250 million years ago. A chemical used by plants to defend their flowers, oleanane, has been detected in fossil plants that old, including gigantopterids, which evolved at that time and bear many of the traits of modern, flowering plants, though they are not known to be flowering plants themselves, because only their stems and prickles have been found preserved in detail; one of the earliest examples of petrification.

The similarity in leaf and stem structure can be very important, because flowers are genetically just an adaptation of normal leaf and stem components on plants, a combination of genes normally responsible for forming new shoots. The most primitive flowers are thought to have had a variable number of flower parts, often separate from (but in contact with) each other. The flowers would have tended to grow in a spiral pattern, to be bisexual (in plants, this means both male and female parts on the same flower), and to be dominated by the ovary (female part). As flowers grew more advanced, some variations developed parts fused together, with a much more specific number and design, and with either specific sexes per flower or plant, or at least 'ovary inferior'.

Flower evolution continues to the present day; modern flowers have been so profoundly influenced by humans that many of them cannot be pollinated in nature. Many modern, domesticated flowers used to be simple weeds, which only sprouted when the ground was disturbed. Some of them tended to grow with human crops, and the prettiest did not get plucked because of their beauty, developing a dependence upon and special adaptation to human affection.

## Symbolism

Many flowers have important symbolic meanings in Western culture. The practice of assigning meanings to flowers is known as floriography. Some of the more common examples include:

- Red oses are given as a symbol of love, beauty, and passion.
- Poppies are a symbol of consolation in time of death. In the United Kingdom, New Zealand, Australia and Canada, red poppies are worn to commemorate soldiers who have died in times of war.
- Irises/Lily are used in burials as a symbol referring to "resurrection/life". It is also associated with stars (sun) and its petals blooming/shining.
- Daisies are a symbol of innocence.

Flowers within art are also representative of the female genitalia, as seen in the works of artists such as Georgia O'Keeffe, Imogen Cunningham, Veronica Ruiz de Velasco, and Judy Chicago, and in fact in Asian and western classical art. Many cultures around the world have a marked tendency to associate flowers with femininity.

The great variety of delicate and beautiful flowers has inspired the works of numerous poets, especially from the 18th-19th century Romantic era. Famous examples include William Wordsworth's *I Wandered Lonely as a Cloud* and William Blake's *Ah! Sun-Flower*.

Because of their varied and colourful appearance, flowers have long been a favorite subject of visual artists as well. Some of the most celebrated paintings from well-known painters are of flowers, such as Van Gogh's sunflowers series or Monet's water lilies. Flowers are also dried, freeze dried and pressed in order to create permanent, three-dimensional pieces of flower art.

The Roman goddess of flowers, gardens, and the season of Spring is Flora. The Greek goddess of spring, flowers and nature is Chloris.

In Hindu mythology, flowers have a significant status. Vishnu, one of the three major gods in the Hindu system, is often depicted standing straight on a lotus flower. Apart from the association with Vishnu, the Hindu tradition also considers the lotus to have spiritual significance. For example, it figures in the Hindu stories of creation.

In modern times, people have sought ways to cultivate, buy, wear, or otherwise be around flowers and blooming plants, partly because of their agreeable appearance and smell. Around the world, people use flowers for a wide range of events and functions that, cumulatively, encompass one's lifetime:

- For new births or Christenings.
- As a corsage or boutonniere to be worn at social functions or for holidays.
- As tokens of love or esteem.
- For wedding flowers for the bridal party, and decorations for the hall.
- As brightening decorations within the home.
- As a gift of remembrance for bon voyage parties, welcome home parties, and 'thinking of you' gifts.
- For funeral flowers and expressions of sympathy for the grieving.
- For worshiping goddesses. in Hindu culture it is very common to bring flowers as a gift to temples.

People therefore grow flowers around their homes, dedicate entire parts of their living space to flower gardens, pick wildflowers, or buy flowers from florists who depend on an entire network of commercial growers and shippers to support their trade.

Flowers provide less food than other major plants parts (seeds, fruits, roots, stems and leaves) but they provide several important foods and spices. Flower vegetables include broccoli, cauliflower and artichoke. The most expensive spice, saffron, consists of dried stigmas of a crocus. Other flower spices are cloves and capers. Hops flowers are used to flavour beer. Marigold flowers are fed to chickens to give their egg yolks a golden yellow colour, which consumers find more desirable. Dandelion flowers are often made into wine. Bee Pollen, pollen collected from bees, is considered a health food by some people. Honey consists of bee-processed flower nectar and is often named for the type of flower, *e.g.* orange blossom honey, clover honey and tupelo honey.

Hundreds of fresh flowers are edible but few are widely marketed as food. They are often used to add colour and flavour to salads. Squash flowers are dipped in breadcrumbs and fried. Edible flowers include nasturtium, chrysanthemum, carnation, cattail, honeysuckle, chicory, cornflower, Canna, and sunflower. Some edible flowers are sometimes candied such as daisy and rose (you may also come across a candied pansy).

Flowers can also be made into herbal teas. Dried flowers such as chrysanthemum, rose, jasmine, camomile are infused into tea both for their fragrance and medical properties. Sometimes, they are also mixed with tea leaves for the added fragrance.

# The Study of Plants

Plants are living organisms belonging to the kingdom Plantae. They include familiar organisms such as trees, flowers, herbs, bushes, grasses, vines, ferns, mosses, and green algae. The scientific study of plants, known as botany, has identified about 350,000 extant species of plants, defined as seed plants, bryophytes, ferns and fern allies. As of 2004, some 287,655 species had been identified, of which 258,650 are flowering and 18,000 bryophytes. Green plants, sometimes called Viridiplantae, obtain most of their energy from sunlight via a process called photosynthesis.

Aristotle divided all living things between plants (which generally do not move), and animals (which often are mobile to catch their food). In Linnaeus' system, these became the Kingdoms Vegetabilia (later Metaphyta or Plantae) and Animalia (also called Metazoa). Since then, it has become clear that the Plantae as originally defined included several unrelated groups, and the fungi and several groups of algae were removed to new kingdoms. However, these are still often considered plants in many contexts, both technical and popular.

Most algae are no longer classified within the Kingdom Plantae. The algae comprise several different groups of organisms that produce energy through photosynthesis, each of which arose independently from separate non-photosynthetic ancestors. Most conspicuous among the algae are the seaweeds, multicellular algae that may roughly resemble terrestrial plants, but are classified among the green, red, and brown algae. Each of these algal groups also includes various microscopic and single-celled organisms.

The two groups of green algae are the closest relatives of land plants (embryophytes). The first of these groups is the Charophyta (desmids and stoneworts), from which the embryophytes developed. The sister group to the combined embryophytes and charophytes is the other group of green algae, Chlorophyta, and this more inclusive group is collectively referred to as the green plants or Viridiplantae. The Kingdom Plantae is often taken to mean this monophyletic grouping. With a few exceptions among the green algae, all such forms have cell walls containing cellulose, have chloroplasts containing chlorophylls *a* and *b*, and store food in the form of starch. They undergo closed mitosis without centrioles, and typically have mitochondria with flat cristae.

The chloroplasts of green plants are surrounded by two membranes, suggesting they originated directly from endosymbiotic cyanobacteria. The same is true of two additional groups of algae: the Rhodophyta (red algae) and Glaucophyta. All three groups together are generally believed to have a common origin, and so are classified together in the taxon Archaeplastida. In contrast, most other algae (*e.g.* heterokonts, haptophytes, dinoflagellates, and euglenids) have chloroplasts with three or four surrounding membranes. They are not close relatives of the green plants, presumably acquiring chloroplasts separately from ingested or symbiotic green and red algae.

## Fungi

The classification of fungi has been controversial until quite recently in the history of biology. Linnaeus' original classification placed the fungi within the Plantae, since they were unquestionably not animalian; this being the only other alternative. With later developments in microbiology, in the 19th century Ernst Haeckel felt that a third kingdom was required to classify newly discovered micro-organisms. The introduction of the new kingdom Protista as an alternative to Animalia, led to uncertainty as to whether fungi truly were best placed in the Plantae or whether they ought to be reclassified as protists. Haeckel himself found it difficult to decide and it was not until 1969 that a solution was found whereby Robert Whittaker proposed the creation of the kingdom Fungi. Molecular evidence has since shown that the concestor (last common ancestor) of the Fungi was probably more similar to that of the Animalia than of any other kingdom, including the Plantae.

Whittaker's original reclassification was based on the fundamental difference in nutrition between the Fungi and the Plantae. Unlike plants, which are generally autotrophic multicellular phototrophs which gain carbon through photosynthesis, fungi are generally heterotrophic uni- or multi-cellular saprotrophs, obtaining carbon by breaking down and absorbing surrounding materials. In addition, the substructure of multicellular fungi takes the form of many chitinous microscopic strands called hyphae, which may be further subdivided into cells or may form a syncytium containing many eukaryotic nuclei. Fruiting bodies, of which mushrooms are most familiar example, are the reproductive structures of fungi.

About 350,000 species of plants, defined as seed plants, bryophytes, ferns and fern allies, are estimated to exist currently. As of 2004, some 287,655 species had been identified, of which 258,650 are flowering plants, 16,000 bryophytes, 11,000 ferns and 8,000 green algae.

## Evolution

The evolution of plants has resulted in increasing levels of complexity, from the earliest algal mats, through bryophytes, lycopods, ferns to the complex gymnosperms and angiosperms of today. While the groups which appeared earlier continue to thrive, especially in the environments in which they evolved, each new grade of organisation has eventually become more 'successful' than its predecessors by most measures.

Evidence suggests that an algal scum formed on the land 1,200 million years ago, but it was not until the Ordovician Period, around 450 million years ago, that land plants appeared. However, new evidence from the study of carbon isotope ratios in Precambrian rocks has suggested that complex photosynthetic plants developed on the earth over 1000 m.y.a . These began to diversify in the late Silurian Period, around 420 million years ago, and the fruits of their diversification are displayed in remarkable detail in an early Devonian fossil assemblage from the Rhynie chert. This chert preserved early plants in cellular detail, petrified in volcanic springs. By the middle of the Devonian Period most of the features recognised in plants today are present, including roots, leaves and secondary wood, and by late Devonian times seeds had evolved. Late Devonian plants had thereby reached a degree of sophistication that allowed them to form forests of tall trees. Evolutionary innovation continued after the Devonian period. Most plant groups were relatively unscathed by the Permo-Triassic extinction event, although the structures of communities changed. This may have set the scene for the evolution of flowering plants in the Triassic (~200 million years ago), which exploded in the Cretaceous and Tertiary. The latest major group of plants to evolve were the grasses, which became important in the mid Tertiary, from around 40 million years ago. The grasses, as well as many other groups, evolved new mechanisms of metabolism to survive the low $CO_2$ and warm, dry conditions of the tropics over the last 10 million years.

The plants that are likely most familiar to us are the multicellular land plants, called embryophytes. They include the vascular plants, plants with full systems of leaves, stems, and roots. They also include a few of their close relatives, often called *bryophytes*, of which mosses and liverworts are the most common.

All of these plants have eukaryotic cells with cell walls composed of cellulose, and most obtain their energy through photosynthesis, using light and carbon dioxide to synthesize food. About three hundred plant species do not photosynthesize but are parasites on other species of photosynthetic plants. Plants are distinguished from green algae, which represent a mode of photosynthetic life similar to the kind modern plants are believed to have evolved from, by having specialized reproductive organs protected by non-reproductive tissues.

Bryophytes first appeared during the early Paleozoic. They can only survive where moisture is available for significant periods, although some species are desiccation tolerant. Most species of bryophyte remain small throughout their life-cycle. This involves an alternation between two generations: a haploid stage, called the gametophyte, and a diploid stage, called the sporophyte. The sporophyte is short-lived and remains dependent on its parent gametophyte.

Vascular plants first appeared during the Silurian period, and by the Devonian had diversified and spread into many different land environments. They have a number of adaptations that allowed them to overcome the limitations of the bryophytes. These include a cuticle resistant to desiccation, and vascular tissues which transport water throughout the organism. In most the sporophyte acts as a separate individual, while the gametophyte remains small.

The first primitive seed plants, Pteridosperms (seed ferns) and Cordaites, both groups now extinct, appeared in the late Devonian and diversified through the Carboniferous, with further evolution through the Permian and Triassic periods. In these the gametophyte stage is completely reduced, and the sporophyte begins life inside an enclosure called a seed, which develops while on the parent plant, and with fertilisation by means of pollen grains. Whereas other vascular plants, such as ferns, reproduce by means of spores and so need moisture to develop, some seed plants can survive and reproduce in extremely arid conditions.

Early seed plants are referred to as gymnosperms (naked seeds), as the seed embryo is not enclosed in a protective structure at pollination, with the pollen landing directly on the embryo. Four surviving groups remain widespread now, particularly the conifers, which are dominant trees in several biomes. The angiosperms, comprising the flowering plants, were the last major group of plants to appear, emerging from within the gymnosperms during the Jurassic and diversifying rapidly during the Cretaceous. These differ in that the seed embryo (angiosperm) is enclosed, so the pollen has to grow a tube to penetrate the protective seed coat; they are the predominant group of flora in most biomes today.

## Fossils

Plant fossils include roots, wood, leaves, seeds, fruit, pollen, spores, phytoliths, and amber (the fossilized resin produced by some plants). Fossil land plants are recorded in terrestrial, lacustrine, fluvial and nearshore marine sediments. Pollen, spores and algae (dinoflagellates and acritarchs) are used for dating sedimentary rock sequences. The remains of fossil plants are not as common as fossil animals, although plant fossils are locally abundant in many regions worldwide.

The earliest fossils clearly assignable to Kingdom Plantae are fossil green algae from the Cambrian. These fossils resemble calcified multicellular members of the Dasycladales. Earlier Precambrian fossils are known which resemble single-cell green algae, but definitive identity with that group of algae is uncertain.

The oldest known fossils of embryophytes date from the Ordovician, though such fossils are fragmentary. By the Silurian, fossils of whole plants are preserved, including the lycophyte *Baragwanathia longifolia*. From the Devonian, detailed fossils of rhyniophytes have been found. Early fossils of these ancient plants show the individual cells within the plant tissue.

The Devonian period also saw the evolution of what many believe to be the first modern tree, *Archaeopteris*. This fern-like tree combined a woody trunk with the fronds of a fern, but produced no seeds.

The Coal measures are a major source of Paleozoic plant fossils, with many groups of plants in existence at this time. The spoil heaps of coal mines are the best places to collect; coal itself is the remains of fossilised plants, though structural detail of the plant fossils is rarely visible in coal. In the Fossil Forest at Victoria Park in Glasgow, Scotland, the stumps of *Lepidodendron* trees are found in their original growth positions.

The fossilized remains of conifer and angiosperm roots, stems and branches may be locally abundant in lake and inshore sedimentary rocks from the Mesozoic and Cenozoic eras. Sequoia and its allies, magnolia, oak, and palms are often found.

Petrified wood is common in some parts of the world, and is most frequently found in arid or desert areas where it is more readily exposed by erosion. Petrified wood is often heavily silicified (the organic material replaced by silicon dioxide), and the impregnated tissue is often preserved in fine detail. Such specimens may be cut and polished using lapidary equipment. Fossil forests of petrified wood have been found in all continents.

Fossils of seed ferns such as *Glossopteris* are widely distributed throughout several continents of the Southern Hemisphere, a fact that gave support to Alfred Wegener's early ideas regarding Continental drift theory.

## Structure, Growth, and Development

Most of the solid material in a plant is taken from the atmosphere. Through a process known as photosynthesis, most plants use the energy in sunlight to convert carbon dioxide from the atmosphere, plus water, into simple sugars. Parasitic plants, on the other hand, use the resources of its host to grow. These sugars are then used as building blocks and form the main structural component of the plant. Chlorophyll, a green-colored, magnesium-containing pigment is essential to this process; it is generally present in plant leaves, and often in other plant parts as well.

Plants usually rely on soil primarily for support and water (in quantitative terms), but also obtain compounds of nitrogen, phosphorus, and other crucial elemental nutrients. Epiphytic and lithophytic plants often depend on rainwater or other sources for nutrients and carnivorous plants supplement their nutrient requirements with insect prey that they capture. For the majority of plants to grow successfully they also require oxygen in the atmosphere and around their roots for respiration. However, some plants grow as submerged aquatics, using oxygen dissolved in the surrounding water, and a few specialized vascular plants, such as mangroves, can grow with their roots in anoxic conditions.

### Factors Affecting Growth

The genotype of a plant affects its growth. For example, selected varieties of wheat grow rapidly, maturing within 110 days, whereas others, in the same environmental conditions, grow more slowly and mature within 155 days.

Growth is also determined by environmental factors, such as temperature, available water, available light, and available nutrients in the soil. Any change in the availability of these external conditions will be reflected in the plants growth.

Biotic factors are also capable of affecting plant growth. Plants compete with other plants for space, water, light and nutrients. Plants can be so crowded that no single individual produces normal growth, causing etiolation and chlorosis. Optimal plant growth can be hampered by grazing animals, suboptimal soil composition, lack of mycorrhizal fungi, and attacks by insects or plant diseases, including those caused by bacteria, fungi, viruses, and nematodes.

Simple plants like algae may have short life spans as individuals, but their populations are commonly seasonal. Other plants may be organized according to their seasonal growth pattern: annual plants live and reproduce within one growing season, biennial plants live for two growing seasons and usually reproduce in second year, and perennial plants live for many growing seasons and continue to reproduce once they are mature. These designations often depend on climate and other environmental factors; plants that are annual in alpine or temperate regions can be biennial or perennial in warmer climates. Among the vascular plants, perennials include both evergreens that keep their leaves the entire year, and deciduous plants which lose their leaves for some part of it. In temperate and boreal climates, they generally lose their leaves during the winter; many tropical plants lose their leaves during the dry season.

The growth rate of plants is extremely variable. Some mosses grow less than 0.001 millimeters per hour (mm/h), while most trees grow 0.025-0.250 mm/h. Some climbing species, such as kudzu, which do not need to produce thick supportive tissue, may grow up to 12.5 mm/h.

Plants protect themselves from frost and dehydration stress with antifreeze proteins, heat-shock proteins and sugars (sucrose is common). LEA (Late Embryogenesis Abundant) protein expression is induced by stresses and protects other proteins from aggregation as a result of desiccation and freezing.

Plant cells are typically distinguished by their large water-filled central vacuole, chloroplasts, and rigid cell walls that are made up of cellulose, hemicellulose, and pectin. Cell division is also characterized by the development of a phragmoplast for the construction of a cell plate in the late stages of cytokinesis. Just as in animals, plant cells differentiate and develop into multiple cell types. Totipotent meristematic cells can differentiate into vascular, storage, protective (*e.g.* epidermal layer), or reproductive tissues, with more primitive plants lacking some tissue types.

Plants are photosynthetic, which means that they manufacture their own food molecules using energy obtained from light. The primary mechanism plants have for capturing light energy is the pigment chlorophyll. All green plants contain two forms of chlorophyll, chlorophyll *a* and chlorophyll *b*. The latter of these pigments is not found in red or brown algae.

## Immune System

By means of cells that behave like nerves, plants receive and distribute within their systems information about incident light intensity and quality. Incident light which stimulates a chemical reaction in one leaf, will cause a chain reaction of signals to the entire plant via a type of cell termed a *'bundle sheath cell'*. Researchers from the Warsaw University of Life Sciences in Poland, found that plants have a specific memory for varying light conditions which prepares their immune systems against seasonal pathogens.

## Internal Distribution

Vascular plants differ from other plants in that they transport nutrients between different parts through specialized structures, called xylem and phloem. They also have roots for taking up water and minerals. The xylem moves water and minerals from the root to the rest of the plant, and the phloem provides the roots with sugars and other nutrient produced by the leaves.

The photosynthesis conducted by land plants and algae is the ultimate source of energy and organic material in nearly all ecosystems. Photosynthesis radically changed the composition of the early Earth's atmosphere, which as a result is now 21 per cent oxygen. Animals and most other organisms are aerobic, relying on oxygen; those that do not are confined to relatively rare anaerobic environments. Plants are the primary producers in most terrestrial ecosystems and form the basis of the food web in those ecosystems. Many animals rely on plants for shelter as well as oxygen and food.

Land plants are key components of the water cycle and several other biogeochemical cycles. Some plants have co-evolved with nitrogen fixing bacteria, making plants an important part of the nitrogen cycle. Plant roots play an essential role in soil development and prevention of soil erosion.

## Distribution

Plants are distributed worldwide in varying numbers. While they inhabit a multitude of biomes and ecoregions, few can be found beyond the tundras at the northernmost regions of continental shelves. At the southern extremes, plants have adapted tenaciously to the prevailing conditions.

Plants are often the dominant physical and structural component of habitats where they occur. Many of the Earth's biomes are named for the type of vegetation because plants are the dominant organisms in those biomes, such as grasslands and forests.

## Ecological Relationships

Numerous animals have coevolved with plants. Many animals pollinate flowers in exchange for food in the form of pollen or nectar. Many animals disperse seeds, often by eating fruit and passing the seeds in their feces. Myrmecophytes are plants that have co-evolved with ants. The plant provides a home, and sometimes food, for the ants. In exchange, the ants defend the plant from herbivores and sometimes competing plants. Ant wastes provide organic fertilizer.

The majority of plant species have various kinds of fungi associated with their root systems in a kind of mutualistic symbiosis known as mycorrhiza. The fungi help the plants gain water and mineral nutrients from the soil, while the plant gives the fungi carbohydrates manufactured in photosynthesis. Some plants serve as homes for endophytic fungi that protect the plant from herbivores by producing toxins. The fungal endophyte, *Neotyphodium coenophialum,* in tall fescue (*Festuca arundinacea*) does tremendous economic damage to the cattle industry in the U.S.

Various forms of parasitism are also fairly common among plants, from the semi-parasitic mistletoe that merely takes some nutrients from its host, but still has photosynthetic leaves, to the fully parasitic broomrape and toothwort that acquire all their nutrients through connections to the roots of other plants, and so have no chlorophyll. Some plants, known as myco-heterotrophs, parasitize mycorrhizal fungi, and hence act as epiparasites on other plants.

Many plants are epiphytes, meaning they grow on other plants, usually trees, without parasitizing them. Epiphytes may indirectly harm their host plant by intercepting mineral nutrients and light that the host would otherwise receive. The weight of large numbers of epiphytes may break tree limbs. Hemiepiphytes like the strangler fig begin as epiphytes but eventually set their own roots and overpower and kill their host. Many orchids, bromeliads, ferns and mosses often grow as epiphytes. Bromeliad epiphytes accumulate water in leaf axils to form phytotelmata, complex aquatic food webs.

Approximately 630 plants are carnivorous, such as the Venus Flytrap (*Dionaea muscipula*) and sundew (*Drosera* species). They trap small animals and digest them to obtain mineral nutrients, especially nitrogen and phosphorus.

## Importance

Potato plant. Potatoes spread to the rest of the world after European contact with the Americas in the late 15th and early 16th centuries and have since become an important field crop.

A section of a Yew branch showing 27 annual growth rings, pale sapwood and dark heartwood, and pith (centre dark spot). The dark radial lines are longitudinal sections of small branches which became included by growth of the tree.

The study of plant uses by people is termed economic botany or ethnobotany; some consider economic botany to focus on modern cultivated plants, while ethnobotany focuses on indigenous plants cultivated and used by native peoples. Human cultivation of plants is part of agriculture, which is the basis of human civilization. Plant agriculture is subdivided into agronomy, horticulture and forestry.

Much of human nutrition depends on land plants, either directly or indirectly. Human nutrition depends to a large extent on cereals, especially maize (or corn), wheat and rice. Other staple crops include potato, cassava, and legumes. Human food also includes vegetables, spices, and certain fruits, nuts, herbs, and edible flowers. Beverages produced from plants include coffee, tea, wine, beer and alcohol. Sugar is obtained mainly from sugar cane and sugar beet. Cooking oils and margarine come from maize, soybean, rapeseed, safflower, sunflower, olive and others. Food additives include gum arabic, guar gum, locust bean gum, starch and pectin. Livestock animals including cows, pigs, sheep, and goats are all herbivores; and feed primarily or entirely on cereal plants, particularly grasses.

## Non-food Products

Wood is used for buildings, furniture, paper, cardboard, musical instruments and sports equipment. Cloth is often made from cotton, flax or synthetic fibres derived from cellulose, such as rayon and acetate. Renewable fuels from plants include firewood, peat and many other biofuels. Coal and petroleum are fossil fuels derived from plants. Medicines derived from plants include aspirin, taxol, morphine, quinine, reserpine, colchicine, digitalis and vincristine. There are hundreds of herbal supplements such as ginkgo, Echinacea, feverfew, and Saint John's wort. Pesticides derived from plants include nicotine, rotenone, strychnine and pyrethrins. Drugs obtained from plants include opium, cocaine and marijuana. Poisons from plants include ricin, hemlock and curare. Plants are the source of many natural products such as fibres, essential oils, natural dyes, pigments, waxes, tannins, latex, gums, resins, alkaloids, amber and cork. Products derived from plants include soaps, paints, shampoos, perfumes, cosmetics, turpentine, rubber, varnish, lubricants, linoleum, plastics, inks, chewing gum and hemp rope. Plants are also a primary source of basic chemicals for the industrial synthesis of a vast array of organic chemicals. These chemicals are used in a vast variety of studies and experiments.

### Aesthetic Uses

Thousands of plant species are cultivated for aesthetic purposes, as well as to provide shade, modify temperatures, reduce wind, abate noise, provide privacy, and prevent soil erosion. People use cut flowers, dried flowers and houseplants indoors or in greenhouses. In outdoor gardens, lawn grasses, shade trees, ornamental trees, shrubs, vines, herbaceous perennials and bedding plants are used. Images of plants are often used in art, architecture, humour, language, and photography and on textiles, money, stamps, flags and coats of arms. Living plant art forms include topiary, bonsai, ikebana and espalier. Ornamental plants have sometimes changed the course of history, as in tulipomania. Plants are the basis of a multi-billion dollar per year tourism industry which includes travel to arboretums, botanical gardens, historic gardens, national parks, tulip festivals, rainforests, forests with colourful autumn leaves and the National Cherry Blossom Festival. Venus Flytrap, sensitive plant and resurrection plant are examples of plants sold as novelties.

### Scientific and Cultural Uses

Tree rings are an important method of dating in archaeology and serve as a record of past climates. Basic biological research has often been done with plants, such as the pea plants used to derive Gregor Mendel's laws of genetics. Space stations or space colonies may one day rely on plants for life support. Plants are used as national and state emblems, including state trees and state flowers. Ancient trees are revered and many are famous. Numerous world records are held by plants. Plants are often used as memorials, gifts and to mark special occasions such as births, deaths, weddings and holidays. Plants figure prominently in mythology, religion and literature. The field of ethnobotany studies plant use by indigenous cultures which helps to conserve endangered species as well as discover new medicinal plants. Gardening is the most popular leisure activity in the U.S. Working with plants or horticulture therapy is beneficial for rehabilitating people with disabilities. Certain plants contain psychotropic chemicals which are extracted and ingested, including tobacco, cannabis (marijuana), and opium.

### Negative Effects

Weeds are plants that grow where people do not want them. People have spread plants beyond their native ranges and some of these introduced plants become invasive, damaging existing ecosystems by displacing native species. Invasive plants cause billions of dollars in crop losses annually by displacing crop plants, they increase the cost of production and the use of chemical means to control them affects the environment.

Plants may cause harm to people and animals. Plants that produce windblown pollen invoke allergic reactions in people who suffer from hay fever. A wide variety of plants are poisonous to people and/or animals. Toxalbumins are plant poisons fatal to most mammals and act as a serious deterrent to consumption. Several plants cause skin irritations when touched, such as poison ivy. Certain plants contain psychotropic chemicals, which are extracted and ingested or smoked, including tobacco, cannabis (marijuana), cocaine and opium. Smoking causes damage to health or even death, while some drugs may also be harmful or fatal to people. Both illegal and legal drugs derived from plants may have negative effects on the economy, affecting worker productivity and law enforcement costs. Some plants cause allergic reactions in people and animals when ingested, while other plants cause food intolerances that negatively affect health.

# 12 Plant Embryogenesis

Plant embryogenesis is the process that produces a plant embryo from a fertilised ovule by asymmetric cell division and the differentiation of undifferentiated cells into tissues and organs. It occurs during seed development, when the single-celled zygote undergoes a programmed pattern of cell division resulting in a mature embryo. A similar process continues during the plant's life within the meristems of the stems and roots.

Embryogenesis occurs naturally as a result of sexual fertilization and the formation of the *zygotic embryos.* The embryo along with other cells from the motherplant develops into the seed or the next generation, which, after germination, grows into a new plant.

Embryogenesis may be divided up into two phases, the first involves morphogenetic events which form the basic cellular pattern for the development of the shoot-root body and the primary tissue layers; it also programmes the regions of meristematic tissue formation. The second phase, or postembryonic development, involves the maturation of cells, which involves cell growth and the storage of macromolecules (such as oils, starches and proteins) required as a 'food and energy supply' during germination and seedling growth.

Embryogenesis involves cell growth and division, cell differentiation and programmeed cellular death. The zygotic embryo is formed following double fertilisation of the ovule, giving rise to two distinct structures: the plant embryo and the endosperm which together go on to develop into a seed. Seeds may also develop without fertilization, which is referred to as apomixis. Plant cells can also be induced to form embryos in plant tissue culture; such embryos are called *somatic embryos*.

Following fertilization, the zygote undergoes an asymmetrical cell division that gives rise to a small apical cell, which becomes the embryo and a large basal cell (called the suspensor), which functions to provide nutrients from the endosperm to the growing embryo. From the eight cell stage (octant) onwards, the zygotic embryo shows clear embryo patterning, which forms the main axis of polarity, and the linear formation of future structures. These structures include the shoot meristem, cotyledons, hypocotyl, and the root and root meristem: they arise from specific groups of cells as the young embryo divides and their formation has been shown to be position-dependent.

In the globular stage , the embryo develops radial patterning through a series of cell divisions, with the outer layer of cells differentiating into the 'protoderm.' The globular embryo can be thought of as two layers of inner cells with distinct developmental fates; the apical layer will go on to produce cotyledons and shoot meristem, while the lower layer produces the hypocotyl and root meristem. Bilateral symmetry is apparent from the heart stage; provascular cells will also differentiate at this stage. In the subsequent torpedo and cotyledonary stages of embryogenesis, the embryo completes its growth by elongating and enlarging.

In a dicot embryo, the hypophysis, which is the uppermost cell of the suspensor, differentiates to form part of the root cap. Plant cells can also be induced to form embryos in plant tissue culture; these embryos are called *somatic embryos,* which are used to generate new plants from single cells.

Embryonic tissue is made up of actively growing cells and the term is normally used to describe the early formation of tissue in the first stages of growth. It can refer to different stages of the sporophyte and gametophyte plant; including the growth of embryos in seedlings, and to meristematic tissues, which are in a persistently embryonic state, to the growth of new buds on stems.

In both gymnosperms and angiosperms, the young plant contained in the seed, begins as a developing egg-cell formed after fertilization (sometimes without fertilization in a process called apomixis) and becomes a plant embryo. This embryonic condition also occurs in the buds that form on stems. The buds have tissue that has differentiated but not grown into complete structures. They can be in a resting state, lying dormant over winter or when conditions are dry, and then commence growth when conditions become suitable. Before they start growing into stem, leaves, or flowers, the buds are said to be in an embryonic state.

## Somatic Embryogenesis

Somatic embryos are formed from plant cells that are not normally involved in the development of embryos, *i.e.* ordinary plant tissue. No endosperm or seed coat is formed around a somatic embryo. Applications of this process include: clonal propagation of genetically uniform plant material; elimination of viruses; provision of source tissue for genetic transformation; generation of whole plants from single cells called protoplasts; development of synthetic seed technology. Cells derived from competent source tissue are cultured to form an undifferentiated mass of cells called a callus. Plant growth regulators in the tissue culture medium can be manipulated to induce callus formation and subsequently changed to induce embryos to form from the callus. The ratio of different plant growth regulators required to induce callus or embryo formation varies with the type of plant. Asymmetrical cell division also seems to be important in the development of somatic embryos, and while failure to form the suspensor cell is lethal to zygotic embryos, it is not lethal for somatic embryos.

## Plant Morphology

Plant morphology or phytomorphology is the study of the physical form and external structure of plants. This is usually considered distinct from plant anatomy, which is the study of the internal structure of plants, especially at the microscopic level. Plant morphology is useful in the identification of plants.

Plant morphology "represents a study of the development, form, and structure of plants, and, by implication, an attempt to interpret these on the basis of similarity of plan and origin." There are four major areas of investigation in plant morphology, and each overlaps with another field of the biological sciences.

*First* of all, morphology is comparative, meaning that the morphologist examines structures in many different plants of the same or different species, then draws comparisons and formulates ideas about similarities. When structures in different species are believed to exist and develop as a result of common, inherited genetic pathways, those structures are termed homologous. For example, the leaves of pine, oak, and cabbage all look very different, but share certain basic structures and arrangement of parts. The homology of leaves is an easy conclusion to make. The plant morphologist goes further, and discovers that the spines of cactus also share the same basic structure and development as leaves in other plants, and therefore cactus spines are homologous to leaves as well. This aspect of plant morphology overlaps with the study of plant evolution and paleobotany.

*Asclepias syriaca* showing complex morphology of the flowers.

*Secondly*, plant morphology observes both the vegetative (somatic) structures of plants, as well as the reproductive structures. The vegetative structures of vascular plants includes the study of the shoot system, composed of stems and leaves, as well as the root system. The reproductive structures are more varied, and are usually specific to a particular group of plants, such as flowers and seeds, fern sori, and moss capsules. The detailed study of reproductive structures in plants led to the discovery of the alternation of generations found in all plants and most algae. This area of plant morphology overlaps with the study of biodiversity and plant systematics.

*Thirdly,* plant morphology studies plant structure at a range of scales. At the smallest scales are ultrastructure, the general structural features of cells visible only with the aid of an electron microscope, and cytology, the study of cells using optical microscopy. At this scale, plant morphology overlaps with plant anatomy as a field of study. At the largest scale is the study of plant growth habit, the overall architecture of a plant. The pattern of branching in a tree will vary from species to species, as will the appearance of a plant as a tree, herb, or grass.

*Fourthly,* plant morphology examines the pattern of development, the process by which structures originate and mature as a plant grows. While animals produce all the body parts they will ever have from early in their life, plants constantly produce new tissues and structures throughout their life. A living plant always has embryonic tissues. The way in which new structures mature as they are produced may be affected by the point in the plants life when they begin to develop, as well as by the environment to which the structures are exposed. A morphologist studies this process, the causes, and its result. This area of plant morphology overlaps with plant physiology and ecology.

## A Comparative Science

A plant morphologist makes comparisons between structures in many different plants of the same or different species. Making such comparisons between similar structures in different plants tackles the question of *why* the structures are similar. It is quite likely that similar underlying causes of genetics, physiology, or response to the environment have led to this similarity in appearance. The result of scientific investigation into these causes can lead to one of two insights into the underlying biology:

- *Homology:* The structure is similar between the two species because of shared ancestry and common genetics.
- *Convergence:* The structure is similar between the two species because of independent adaptation to common environmental pressures.

Understanding which characteristics and structures belong to each type is an important part of understanding plant evolution. The evolutionary biologist relies on the plant morphologist to interpret structures, and in turn provides phylogenies of plant relationships that may lead to new morphological insights.

## Homology

When structures in different species are believed to exist and develop as a result of common, inherited genetic pathways, those structures are termed *homologous*. For example, the leaves of pine, oak, and cabbage all look very different, but share certain basic structures and arrangement of parts. The homology of leaves is an easy conclusion to make. The plant morphologist goes further, and discovers that the spines of cactus also share the same basic structure and development as leaves in other plants, and therefore cactus spines are homologous to leaves as well.

## Convergence

When structures in different species are believed to exist and develop as a result of common adaptive responses to environmental pressure, those structures are termed *convergent*. For example, the fronds of *Bryopsis plumosa* and stems of *Asparagus setaceus* both have the same feathery branching appearance, even though one is an alga and one is a flowering plant. The similarity in overall structure occurs independently as a result of convergence. The growth form of many cacti and species of *Euphorbia* is very similar, even though they belong to widely distant families. The similarity results from common solutions to the problem of surviving in a hot, dry environment.

## Vegetative and Reproductive Characters

Plant morphology treats both the vegetative structures of plants, as well as the reproductive structures.

The vegetative (somatic) structures of vascular plants include two major organ systems:

1. a shoot system, composed of stems and leaves; and
2. a root system.

These two systems are common to nearly all vascular plants, and provide a unifying theme for the study of plant morphology.

By contrast, the reproductive structures are varied, and are usually specific to a particular group of plants. Structures such as flowers and fruits are only found in the angiosperms; sori are only found in ferns; and seed cones are only found in conifers and other gymnosperms. Reproductive characters are therefore regarded as more useful for the classification of plants than vegetative characters.

## Use in Identification

Plant biologists use morphological characters of plants which can be compared, measured counted and described to assess the differences or similarities in plant taxa and use these characters for plant identification, classification and descriptions.

When characters are used in descriptions or for identification they are called diagnostic or key characters which can be either qualitative and quantitative.

Quantitative characters are morphological features that can be counted or measured for example a plant species has flower petals 10-12 mm wide.

Qualitative characters are morphological features such as leaf shape, flower colour or pubescence.

Both kinds of characters can be very useful for the identification of plants.

## Alternation of Generations

The detailed study of reproductive structures in plants led to the discovery of the alternation of generations, found in all plants and most algae, by the German botanist Wilhelm Hofmeister. This discovery is one of the most important made in all of plant morphology, since it provides a common basis for understanding the life cycle of all plants.

## Development

Plant development is the process by which structures originate and mature as a plant grows. It is a subject studies in plant anatomy and plant physiology as well as plant morphology.

The process of development in plants is fundamentally different from that seen in vertebrate animals. When an animal embryo begins to develop, it will very early produce all of the body parts that it will ever have in its life. When the animal is born (or hatches from its egg), it has all its body parts and from that point will only grow larger and more mature. By contrast, plants constantly produce new tissues and structures throughout their life from meristems located at the tips of organs, or between mature tissues. Thus, a living plant always has embryonic tissues.

The properties of organization seen in a plant are emergent properties which are more than the sum of the individual parts. "The assembly of these tissues and functions into an integrated multicellular organism yields not only the characteristics of the separate parts and processes but also quite a new set of characteristics which would not have been predictable on the basis of examination of the separate parts." In other words, knowing everything about the molecules in a plant are not enough to predict characteristics of the cells; and knowing all the properties of the cells will not predict all the properties of a plant's structure.

A vascular plant begins from a single celled zygote, formed by fertilisation of an egg cell by a sperm cell. From that point, it begins to divide to form a plant embryo through the process of embryogenesis. As this happens, the resulting cells will organize so that one end becomes the first root, while the other end forms the tip of the shoot. In seed plants, the embryo will develop one or more 'seed leaves' (cotyledons). By the end of embryogenesis, the young plant will have all the parts necessary to begin in its life.

Once the embryo germinates from its seed or parent plant, it begins to produce additional organs (leaves, stems, and roots) through the process of organogenesis. New roots grow from root meristems located at the tip of the root, and new stems and leaves grow from shoot meristems located at the tip of the shoot . Branching occurs when small clumps of cells left behind by the meristem, and which have not yet undergone cellular differentiation to form a specialized tissue, begin to grow as the tip of a new root or shoot. Growth from any such meristem at the tip of a root or shoot is termed primary growth and results in the lengthening of that root or shoot. Secondary growth results in widening of a root or shoot from divisions of cells in a cambium.

In addition to growth by cell division, a plant may grow through cell elongation. This occurs when individual cells or groups of cells grow longer. Not all plant cells will grow to the same length. When cells on one side of a stem grow longer and faster than cells on the other side, the stem will bend to the side of the slower growing cells as a result. This directional growth can occur via a plant's response to a particular stimulus, such as light (phototropism), gravity (gravitropism), water, (hydrotropism), and physical contact (thigmotropism).

### Morphological Variation

Plants exhibit natural variation in their form and structure. While all organisms vary from individual to individual, plants exhibit an additional type of variation. Within a single individual, parts are repeated which may differ in form and structure from other similar parts. This variation is most easily seen in the leaves of a plant, though other organs such as stems and flowers may show similar variation. There are three primary causes of this variation: positional effects, environmental effects, and juvenility.

## Positional Effects

Variation in leaves from the giant ragweed illustrating positional effects. The lobed leaves come from the base of the plant, while the unlobed leaves come from the top of the plant.

Although plants produce numerous copies of the same organ during their lives, not all copies of a particular organ will be identical. There is variation among the parts of a mature plant resulting from the relative position where the organ is produced. For example, along a new branch the leaves may vary in a consistent pattern along the branch. The form of leaves produced near the base of the branch will differ from leaves produced at the tip of the plant, and this difference is consistent from branch to branch on a given plant and in a given species. This difference persists after the leaves at both ends of the branch have matured, and is not the result of some leaves being younger than others.

## Environmental Effects

The way in which new structures mature as they are produced may be affected by the point in the plants life when they begin to develop, as well as by the environment to which the structures are exposed. This can be seen in aquatic plants and emergent plants.

## Juvenility

Juvenility in a seedling of European beech. Notice the difference in shape between the first dark green 'seed leaves' and the lighter second pair of leaves.

The organs and tissues produced by a young plant, such as a seedling, are often different from those that are produced by the same plant when it is older. This phenomenon is known as juvenility. For example, young trees will produce longer, leaner branches that grow upwards more than the branches they will produce as a fully grown tree. In addition, leaves produced during early growth tend to be larger, thinner, and more irregular than leaves on the adult plant. Species of juvenile plants may look so completely different from the adult leaves that egg-laying insects do not recognize the plant as food for their young.

## Some Recent Developments

Rolf Sattler has revised fundamental concepts of comparative morphology such as the concept of homology. He emphasized that homology should also include partial homology and quantitative homology. This leads to a continuum morphology that demonstrates a continuum between the morphological categories of root, shoot, stem (caulome), leaf (phyllome), and hair (trichome). How intermediates between the categories are best described has been discussed.

Researcher of the partial-shoot theory of the leaf, Rutishauser and Isler called the continuum approach Fuzzy Arberian Morphology (FAM). 'Fuzzy' refers to fuzzy logic, 'Arberian' to Agnes Arber. Rutishauser and Isler emphasized that this approach is not only supported by many morphological data but also by evidence from molecular genetics.

Process morphology (dynamic morphology) describes and analyzes the dynamic continuum of plant form.

According to this approach, structures do not *have* process(es), they *are* process(es). Thus, the structure/process dichotomy is overcome by "an enlargement of our concept of 'structure' so as to include and recognize that in the living organism it is not merely a question of spatial structure with an 'activity' as something over or against it, but that the concrete organism is a spatio-*temporal* structure and that this spatio-temporal structure is the activity itself."

For Jeune, Barabé and Lacroix, classical morphology (that is, mainstream morphology, based on a qualitative homology concept implying mutually exclusive categories) and continuum morphology are sub-classes of the more encompassing process morphology (dynamic morphology).

# Meristem

A meristem is the tissue in most plants consisting of undifferentiated cells (meristematic cells), found in zones of the plant where growth can take place.

The meristematic cells give rise to various organs of the plant, and keep the plant growing. The Shoot Apical Meristem (SAM) gives rise to organs like the leaves and flowers. The cells of the apical meristems — SAM and RAM (Root Apical Meristem) — divide rapidly and are considered to be indeterminate, in that they do not possess any defined end fate. In that sense, the meristematic cells are frequently compared to the stem cells in animals, that have an analogous behaviour and function.

The term *meristem* was first used in 1858 by Karl Wilhelm von Nägeli (1817-1891) in his book *Beiträge zur Wissenschaftlichen Botanik*. It is derived from the Greek word *merizein*, meaning to divide, in recognition of its inherent function.

Differentiated plant cells generally cannot divide or produce cells of a different type. Therefore, cell division in the meristem is required to provide new cells for expansion and differentiation of tissues and initiation of new organs, providing the basic structure of the plant body.

Meristematic cells are analogous in function to stem cells in animals, are incompletely or not at all differentiated, and are capable of continued cellular division (youthful). Furthermore, the cells are small and protoplasm fills the cell completely. The vacuoles are extremely small. The cytoplasm does not contain differentiated plastids (chloroplasts or chromoplasts), although they are present in rudimentary form (proplastids). Meristematic cells are packed closely together without intercellular cavities. The cell wall is a very thin *primary cell wall.*

Maintenance of the cells requires a balance between two antagonistic processes: organ initiation and stem cell population renewal.

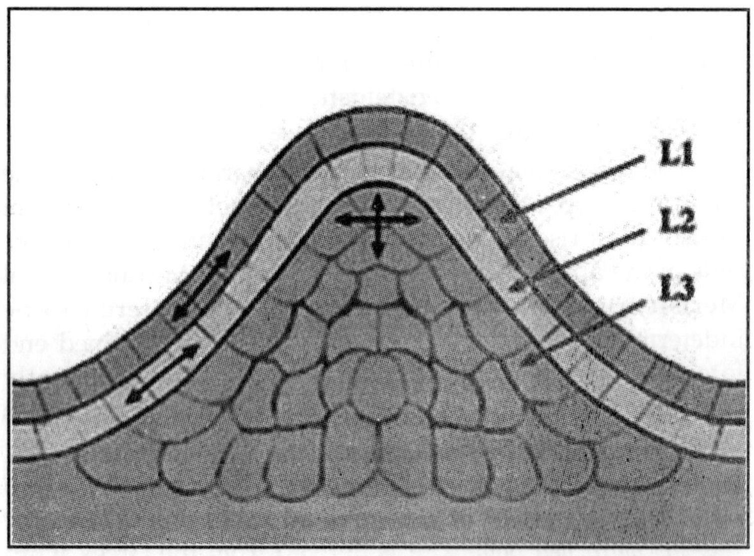


**Tunica-Corpus Model of the Apical Meristem (Growing Tip). The Epidermal (L1) and Subepidermal (L2) Layers form the Outer Layers Called the Tunica. The Inner L3 Layer is Called the Corpus. Cells in the L1 and L2 Layers Divide in a Sideways Fashion, Which Keeps These Layers Distinct, Whereas the L3 Layer Divides in a More Random Fashion**

Apical meristems are the completely undifferentiated (indeterminate) meristems in a plant. These differentiate into three kinds of primary meristems. The primary meristems in turn produce the two secondary meristem types. These secondary meristems are also known as lateral meristems because they are involved in lateral growth.

At the meristem summit, there is a small group of slowly dividing cells, which is commonly called the central zone. Cells of this zone have a stem cell function and are essential for meristem maintenance. The proliferation and growth rates at the meristem summit usually differ considerably from those at the periphery.

Meristems also are induced in the roots of legumes such as soybean, *Lotus japonicus*, pea, and *Medicago truncatula* after infection with soil bacteria commonly called Rhizobium. Cells of the inner or outer cortex in the so-called "window of nodulation" just behind the developing root tip are induced to divide. The critical signal substance is the lipo-oligosaccharide Nod-factor, decorated with side groups to allow specificity of interaction. The Nod factor receptor proteins NFR1 and NFR5 were cloned from several legumes including *Lotus japonicus, Medicago truncatula* and soybean (Glycine max). Regulation of nodule meristems utilizes long distance regulation commonly called "Autoregulation of Nodulation" (AON). This process involves a leaf-vascular tissue located LRR receptor kinases (LjHAR1, GmNARK and MtSUNN), CLE peptide signalling , and KAPP interaction, similar to that seen in the CLV1,2,3 system. LjKLAVIER also exhibits a nodule regulation phenotype though it is not yet known how this relates to the other AON receptor kinases.

The apical meristem, or growing tip, is a completely undifferentiated meristematic tissue found in the buds and growing tips of roots in plants. Its main function is to begin growth of new cells in young seedlings at the tips of roots and shoots (forming buds, among other things). Specifically, an active apical meristem lays down a growing root or shoo behind itself, pushing itself forward. Apical meristems are very small, compared to the cylinder-shaped lateral meristems (see 'Secondary Meristems' below).

Apical meristems are composed of several layers. The number of layers varies according to plant type. In general the outermost layer is called the tunica while the innermost layers are the corpus. In monocots, the tunica determine the physical characteristics of the leaf edge and margin. In dicots, layer two of the corpus determine the characteristics of the edge of the leaf. The corpus and tunica play a critical part of the plant physical appearance as all plant cells are formed from the meristems. Apical meristems are found in two locations: the root and the stem. Some Arctic plants have an apical meristem in the lower/middle parts of the plant. It is thought that this kind of meristem evolved because it is advantageous in Arctic conditions.

### Shoot Apical Meristems

The source of all above-ground organs. Cells at the shoot apical meristem summit serve as stem cells to the surrounding peripheral region, where they proliferate rapidly and are incorporated into differentiating leaf or flower primordia.

The shoot apical meristem is the site of most of the embryogenesis in flowering plants. Primordia of leaves, sepals, petals, stamens and ovaries are initiated here at the rate of one every time interval, called a plastochron. It is where the first indications that flower development has been evoked are manifested. One of these indications might be the loss of apical dominance and the release of otherwise dormant cells to develop as axillary shoot meristems, in some species in axils of primordia as close as two or three away from the apical dome. The shoot apical meristem consists of four distinct cell groups:

1. Stem cells
2. The immediate daughter cells of the stem cells
3 A subjacent organising centre
4. Founder cells for organ initiation in surrounding regions

The four distinct zones mentioned above are maintained by a complex signalling pathway. In *Arabidopsis thaliana* , 3 interacting *CLAVATA* genes are required to regulate the size of the stem cell reservoir in the shoot apical meristem by controlling the rate of cell division. CLV1 and CLV2 are predicted to form a receptor complex (of the LRR receptor like kinase family) to which CLV3 is a ligand. CLV3 shares some homology with the ESR proteins of maize, with a short 14 amino acid region being conserved between the proteins. Proteins that contain these conserved regions have been grouped into the CLE family of proteins.

CLV1 has been shown to interact with several cytoplasmic proteins that are most likely involved in downstream signalling. For example, the CLV complex has been found to be associated with Rho/Rac small GTPase-related proteins. These proteins may act as an intermediate between the CLV complex and a mitogen-activated protein kinase (MAPK), which is often involved in signalling cascades. KAPP is a kinase-associated protein phosphatase that has been shown to interact with CLV1. KAPP is thought to act as a negative regulator of CLV1 by dephosphorylating it.

Another important gene in plant meristem maintenance is *WUSCHEL* (shortened to *WUS*), which is a target of CLV signalling. *WUS* is expressed in the cells below the stem cells of the meristem and its presence prevents the differentiation of the stem cells. CLV1 acts to promote cellular differentiation by repressing *WUS* activity outside of the central zone containing the stem cells. *STM* also acts to prevent the differentiation of stem cells by repressing the expression of Myb genes that are involved in cellular differentiation.

## Root Apical Meristems

Unlike the shoot apical meristem, the root apical meristem produces cells in two dimensions. It is covered by the root cap, which protects the apical meristem from the rocks, dirt and pathogens. Cells are continuously sloughed off the outer surface of the root cap. The center of the root apical meristem is occupied by a quiescent center which has low mitotic activity. Evidence suggests the quiescent center does function as the zone of initials. Infrequent division of initial cells in the quiescent center is the source of cells for the root apical meristem. These initial cells and tissue patterns become established in the embryo in the case of the primary root, and in the new lateral meristems in the case of secondary roots.

### Intercalary Meristem

In angiosperms, intercalary meristems occur only in monocot (in particular, grass) stems at the base of nodes and leaf blades. Horsetails also exhibit intercalary growth. Intercalary meristems are capable of cell division and allow for rapid growth and regrowth of many monocots. Intercalary meristems at the nodes of bamboo allow for rapid stem elongation, while those at the base of most grass leaf blades allow damaged leaves to rapidly regrow. This leaf regrowth in grasses evolved in response to damage by grazing herbivores, but is more familiar to us in response to lawnmowers.

### Floral Meristem

When plants begin the developmental process known as flowering, the shoot apical meristem is transformed into an inflorescence meristem, which goes on to produce the floral meristem, which produces the familiar sepals, petals, stamens, and carpels of the flower.

In contrast to vegetative apical meristems and some exflorescence meristems, floral meristems are responsible for determinate growth, the limited growth of the flower to a particular size and form. The transition from shoot meristem to floral meristem requires floral meristem identity genes, that both specify the floral organs and cause the termination of the production of stem cells. *AGAMOUS* (*AG*) is a floral homeotic gene required for floral meristem termination and necessary for proper development of the stamens and carpels. *AG* is necessary to prevent the conversion of floral meristems to inflorescence shoot meristems, but is not involved in the transition from shoot to floral meristem. AG is turned on by the floral meristem identity gene *LEAFY* (*LFY*) and *WUS* and is restricted to the centre of the floral meristem or the inner two whorls. This way floral identity and region specificity is achieved. WUS activates AG by binding to a consensus sequence in the AG's second intron and LFY binds to adjacent recognition sites. Once AG is activated it represses expression of WUS leading to the termination of the meristem.

Through the years, scientists have manipulated floral meristems for economics reasons. An example is the mutant tobacco plant 'Maryland Mammoth'. In 1936, the department of agriculture of Switzerland performed several scientific tests with this plant. 'Maryland Mammoth' is peculiar in this sense that it grows much faster than other tobacco plants.

## Apical Dominance

Apical dominance is phenomenon where one meristem prevents or inhibits the growth of other meristems. As a result the plant will have one clearly defined main trunk. For example, in trees, the tip of the main trunk bears the dominant meristem. Therefore, the tip of the trunk grows rapidly and is not shadowed by branches. If the dominant meristem is cut off, one or more branch tips will assume dominance. The branch will start growing faster and the new growth will be vertical. Over the years, the branch may begin to look more and more like an extension of the main trunk. Often several branches will exhibit this behaviour after the removal of apical meristem, leading to a bushy growth.

The mechanism of apical dominance is based on the plant hormone auxin. It is produced in the apical meristem and transported towards the roots in the cambium. If apical dominance is complete, it prevents any branches from forming as long as apical meristem is active. If the dominance is incomplete, side branches will develop.

Recent investigations into apical dominance and the control of branching have revealed a new plant hormone family termed strigolactones. These compounds were previously known to be involved in seed germination and communication with mycorrhizal fungi and are now shown to be involved in inhibition of branching.

**Diversity in Meristem Architectures**

Is the mechanism of being *indeterminate* conserved in the SAM's of the plant world? The SAM contains a population of stem cells that also produce the lateral meristems while the stem elongates. It turns out that the mechanism of regulation of the stem cell number might indeed be evolutionarily conserved. The *CLAVATA* gene *CLV2* responsible for maintaining the stem cell population in *Arabidopsis thaliana* is very closely related to the Maize gene *FASCIATED EAR 2*(*FEA2*) also involved in the same function. Similarly, in Rice, the *FON1-FON2* system seems to bear a close relationship with the CLV signaling system in *Arabidopsis thaliana*. These studies suggest that the regulation of stem cell number, identity and differentiation might be an evolutionarily conserved mechanism in monocots, if not in angiosperms. Rice also contains another genetic system distinct from *FON1-FON2*, that is involved in regulating stem cell number. This example underlines the innovation that goes about in the living world all the time.

Genetic screens have identified genes belonging to the KNOX family in this function. These genes essentially maintain the stem cells in an undifferentiated state. The KNOX family has undergone quite a bit of evolutionary diversification, while keeping the overall mechanism more or less similar. Members of the KNOX family have been found in plants as diverse as Arabidopsis thaliana, rice, barley and tomato. KNOX-like genes are also present in some algae, mosses, ferns and gymnosperms. Misexpression of these genes leads to formation of interesting morphological features. For example, among members of *Antirrhinae*, only the species of genus *Antirrhinum* lack a structure called spur in the floral region. A spur is considered an evolutionary innovation because it defines pollinator specificity and attraction. Researchers carried out transposon mutagenesis in *Antirrhinum majus*, and saw that some insertions led to formation of spurs that were very similar to the other members of *Antirrhinae*, indicating that the loss of spur in wild *Antirrhinum majus* populations could probably be an evolutionary innovation.

The KNOX family has also been implicated in leaf shape evolution *(See below for a more detailed discussion)*. One study looked at the pattern of KNOX gene expression in *A. thaliana*, that has simple leaves and *Cardamine hirsuta*, a plant having complex leaves. In *A. thaliana*, the KNOX genes are completely turned off in leaves, but in *C.hirsuta*, the expression continued, generating complex leaves. Also, it has been proposed that the mechanism of KNOX gene action is conserved across all vascular plants, because there is a tight correlation between KNOX expression and a complex leaf morphology.

## Primary Meristems

Apical meristems may differentiate into three kinds of primary meristem:

1. *Protoderm* — lies around the outside of the stem and develops into the epidermis;
2. *Procambium* — lies just inside of the protoderm and develops into primary xylem and primary phloem. It also produces the vascular cambium, a secondary meristem;
3. Ground meristem develops into the pith. It produces the cork cambium, another secondary meristem.

These meristems are responsible for primary growth, or an increase in length or height which were discovered by scientist Joseph D. Carr of North Carolina in 1943.

## Secondary meristems

There are two types of secondary meristems, these are also called the *lateral meristems* because they surround the established stem of a plant and cause it to grow laterally (*i.e.*, larger in diameter).

1. Vascular cambium, which produces secondary xylem and secondary phloem. This is a process that may continue

throughout the life of the plant. This is what gives rise to wood in plants. Such plants are called arborescent. This does not occur in plants that do not go through secondary growth (known as herbaceous plants).

2. Cork cambium, which gives rise to the periderm, which replaces the epidermis.

## Indeterminate Growth of Meristems

Though each plant grows according to a certain set of rules, each new root and shoot meristem can go on growing for as long as it is alive. In many plants meristematic growth is potentially indeterminate, making the overall shape of the plant not determinate in advance. This is the primary growth. Primary growth leads to lengthening of the plant body and organ formation. All plant organs arise ultimately from cell divisions in the apical meristems, followed by cell expansion and differentiation. Primary growth gives rise to the apical part of many plants.

The growth of nitrogen fixing nodules on legume plants such as soybean and pea is either determinate or indeterminate. Thus, soybean (or bean and Lotus japonicus) produce determinate nodules (spherical), with a branched vascular system surrounding the central infected zone. Often, Rhizobium infected cells have only small vacuoles. In contrast, nodules on pea, clovers, and Medicago truncatula are indeterminate; to maintain (at least for some time) an active meristem that yields new cells for Rhizobium infection. Thus zones of maturity exist in the nodule. Infected cells usually possess a large vacuole. The plant vascular system is branched and peripheral.

## Cloning

Under appropriate conditions, each shoot meristem can develop into a complete new plant or clone. Such new plants can be grown from shoot cuttings that contain an apical meristem. Root apical meristems are not readily cloned, however. This cloning is called asexual reproduction or vegetative reproduction and is widely practiced in horticulture to mass-produce plants of a desirable genotype. This process is also known as mericloning.

Propagating through cuttings is another form of vegetative propogation that initiates root or shoot production from secondary meristematic cambial cells. This explains why basal 'wounding' of shoot-borne cuttings often aids root formation.

# Plant Anatomy

Plant anatomy or phytotomy is the general term for the study of the internal structure of plants. While originally it included plant morphology, which is the description of the physical form and external structure of plants, since the mid-20th century the investigations of plant anatomy are considered a separate, distinct field, and plant anatomy refers to *just* the internal plant structures. Plant anatomy is now frequently investigated at the cellular level, and often involves the sectioning of tissues and microscopy.

## Structural Divisions

Plant anatomy is sometimes divided into the following categories:

- Flower anatomy
- Calyx
- Corolla
- Androecium
- Gynoecium
- Leaf anatomy
- Stem anatomy
- Stem structure

- Fruit/Seed anatomy
- Ovule
- Seed structure
- Pericarp
- Accessory fruit
- Wood anatomy
- Bark
- Cork
- Phloem
- Vascular cambium
- Heartwood and sapwood
- Branch collar
- Root anatomy
- Root structure

About 300 BCE Theophrastus wrote a number of plant treatises, only two of which survive. He developed concepts of plant morphology and classification, which did not withstand the scientific scrutiny of the Renaissance.

A Swiss physician and botanist, Gaspard Bauhin, introduced binomial nomenclature into plant taxonomy. He published *Pinax theatri botanici* in 1596, which was the first to use this convention for naming of species. His criteria for classification included natural relationships, or 'affinities', which in many cases were structural.

Italian doctor and microscopist, Marcello Malpighi, was one of the two founders of plant anatomy. In 1671 he published his *Anatomia Plantarum*, the first major advance in plant physiogamy since Aristotle.

The British doctor, Nehemiah Grew was one of the two founders of plant anatomy. He published *An Idea of a Philosophical History of Plants* in 1672 and *The Anatomy of Plants* in 1682. Grew is credited with the recognition of plant cells, although he called them 'vesicles' and 'bladders'. He correctly identified and described the sexual organs of plants (flowers) and their parts.

In the Eighteenth Century, Carolus Linnaeus established taxonomy based on structure, and his early work was with plant anatomy. While the exact structural level which is to be considered to be scientifically valid for comparison and differentiation has changed with the growth of knowledge, the basic principles were established by Linnaeus. He published his master work, *Species Plantarum* in 1753.

In 1802, French botanist, Charles-François Brisseau de Mirbel, published *Traité d'anatomie et de physiologie végétale* (*Treatise on Plant Anatomy and Physiology*) establishing the beginnings of the science of plant cytology.

In 1812, Johann Jacob Paul Moldenhawer published *Beyträge zur Anatomie der Pflanzen*, describing microscopic studies of plant tissues.

In 1813 a Swiss botanist, Augustin Pyrame de Candolle, published *Théorie élémentaire de la botanique*, in which he argued that plant anatomy, not physiology, ought to be the sole basis for plant classification. Using a scientific basis, he established structural criteria for defining and separating plant genera.

In 1830, Franz Meyen published *Phytotomie*, the first comprehensive review of plant anatomy.

In 1838 German botanist, Matthias Jakob Schleiden, published *Contributions to Phytogenesis*, stating, "the lower plants all consist of one cell, while the higher plants are composed of (many) individual cells" thus confirming and continuing Mirabel's work.

A German-Polish botanist, Eduard Strasburger, described the mitotic process in plant cells and further demonstrated that new cell nuclei can only arise from the division of other pre-existing nuclei. His *Studien über Protoplasma* was published in 1876.

Gottlieb Haberlandt, a German botanist, studied plant physiology and classified plant tissue based upon function. On this basis, in 1884 he published *Physiologische Pflanzenanatomie* (*Physiological Plant Anatomy*) in which he described twelve types of tissue systems (absorptive, mechanical, photosynthetic, etc.).

British paleobotanists Dunkinfield Henry Scott and William Crawford Williamson described the structures of fossilized plants at the end of the Nineteenth Century. Scott's *Studies in Fossil Botany* was published in 1900.

Following Charles Darwin's *Origin of Species* a Canadian botanist, Edward Charles Jeffrey, who was studying the comparative anatomy and phylogeny of different vascular plant groups, applied the theory to plants using the form and structure of plants to establish a number of evolutionary lines. He published his *The Anatomy of Woody Plants* in 1917.

The growth of comparative plant anatomy was spearheaded by a British botanist, Agnes Arber. She published *Water Plants: A Study of Aquatic Angiosperms* in 1920, *Monocotyledons: A Morphological Study* in 1925, and *The Gramineae: A Study of Cereal, Bamboo and Grass* in 1934.

Following the Second World War, Katherine Esau published, Plant Anatomy (1953), which became the definitive textbook on plant structure in North American universities and elsewhere, it was still in print as of 2006. She followed up with her Anatomy of seed plants in 1960.

# Plant Physiology

Plant physiology is a subdiscipline of botany concerned with the functioning, or physiology, of plants. Closely related fields include plant morphology (structure of plants), plant ecology (interactions with the environment), phytochemistry (biochemistry of plants), cell biology and molecular biology.

Fundamental processes such as photosynthesis, respiration, plant nutrition, plant hormone functions, tropisms, nastic movements, photoperiodism, photomorphogenesis, circadian rhythms, environmental stress physiology, seed germination, dormancy and stomata function and transpiration, both part of plant water relations, are studied by plant physiologists.

The field of plant physiology includes the study of all the internal activities of plants—those chemical and physical processes associated with life as they occur in plants. This includes study at many levels of scale of size and time. At the smallest scale are molecular interactions of photosynthesis and internal diffusion of water, minerals, and nutrients. At the largest scale are the processes of plant development, seasonality, dormancy, and reproductive control. Major subdisciplines of plant physiology include phytochemistry (the study of the biochemistry of plants) and phytopathology (the study of disease in plants). The scope of plant physiology as a discipline may be divided into several major areas of research.

*First*, the study of phytochemistry (plant chemistry) is included within the domain of plant physiology. In order to function and survive, plants produce a wide array of chemical compounds not found in other organisms. Photosynthesis requires a large array of pigments, enzymes, and other compounds to function. Because they cannot move, plants must also defend themselves chemically from herbivores, pathogens and competition from other plants. They do this by producing toxins and foul-tasting or smelling chemicals. Other compounds defend plants against disease, permit survival during drought, and prepare plants for dormancy. While other compounds are used to attract pollinators or herbivores to spread ripe seeds.

*Secondly*, plant physiology includes the study of biological and chemical processes of individual plant cells. Plant cells have a number of features that distinguish them from cells of animals, and which lead to major differences in the way that plant life behaves and responds differently from animal life. For example, plant cells have a cell wall which restricts the shape of plant cells and thereby limits the flexibility and mobility of plants. Plant cells also contain chlorophyll, a chemical compound that interacts with light in a way that enables plants to manufacture their own nutrients rather than consuming other living things as animals do.

*Thirdly*, plant physiology deals with interactions between cells, tissues, and organs within a plant. Different cells and tissues are physically and chemically specialized to perform different functions. Roots and rhizoids function to anchor the plant and acquire minerals in the soil. Leaves function to catch light in order to manufacture nutrients. For both of these organs to remain living, the minerals acquired by the roots must be transported to the leaves and the nutrients manufactured in the leaves must be transported to the roots. Plants have developed a number of means by which this transport may occur, such as vascular tissue, and the functioning of the various modes of transport is studied by plant physiologists.

*Fourthly,* plant physiologists study the ways that plants control or regulate internal functions. Like animals, plants produce chemicals called hormones which are produced in one part of the plant to signal cells in another part of the plant to respond. Many flowering plants bloom at the appropriate time because of light-sensitive compounds that respond to the length of the night, a phenomenon known as photoperiodism. The ripening of fruit and loss of leaves in the winter are controlled in part by the production of the gas ethylene by the plant.

*Finally,* plant physiology includes the study of how plants respond to conditions and variation in the environment, a field known as environmental physiology. Stress from water loss, changes in air chemistry, or crowding by other plants can lead to changes in the way a plant functions. These changes may be affected by genetic, chemical, and physical factors.

The list of simple elements of which plants are primarily constructed—carbon, oxygen, hydrogen, calcium, phosphorus, etc.—is not different from similar lists for animals, fungi, or even bacteria. The fundamental atomic components of plants are the same as for all life; only the details of the way in which they are assembled differs.

Despite this underlying similarity, plants produce a vast array of chemical compounds with unusual properties which they use to cope with their environment. Pigments are used by plants to absorb or detect light, and are extracted by humans for use in dyes. Other plant products may be used for the manufacture of commercially important rubber or biofuel. Perhaps the most celebrated compounds from plants are those with pharmacological activity, such as salicylic acid (aspirin), morphine, and digitalis. Drug companies spend billions of dollars each year researching plant compounds for potential medicinal benefits.

Plants require some nutrients, such as carbon and nitrogen, in large quantities to survive. Such nutrients are termed macronutrients, where the prefix *macro-* (large) refers to the quantity needed, not the size of the nutrient particles themselves. Other nutrients, called micronutrients, are required only in trace amounts for plants to remain healthy. Such micronutrients are usually absorbed as ions dissolved in water taken from the soil, though carnivorous plants acquire some of their micronutrients from captured prey.

The following tables list element nutrients essential to plants. Uses within plants are generalized.

Among the most important molecules for plant function are the pigments. Plant pigments include a variety of different kinds of molecules, including porphyrins, carotenoids, and anthocyanins. All biological pigments selectively absorb certain wavelengths of light while reflecting others. The light that is absorbed may be used by the plant to power chemical reactions, while the reflected wavelengths of light determine the colour the pigment will appear to the eye.

Chlorophyll is the primary pigment in plants; it is a porphyrin that absorbs red and blue wavelengths of light while reflecting green. It is the presence and relative abundance of chlorophyll that gives plants their green colour. All land plants and green algae possess two forms of this pigment: chlorophyll *a* and chlorophyll *b*. Kelps, diatoms, and other photosynthetic heterokonts contain chlorophyll *c* instead of *b*, while red algae possess only chlorophyll *a*. All chlorophylls serve as the primary means plants use to intercept light in order to fuel photosynthesis.

Carotenoids are red, orange, or yellow tetraterpenoids. They function as accessory pigments in plants, helping to fuel photosynthesis by gathering wavelengths of light not readily absorbed by chlorophyll. The most familiar carotenoids are carotene (an orange pigment found in carrots), lutein (a yellow pigment found in fruits and vegetables), and lycopene (the red pigment responsible for the colour of tomato^).

Carotenoids have been shown to act as antioxidants and to promote healthy eyesight in humans.

Anthocyanins (literally 'flower blue') are water-soluble flavonoid pigments that appear red to blue, according to pH. They occur in all tissues of higher plants, providing color in leaves, stems, roots, flowers, and fruits, though not always in sufficient quantities to be noticeable. Anthocyanins are most visible in the petals of flowers, where they may make up as much as 30 per cent of the dry weight of the tissue. They are also responsible for the purple color seen on the underside of tropical shade plants such as *Tradescantia zebrina*; in these plants, the anthocyanin catches light that has passed through the leaf and reflects it back towards regions bearing chlorophyll, in order to maximize the use of available light.

Betalains are red or yellow pigments. Like anthocyanins they are water-soluble, but unlike anthocyanins they are indole-derived compounds synthesized from tyrosine. This class of pigments is found only in the Caryophyllales (including cactus and amaranth), and never co-occur in plants with anthocyanins. Betalains are responsible for the deep red colour of beets, and are used commercially as food-coloring agents. Plant physiologists are uncertain of the function that betalains have in plants which possess them, but there is some preliminary evidence that they may have fungicidal properties.

## Signals and Regulators

Plants produce hormones and other growth regulators which act to signal a physiological response in their tissues. They also produce compounds such as phytochrome that are sensitive to light and which serve to trigger growth or development in response to environmental signals.

## Plant Hormones

Plant hormones, known as plant growth regulators (PGRs) or phytohormones, are chemicals that regulate a plant's growth. According to a standard animal definition, hormones are signal molecules produced at specific locations, that occur in very low concentrations, and cause altered processes in target cells at other locations. Unlike animals, plants lack specific hormone-producing tissues or organs. Plant hormones are often not transported to other parts of the plant and production is not limited to specific locations.

Plant hormones are chemicals that in small amounts promote and influence the growth, development and differentiation of cells and tissues. Hormones are vital to plant growth; affecting processes in plants from flowering to seed development, dormancy, and germination. They regulate which tissues grow upwards and which grow downwards, leaf formation and stem growth, fruit development and ripening, as well as leaf abscission and even plant death.

The most important plant hormones are abscissic acid (ABA), auxins, ethylene, gibberellins, and cytokinins, though there are many other substances that serve to regulate plant physiology.

## Photomorphogenesis

While most people know that light is important for photosynthesis in plants, few realize that plant sensitivity to light plays a role in the control of plant structural development (morphogenesis). The use of light to control structural development is called photomorphogenesis, and is dependent upon the presence of specialized photoreceptors, which are chemical pigments capable of absorbing specific wavelengths of light.

Plants use four kinds of photoreceptors: phytochrome, cryptochrome, a UV-B photoreceptor, and protochlorophyllide *a*. The first two of these, phytochrome and cryptochrome, are photoreceptor proteins, complex molecular structures formed by joining a protein with a light-sensitive pigment.

Cryptochrome is also known as the UV-A photoreceptor, because it absorbs ultraviolet light in the long wave 'A' region. The UV-B receptor is one or more compounds that have yet to be identified with certainty, though some evidence suggests carotene or riboflavin as candidates. Protochlorophyllide *a*, as its name suggests, is a chemical precursor of chlorophyll.

The most studied of the photoreceptors in plants is phytochrome. It is sensitive to light in the red and far-red region of the visible spectrum. Many flowering plants use it to regulate the time of flowering based on the length of day and night (photoperiodism) and to set circadian rhythms.

It also regulates other responses including the germination of seeds, elongation of seedlings, the size, shape and number of leaves, the synthesis of chlorophyll, and the straightening of the epicotyl or hypocotyl hook of dicot seedlings.

Many flowering plants use the pigment phytochrome to sense seasonal changes in day length, which they take as signals to flower. This sensitivity to day length is termed photoperiodism. Broadly speaking, flowering plants can be classified as long day plants, short day plants, or day neutral plants, depending on their particular response to changes in day length.

Long day plants require a certain minimum length of daylight to initiate flowering, so these plants flower in the spring or summer. Conversely, short day plants will flower when the length of daylight falls below a certain critical level. Day neutral plants do not initiate flowering based on photoperiodism, though some may use temperature sensitivity (vernalization) instead.

Although a short day plant cannot flower during the long days of summer, it is not actually the period of light exposure that limits flowering. Rather, a short day plant requires a minimal length of uninterrupted darkness in each 24 hour period (a short daylength) before floral development can begin. It has been determined experimentally that a short day plant (long night) will not flower if a flash of phytochrome activating light is used on the plant during the night.

Plants make use of the phytochrome system to sense day length or photoperiod. This fact is utilized by florists and greenhouse gardeners to control and even induce flowering out of season, such as the *Poinsettia*.

Paradoxically, the subdiscipline of environmental physiology is on the one hand a recent field of study in plant ecology and on the other hand one of the oldest. Environmental physiology is the preferred name of the subdiscipline among plant physiologists, but it goes by a number of other names in the applied sciences.

It is roughly synonymous with ecophysiology, crop ecology, horticulture and agronomy. The particular name applied to the subdiscipline is specific to the viewpoint and goals of research. Whatever name is applied, it deals with the ways in which plants respond to their environment and so overlaps with the field of ecology.

Environmental physiologists examine plant response to physical factors such as radiation (including light and ultraviolet radiation), temperature, fire, and wind. Of particular importance are water relations (which can be measured with the Pressure bomb) and the stress of drought or inundation, exchange of gases with the atmosphere, as well as the cycling of nutrients such as nitrogen and carbon.

Environmental physiologists also examine plant response to biological factors. This includes not only negative interactions, such as competition, herbivory, disease and parasitism, but also positive interactions, such as mutualism and pollination.

## Tropisms and Nastic Movements

Plants may respond both to directional and nondirectional stimuli. A response to a directional stimulus, such as gravity or sunlight, is called a tropism. A response to a non-directional stimulus, such as temperature or humidity, is a nastic movement.

Tropisms in plants are the result of differential cell growth, in which the cells on one side of the plant elongate more than those on the other side, causing the part to bend toward the side with less growth. Among the common tropisms seen in plants is phototropism, the bending of the plant toward a source of light.

Phototropism allows the plant to maximize light exposure in plants which require additional light for photosynthesis, or to minimize it in plants subjected to intense light and heat. Geotropism allows the roots of a plant to determine the direction of gravity and grow downwards. Tropisms generally result from an interaction between the environment and production of one or more plant hormones.

In contrast to tropisms, nastic movements result from changes in turgor pressure within plant tissues, and may occur rapidly. A familiar example is thigmonasty (response to touch) in the Venus fly trap, a carnivorous plant. The traps consist of modified leaf blades which bear sensitive trigger hairs. When the hairs are touched by an insect or other animal, the leaf folds shut. This mechanism allows the plant to trap and digest small insects for additional nutrients. Although the trap is rapidly shut by changes in internal cell pressures, the leaf must grow slowly in order to reset for a second opportunity to trap insects.

## Plant Disease

Economically, one of the most important areas of research in environmental physiology is that of phytopathology, the study of diseases in plants and the manner in which plants resist or cope with infection. Plant are susceptible to the same kinds of disease organisms as animals, including viruses, bacteria, and fungi, as well as physical invasion by insects and roundworms.

Because the biology of plants differs from animals, their symptoms and responses are quite different. In some cases, a plant can simply shed infected leaves or flowers to prevent to spread of disease, in a process called abscission.

Most animals do not have this option as a means of controlling disease. Plant diseases organisms themselves also differ from those causing disease in animals because plants cannot usually spread infection through casual physical contact. Plant pathogens tend to spread via spores or are carried by animal vectors.

One of the most important advances in the control of plant disease was the discovery of Bordeaux mixture in the nineteenth century. The mixture is the first known fungicide and is a combination of copper sulfate and lime. Application of the mixture served to inhibit the growth of downy mildew that threatened to seriously damage the French wine industry.

Sir Francis Bacon published one of the first plant physiology experiments in 1627 in the book, *Sylva Sylvarum.* Bacon grew several terrestrial plants, including a rose, in water and concluded that soil was only needed to keep the plant upright. Jan Baptist van Helmont published what is considered the first quantitative experiment in plant physiology in 1648. He grew a willow tree for five years in a pot containing 200 pounds of oven-dry soil. The soil lost just two ounces of dry weight and van Helmont concluded that plants get all their weight from water, not soil. In 1699, John Woodward published experiments on growth of spearmint in different sources of water. He found that plants grew much better in water with soil added than in distilled water.

Stephen Hales is considered the Father of Plant Physiology for the many experiments in the 1727 book; though Julius von Sachs unified the pieces of plant physiology and put them together as a discipline. His *Lehrbuch der Botanik* was the plant physiology bible of its time.

Researchers discovered in the 1800s that plants absorb essential mineral nutrients as inorganic ions in water. In natural conditions, soil acts as a mineral nutrient reservoir but the soil itself is not essential to plant growth. When the mineral nutrients in the soil are dissolved in water, plant roots absorb nutrients readily, soil is no longer required for the plant to thrive.

This observation is the basis for hydroponics, the growing of plants in a water solution rather than soil, which has become a standard technique in biological research, teaching lab exercises, crop production and as a hobby.

## Current Research

One of the leading journals in the field is *Plant Physiology,* started in 1926. All its back issues are available online for free. Many other journals often carry plant physiology articles, including: *Physiologia Plantarum, Journal of Experimental Botany, American Journal of Botany, Annals of Botany, Journal of Plant Nutrition* and *Proceedings of the National Academy of Science.*

In horticulture and agriculture along with food science, plant physiology is an important topic relating to fruits, vegetables, and other consumable parts of plants. Topics studied include: *climatic* requirements, fruit drop, nutrition, ripening, fruit set. The production of food crops also hinges on the study of plant physiology covering such topics as Optimal planting and harvesting times and post harvest storage of plant products for human consumption and the production of secondary products like drugs and cosmetics.

# 16 Plant Nutrition

Plant nutrition is the study of the chemical elements that are necessary for growth. In 1972, E. Epstein defined two criteria for an element to be essential for plant growth:

1. in its absence the plant is unable to complete a normal life cycle; or
2. that the element is part of some essential plant constituent or metabolite, this is all in accordance with Liebig's law of the minimum.

There are seventeen essential plant nutrients. Carbon and oxygen are absorbed from the air, while other nutrients including water are obtained from the soil. Plants must obtain the following mineral nutrients from the growing media:

- the primary macronutrients: nitrogen (N), phosphorus (P), potassium (K)
- the three secondary macronutrients such as calcium (Ca), sulphur (S), magnesium (Mg).
- the macronutrient Silicon (Si); and
- micronutrients or trace minerals: boron (B), chlorine (Cl), manganese (Mn), iron (Fe), zinc (Zn), copper (Cu), molybdenum (Mo), nickel (Ni), selenium (Se), and sodium (Na).

The macronutrients are consumed in larger quantities and are present in plant tissue in quantities from 0.2 per cent to 4.0 per cent (on a dry matter weight basis). Micronutrients are present in plant tissue in quantities measured in parts per million, ranging from 5 to 200 ppm, or less than 0.02 per cent dry weight.

Most soil conditions across the world can provide plants with adequate nutrition and do not require fertilizer for a complete life cycle. However, man can artificially modify soil through the addition of fertilizer to promote vigorous growth and increase yield. The plants are able to obtain their required nutrients from the fertilizer added to the soil. A colloidal carbonaceous residue, known as humus, can serve as a nutrient reservoir. Besides lack of water and sunshine, nutrient deficiency is a major growth limiting factor.

Nutrient uptake in the soil is achieved by cation exchange, where in root hairs pump hydrogen ions ($H^+$) into the soil through proton pumps. These hydrogen ions displace cations attached to negatively charged soil particles so that the cations are available for uptake by the root.

Plant nutrition is a difficult subject to understand completely, partially because of the variation between different plants and even between different species or individuals of a given clone. An element present at a low level may cause deficiency symptoms, while the same element at a higher level may cause toxicity. Further, deficiency of one element may present as symptoms of toxicity from another element. An abundance of one nutrient may cause a deficiency of another nutrient. Also a lowered availability of a given nutrient, such as $SO_2^{-4}$ can affect the uptake of another nutrient, such as $NO_3^-$. Also, $K^+$ uptake can be influenced by the amount $NH_4^+$ available.

The root, especially the root hair, is the most essential organ for the uptake of nutrients. The structure and architecture of the root can alter the rate of nutrient uptake. Nutrient ions are transported to the center of the root, the stele in order for the nutrients to reach the conducting tissues, xylem and phloem. The Casparian strip, a cell wall outside of the stele but within the root, prevents passive flow of water and nutrients to help regulate the uptake of nutrients and water. Xylem moves water and inorganic molecules within the plant and phloem counts organic molecule transportation. Water potential plays a key role in a plants nutrient uptake. If the water potential is more negative within the plant than the surrounding soils, the nutrients will move from the more higher solute (soil) concentration to lower solute concentration (plant).

There are three fundamental ways plants uptake nutrients through the root:

1. *Simple diffusion*, occurs when a nonpolar molecule, such as $O_2$, $CO_2$, and $NH_3$ that follow a concentration gradient, can passively move through the lipid bilayer membrane without the use of transport proteins;
2. *Facilitated diffusion*, is the rapid movement of solutes or ions following a concentration gradient, facilitated by transport proteins;
3. *Active transport*, is the active transport of ions or molecules against a concentration gradient that requires an energy source, usually ATP, to pump the ions or molecules through the membrane.

Nutrients are moved inside a plant to where they are most needed. For example, a plant will try to supply more nutrients to its younger leaves than its older ones. So when nutrients are mobile, the lack of nutrients is first visible on older leaves. However, not all nutrients are equally mobile. When a less mobile nutrient is lacking, the younger leaves suffer because the nutrient does not move up to them but stays lower in the older leaves. Nitrogen, phosphorus, and potassium are mobile nutrients, while the others have varying degrees of mobility. This phenomenon is helpful in determining what nutrients a plant may be lacking.

A symbiotic relationship may exist with:

1. Nitrogen-fixing bacteria, like rhizobia which are involved with nitrogen fixation; and
2. Mycorrhiza, which help to create a larger root surface area.

Both of these mutualistic relationships enhance nutrient uptake.

Though nitrogen is plentiful in the Earth's atmosphere, relatively few plants engage in nitrogen fixation (conversion of atmospheric nitrogen to a biologically useful form). Most plants therefore require nitrogen compounds to be present in the soil in which they grow. These can either be supplied by decaying matter, nitrogen fixing bacteria, animal waste, or through the agricultural application of purpose made fertilizers.

Hydroponics, is growing plants in a water-nutrient solution without the use of nutrient-rich soil. It allows researchers and home gardeners to grow their plants in a controlled environment. The most common solution, is the Hoagland Solution, developed by D.R. Hoagland in 1933, the solution consists of all the essential nutrients in the correct proportions necessary for most plant growth. An aerator is used to prevent an anoxic event or hypoxia. Hypoxia can affect nutrient uptake of a plant because without oxygen present, respiration becomes inhibited within the root cells. The Nutrient film technique is a variation of hydroponic technique. The roots are not fully submerged which allows for adequate aeration of the roots, while a 'film' thin layer of nutrient rich water is pumped through the system to provide nutrients and water to the plant.

Plants uptake essential elements from the soil through their roots and from the air (mainly consisting of carbon and oxygen) through their leaves.

In the leaves, transpiration occurs, where stomata open to take in carbon dioxide and expel oxygen that drives the movement of water and nutrients to the plant Green plants obtain their carbohydrate supply from the carbon dioxide in the air by the process of photosynthesis.

## Functions of Nutrients

Each of these nutrients is used in a different place for a different essential function.

### Carbon

Carbon forms the backbone of many plants biomolecules, including starches and cellulose. Carbon is fixed through photosynthesis from the carbon dioxide in the air and is a part of the carbohydrates that store energy in the plant.

### Hydrogen

Hydrogen also is necessary for building sugars and building the plant. It is obtained almost entirely from water. Hydrogen ions are imperative for a proton gradient to help drive the electron transport chain in photosynthesis and for respiration.

### Oxygen

Oxygen is necessary for cellular respiration. Cellular respiration is the process of generating energy-rich adenosine triphosphate (ATP) via the consumption of sugars made in photosynthesis. Plants produce oxygen gas during photosynthesis to produce glucose but then require oxygen to undergo aerobic cellular respiration and break down this glucose and produce ATP.

### Phosphorus

Phosphorus is important in plant bioenergetics. As a component of ATP, phosphorus is needed for the conversion of light energy to chemical energy (ATP) during photosynthesis. Phosphorus can also be used to modify the activity of various enzymes by phosphorylation, and can be used for cell signalling. Since ATP can be used for the biosynthesis of many plant biomolecules, phosphorus is important for plant growth and flower/seed formation. Phosphate esters make up DNA, RNA, and phospholipids. Most common in the form of polyprotic phosphoric acid ($H_3PO_4$) in soil, but it is taken up most readily in the form of

$H_2PO_4$. Phosphorus is limited in most soils because it is released very slowly from insoluble phosphates. Under most environmental conditions it is the limiting element because of its small concentration in soil and high demand by plants and microorganisms. Plants can increase phosphorus uptake by a mutualism with mycorrhiza.

A Phosphorus deficiency in plants is characterized by an intense green colouration in leaves. If the plant is experiencing high phosphorus deficiencies the leaves may become denatured and show signs of necrosis. Occasionally the leaves may appear purple from an accumulation of anthocyanin. Because phosphorus is a mobile nutrient, older leaves will show the first signs of deficiency.

High phosphorus content fertilizers, such as bone meal, is useful to apply to perennials to help with successful root formation.

### Potassium

Potassium regulates the opening and closing of the stomata by a potassium ion pump. Since stomata are important in water regulation, potassium reduces water loss from the leaves and increases drought tolerance. Potassium deficiency may cause necrosis or interveinal chlorosis. $K^+$ is highly mobile and can aid in balancing the anion charges within the plant. It also has high solubility in water and leaches out of soils that rocky or sandy that can result in potassium deficiency. It serves as an activator of enzymes used in photosynthesis and respiration Potassium is used to build cellulose and aids in photosynthesis by the formation of a chlorophyll precursor.

Potassium deficiency may result in higher risk of pathogens, wilting, chlorosis, brown spotting, and higher chances of damage from frost and heat.

### Nitrogen

Nitrogen is an essential component of all proteins. Nitrogen deficiency most often results in stunted growth, slow growth, and chlorsis. Nitrogen deficient plants will also exhibit a purple appearance on the stems, petioles and underside of leaves from an accumulation of anthocyanin pigements.

Most of the nitrogen taken up by plants is from the soil in the forms of $NO_3^-$. Amino acids and proteins can only be built from $NH_4^+$ so $NO_3^-$ must be reduced. Under many agricultural settings, nitrogen is the limiting nutrient of high growth. Some plants require more nitrogen than others, such as corn (*Zea mays*). Because nitrogen is mobile, the older leaves exhibit chlorosis and necrosis earlier than the younger leaves. Soluble forms of nitrogen are transported as amines and amides.

**Sulphur**

Sulphur is a structural component of some amino acids and vitamins, and is essential in the manufacturing of chloroplasts.

**Calcium**

Calcium regulates transport of other nutrients into the plant and is also involved in the activation of certain plant enzymes. Calcium deficiency results in stunting.

**Magnesium**

Magnesium is an important part of chlorophyll, a critical plant pigment important in photosynthesis. It is important in the production of ATP through its role as an enzyme cofactor. There are many other biological roles for magnesium—Magnesium deficiency can result in interveinal chlorosis.

**Silicon**

Silicon is deposited in cell walls and contributes to its mechanical properties including rigidity and elasticity.

**Iron**

Iron is necessary for photosynthesis and is present as an enzyme cofactor in plants. Iron deficiency can result in interveinal chlorosis and necrosis.

## Molybdenum

Molybdenum is a cofactor to enzymes important in building amino acids.

## Boron

Boron is important for binding of pectins in the RGII region of the primary cell wall, secondary roles may be in sugar transport, cell division, and synthesizing certain enzymes. Boron deficiency causes necrosis in young leaves and stunting.

## Copper

Copper is important for photosynthesis. Symptoms for copper deficiency include chlorosis. Involved in many enzyme processes. Necessary for proper photosythesis. Involved in the manufacture of lignin (cell walls). Involved in grain production.

## Manganese

Manganese is necessary for building the chloroplasts. Manganese deficiency may result in coloration abnormalities, such as discoloured spots on the foliage.

## Sodium

Sodium is involved in the regeneration of phosphoenolpyruvate in CAM and C4 plants. It can also substitute for potassium in some circumstances.

## Zinc

Zinc is required in a large number of enzymes and plays an essential role in DNA transcription. A typical symptom of zinc deficiency is the stunted growth of leaves, commonly known as 'little leaf' and is caused by the oxidative degradation of the growth hormone auxin.

## Nickel

In higher plants, Nickel is essential for activation of urease, an enzyme involved with nitrogen metabolism that is required to process urea. Without Nickel, toxic levels of urea accumulate, leading to the formation of necrotic lesions. In lower plants, Nickel activates several enzymes involved in a variety of processes, and can substitute for Zinc and Iron as a cofactor in some enzymes.

## Chlorine

Chlorine is necessary for osmosis and ionic balance; it also plays a role in photosynthesis.

Cobalt has proven to be beneficial to at least some plants, but is essential in others, such as legumes where it is required for nitrogen fixation for the symbiotic relationship it has with nitrogen-fixing bacteria. Vanadium may be required by some plants, but at very low concentrations. It may also be substituting for molybdenum. Selenium and sodium may also be beneficial. Sodium can replace potassium's regulation of stomatal opening and closing.

Some elements are directly involved in plant metabolism. However, this principle does not account for the so-called beneficial elements, whose presence, while not required, has clear positive effects on plant growth.

# Leaf

In botany, a leaf is an above-ground plant organ specialized for the process of photosynthesis. For this purpose, a leaf is typically flat (laminar) and thin. As an evolutionary trait, the flatness of leaves works to expose the chloroplasts to more light and to increase the absorption of carbon dioxide at the expense of water loss. In the Devonian period, when carbon dioxide concentration was at several times its present value, plants did not have leaves or flat stems. Many bryophytes have flat, photosynthetic organs, but these are not true leaves. Neither are the microphylls of lycophytes. The leaves of ferns, gymnosperms, and angiosperms are variously referred to as macrophyll, megaphylls, or euphylls.

Leaves are also the sites in most plants where transpiration and guttation take place. Leaves can store food and water, and are modified in some plants for other purposes. The comparable structures of ferns are correctly referred to as fronds. Furthermore, leaves are prominent in the human diet as leaf vegetables.

A structurally complete leaf of an angiosperm consists of a petiole (leaf stalk), a *lamina* (leaf blade), and stipules (small processes located to either side of the base of the petiole). The petiole attaches to the stem at a point called the 'leaf axil'. Not every species produces leaves with all of the aforementioned structural components. In certain species, paired stipules are not obvious or are absent altogether. A petiole may be absent, or the blade may not be laminar (flattened). The tremendous variety shown in leaf structure (anatomy) from species to species is presented in detail below under Leaf morphology. Periodically (*i.e.* seasonally, during the autumn), deciduous trees shed their leaves. These leaves then decompose into the soil.

A leaf is considered a plant organ and typically consists of the following tissues:

- An epidermis that covers the upper and lower surfaces.
- An interior *chlorenchyma* called the mesophyll.
- An arrangement of veins (the vascular tissue).

The epidermis is the outer layer of cells covering the leaf. It forms the boundary separating the plant's inner cells from the external world. The epidermis serves several functions: protection against water loss by way of transpiration, regulation of gas exchange, secretion of metabolic compounds, and (in some species) absorption of water. Most leaves show dorsoventral anatomy: the upper (adaxial) and lower (abaxial) surfaces have somewhat different construction and may serve different functions.

The epidermis is usually transparent (epidermal cells lack chloroplasts) and coated on the outer side with a waxy cuticle that prevents water loss. The cuticle is in some cases thinner on the lower epidermis than on the upper epidermis, and is thicker on leaves from dry climates as compared with those from wet climates.

The epidermis tissue includes several differentiated cell types: epidermal cells, guard cells, subsidiary cells, and epidermal hairs (trichomes). The epidermal cells are the most numerous, largest, and least specialized. These are typically more elongated in the leaves of monocots than in those of dicots.

The epidermis is covered with pores called *stomata*, part of a stoma complex consisting of a pore surrounded on each side by chloroplast-containing guard cells, and two to four subsidiary cells that lack chloroplasts. The stoma complex regulates the exchange of gases and water vapor between the outside air and the interior of the leaf. Typically, the stomata are more numerous over the abaxial (lower) epidermis than the adaxial (upper) epidermis.

## Mesophyll

Most of the interior of the leaf between the upper and lower layers of epidermis is a *parenchyma* (ground tissue) or *chlorenchyma* tissue called the mesophyll (Greek for 'middle leaf'). This assimilation tissue is the primary location of photosynthesis in the plant. The products of photosynthesis are called 'assimilates'.

## Palisade Layer

An upper *palisade layer* of tightly packed, vertically elongated cells, one to two cells thick, directly beneath the adaxial epidermis. Its cells contain many more chloroplasts than the spongy layer. These long cylindrical cells are regularly arranged in one to five rows. Cylindrical cells, with the *chloroplasts* close to the walls of the cell, can take optimal advantage of light. The slight separation of the cells provides maximum absorption of carbon dioxide. This separation must be minimal to afford capillary action for water distribution. In order to adapt to their different environment (such as sun or shade), plants had to adapt this structure to obtain optimal result. Sun leaves have a multi-layered palisade layer, while shade leaves or older leaves closer to the soil, are single-layered.

## Spongy Cells

Beneath the palisade layer is the spongy layer. The cells of the spongy layer are more rounded and not so tightly packed. There are large intercellular air spaces. These cells contain fewer chloroplasts than those of the palisade layer.

The pores or *stomata* of the epidermis open into substomatal chambers, connecting to air spaces between the spongy layer cells.

These two different layers of the mesophyll are absent in many aquatic and marsh plants. Even an epidermis and a mesophyll may be lacking. Instead for their gaseous exchanges they use a homogeneous aerenchyma (thin-walled cells separated by large gas-filled spaces). Their stomata are situated at the upper surface.

Leaves are normally green in colour, which comes from chlorophyll found in plastids in the chlorenchyma cells. Plants that lack chlorophyll cannot photosynthesize.

Leaves in temperate, boreal, and seasonally dry zones may be seasonally deciduous (falling off or dying for the inclement season). This mechanism to shed leaves is called abscission. After the leaf is shed, a leaf scar develops on the twig. In cold autumns they sometimes change colour, and turn yellow, bright orange or red as various accessory pigments (carotenoids and xanthophylls) are revealed when the tree responds to cold and reduced sunlight by curtailing chlorophyll production. Red anthocyanin pigments are now thought to be produced in the leaf as it dies, possibly to mask the yellow hue left when the chlorophyll is lost — yellow leaves appear to attract herbivores such as aphids.

## Veins

The veins are the vascular tissue of the leaf and are located in the spongy layer of the mesophyll. They are typical examples of pattern formation through ramification. The pattern of the veins is called venation.

The veins are made up of:

- *Xylem:* tubes that brings water and minerals from the roots into the leaf;
- *Phloem:* tubes that usually move sap, with dissolved sucrose, produced by photosynthesis in the leaf, out of the leaf;

The xylem typically lies over the phloem. Both are embedded in a dense parenchyma tissue, called 'pith', with usually some structural collenchyma tissue present.

## Morphology

External leaf characteristics (such as shape, margin, hairs, etc.) are important for identifying plant species, and botanists have developed a rich terminology for describing leaf characteristics. These structures are a part of what makes leaves determinant; they grow and achieve a specific pattern and shape, then stop. Other plant parts like stems or roots are non-determinant, and will usually continue to grow as long as they have the resources to do so.

Classification of leaves can occur through many different designative schema, and the type of leaf is usually characteristic of a species, although some species produce more than one type of leaf. The longest type of leaf is a leaf from palm trees, measuring at nine feet long. The terminology associated with the description of leaf morphology is presented, in illustrated form, at Wikibooks.

## Basic Types

Leaves of the White Spruce (Picea glauca) are needle-shaped and their arrangement is spiral:

- Ferns have fronds
- Conifer leaves are typically needle-, awl-, or scale-shaped.
- Angiosperm (flowering plant) leaves: the standard form includes stipules, a petiole, and a lamina.
- Lycophytes have microphyll leaves.
- Sheath leaves (type found in most grasses).
- Other specialized leaves (such as those of *Nepenthes*).

## Arrangement on the Stem

Different terms are usually used to describe leaf placement (phyllotaxis).

The leaves on this plant are arranged in pairs opposite one another, with successive pairs at right angles to each other ('decussate') along the red stem. Note developing buds in the axils of these leaves.

Alternate — leaf attachments are singular at nodes, and leaves alternate direction, to a greater or lesser degree, along the stem.

- *Opposite* — Two structures, one on each opposite side of the stem, typically leaves, branches, or flower parts. Leaf attachments are paired at each node; decussate if, as typical, each successive pair is rotated 90° progressing along the stem; or distichous if not rotated, but two-ranked (in the same geometric flat-plane).
- *Whorled* — three or more leaves attach at each point or node on the stem. As with opposite leaves, successive whorls may or may not be decussate, rotated by half the angle between the leaves in the whorl (*i.e.*, successive whorls of three rotated 60°, whorls of four rotated 45°, etc.). Opposite leaves may appear whorled near the tip of the stem.
- *Rosulate* — leaves form a rosette.

As a *stem* grows, leaves tend to appear arranged around the stem in a way that optimizes yield of light. In essence, leaves form a helix pattern centred around the stem, either clockwise or counterclockwise, with (depending upon the species) the same angle of divergence. There is a regularity in these angles and they follow the numbers in a Fibonacci sequence: 1/2, 2/3, 3/5, 5/8, 8/13, 13/21, 21/34, 34/55, 55/89. This series tends to a limit close to 360° × 34/89 = 137.52 or 137° 30′, an angle known mathematically as the golden angle. In the series, the numerator indicates the number of complete turns or 'gyres' until a leaf arrives at the initial position. The denominator indicates the number of leaves in the arrangement. This can be demonstrated by the following:

- alternate leaves have an angle of 180° (or 1/2)
- 120° (or 1/3): three leaves in one circle

- 144° (or 2/5): five leaves in two gyres
- 135° (or 3/8): eight leaves in three gyres.

Two basic forms of leaves can be described considering the way the blade (lamina) is divided. A simple leaf has an undivided blade. However, the leaf shape may be formed of lobes, but the gaps between lobes do not reach to the main vein. A compound leaf has a fully subdivided blade, each leaflet of the blade separated along a main or secondary vein. Because each leaflet can appear to be a simple leaf, it is important to recognize where the petiole occurs to identify a compound leaf. Compound leaves are a characteristic of some families of higher plants, such as the Fabaceae. The middle vein of a compound leaf or a frond, when it is present, is called a rachis.

- *Palmately compound* leaves have the leaflets radiating from the end of the petiole, like fingers off the palm of a hand, *e.g. Cannabis* (hemp) and *Aesculus* (buckeyes).
- *Pinnately compound* leaves have the leaflets arranged along the main or mid-vein.
- *Odd pinnate* with a terminal leaflet, *e.g. Fraxinus* (ash).
- *Even pinnate:* lacking a terminal leaflet, *e.g. Swietenia* (mahogany).
- *Bipinnately compound* leaves are twice divided: the leaflets are arranged along a secondary vein that is one of several branching off the rachis. Each leaflet is called a 'pinnule'. The pinnules on one secondary vein are called 'pinna'; e.g. *Albizia* (silk tree).
- *Trifoliate* (or *trifoliolate*): a pinnate leaf with just three leaflets, e.g. *Trifolium* (clover), *Laburnum* (laburnum).
- *Pinnatifid:* pinnately dissected to the central vein, but with the leaflets not entirely separate, *e.g. Polypodium,* some *Sorbus* (whitebeams). In pinnately veined leaves the central vein in known as the *midrib*. Characteristics of the petiole.

The overgrown petioles of Rhubarb (*Rheum rhabarbarum*) are edible.

Petiolated leaves have a petiole (leaf stem). Sessile leaves do not: the blade attaches directly to the stem. In clasping or decurrent leaves, the blade partially or wholly surrounds the stem, often giving the impression that the shoot grows through the leaf. When this is actually the case, the leaves are called 'perfoliate', such as in *Claytonia perfoliata*. In peltate leaves, the petiole attaches to the blade inside from the blade margin.

In some *Acacia* species, such as the Koa Tree (*Acacia koa*), the petioles are expanded or broadened and function like leaf blades; these are called phyllodes. There may or may not be normal pinnate leaves at the tip of the phyllode.

A stipule, present on the leaves of many dicotyledons, is an appendage on each side at the base of the petiole resembling a small leaf. Stipules may be lasting and not be shed (a stipulate leaf, such as in roses and beans), or be shed as the leaf expands, leaving a stipule scar on the twig (an exstipulate leaf).

- The situation, arrangement, and structure of the stipules is called the 'stipulation'.
- Free
- *Adnate:* fused to the petiole base.
- *Ochreate:* provided with ochrea, or sheath-formed stipules, *e.g.* rhubarb, encircling the petiole base.
- *Interpetiolar:* between the petioles of two opposite leaves.
- *Intrapetiolar:* between the petiole and the subtending stem.

There are two subtypes of venation, namely, *craspedodromous*, where the major veins stretch up to the margin of the leaf, and *camptodromous*, when major veins extend close to the margin, but bend before they intersect with the margin.

Feather-veined, reticulate (also called pinnate-netted, penniribbed, penninerved, or penniveined)—the veins arise pinnately from a single mid-vein and subdivide into veinlets. These, in turn, form a complicated network. This type of venation is typical for (but by no means limited to) dicotyledons.

Three main veins branch at the base of the lamina and run essentially parallel subsequently, as in *Ceanothus*. A similar pattern (with 3-7 veins) is especially conspicuous in Melastomataceae.

1. Palmate-netted, palmate-veined, fan-veined; several main veins diverge from near the leaf base where the petiole attaches, and radiate toward the edge of the leaf; *e.g.* most *Acer* (maples).
2. Parallel-veined, parallel-ribbed, parallel-nerved, penniparallel—veins run parallel for the length of the leaf, from the base to the apex. Commissural veins (small veins) connect the major parallel veins. Typical for most monocotyledons, such as grasses.
3. Dichotomous—There are no dominant bundles, with the veins forking regularly by pairs; found in *Ginkgo* and some pteridophytes.

Note that although it is the more complex pattern, branching veins appear to be plesiomorphic and in some form were present in ancient seed plants as long as 250 million years ago. A pseudo-reticulate venation that is actually a highly modified penniparallel one is an autapomorphy of some Melanthiaceae which are monocots, e.g. *Paris quadrifolia* (True-lover's Knot).

## Morphology Changes within a Single Plant

- Homoblasty — Characteristic in which a plant has small changes in leaf size, shape, and growth habit between juvenile and adult stages.
- Heteroblasty — Characteristic in which a plant has marked changes in leaf size, shape, and growth habit between juvenile and adult stages. Edge (margin).
- *ciliate:* fringed with hairs.
- *crenate:* wavy-toothed; dentate with rounded teeth, such as *Fagus* (beech).
- *crenulate* finely or shallowly crenate.
- *dentate:* toothed, such as *Castanea* (chestnut).

- *coarse-toothed:* with large teeth.
- *glandular toothed:* with teeth that bear glands.
- *denticulate:* finely toothed.
- *doubly toothed:* each tooth bearing smaller teeth, such as *Ulmus* (elm).
- *entire:* even; with a smooth margin; without toothing.
- *lobate:* indented, with the indentations not reaching to the center, such as many *Quercus* (oaks).
- *palmately lobed:* indented with the indentations reaching to the center, such as *Humulus* (hop).
- *serrate:* saw-toothed with asymmetrical teeth pointing forward, such as *Urtica* (nettle).
- *serrulate:* finely serrate.
- *sinuate:* with deep, wave-like indentations; coarsely crenate, such as many *Rumex* (docks).
- *spiny* or *pungent:* with stiff, sharp points, such as some *Ilex* (hollies) and *Cirsium* (thistles).

## Tip

Leaves showing various morphologies. Clockwise from upper left: tripartite lobation, elliptic with serrulate margin, peltate with palmate venation, acuminate odd-pinnate (center), pinnatisect, lobed, elliptic with entire margin.

- *acuminate:* long-pointed, prolonged into a narrow, tapering point in a concave manner.
- *acute:* ending in a sharp, but not prolonged point.
- *cuspidate:* with a sharp, elongated, rigid tip; tipped with a cusp.
- *emarginate:* indented, with a shallow notch at the tip.
- *mucronate:* abruptly tipped with a small short point, as a continuation of the midrib; tipped with a mucro.
- *mucronulate:* mucronate, but with a smaller spine.
- *obcordate:* inversely heart-shaped, deeply notched at the top.

- *obtuse:* rounded or blunt.
- *truncate:* ending abruptly with a flat end, that looks cut off.

## Base

- *acuminate:* coming to a sharp, narrow, prolonged point.
- *acute:* coming to a sharp, but not prolonged point.
- *auriculate:* ear-shaped.
- *cordate:* heart-shaped with the notch towards the stalk.
- *cuneate:* wedge-shaped.
- *hastate:* shaped like an halberd and with the basal lobes pointing outward.
- *oblique:* slanting.
- *reniform:* kidney-shaped but rounder and broader than long.
- *rounded:* curving shape.
- *sagittate:* shaped like an arrowhead and with the acute basal lobes pointing downward.
- *truncate:* ending abruptly with a flat end, that looks cut off.

## Surface

- *farinose:* bearing farina; mealy, covered with a waxy, whitish powder.
- *glabrous:* smooth, not hairy.
- *glaucous:* with a whitish bloom; covered with a very fine, bluish-white powder.
- *glutinous:* sticky, viscid.
- *papillate*, or *papillose:* bearing papillae (minute, nipple-shaped protuberances).
- *pubescent:* covered with erect hairs (especially soft and short ones).
- *punctate:* marked with dots; dotted with depressions or with translucent glands or colored dots.
- *rugose:* deeply wrinkled; with veins clearly visible.

- *scurfy:* covered with tiny, broad scalelike particles.
- *tuberculate:* covered with tubercles; covered with warty prominences.
- *verrucose:* warted, with warty outgrowths.
- *viscid*, or *viscous:* covered with thick, sticky secretions.

The leaf surface is also host to a large variety of microorganisms; in this context it is referred to as the phyllosphere.

## Hairiness

Scanning electron microscope image of trichomes on the lower surface of a *Coleus blumei* (coleus) leaf.

'Hairs' on plants are properly called trichomes. Leaves can show several degrees of hairiness. The meaning of several of the following terms can overlap.

- *arachnoid*, or *arachnose:* with many fine, entangled hairs giving a cobwebby appearance.
- *barbellate:* with finely barbed hairs (barbellae).
- *bearded:* with long, stiff hairs.
- *bristly:* with stiff hair-like prickles.
- *canescent:* hoary with dense grayish-white pubescence.
- *ciliate:* marginally fringed with short hairs (cilia).
- *ciliolate:* minutely ciliate.
- *floccose:* with flocks of soft, woolly hairs, which tend to rub off.
- *glabrous:* no hairs of any kind present.
- *glandular:* with a gland at the tip of the hair.
- *hirsute:* with rather rough or stiff hairs.
- *hispid:* with rigid, bristly hairs.
- *hispidulous:* minutely hispid.
- *hoary:* with a fine, close grayish-white pubescence.
- *lanate*, or *lanose:* with woolly hairs.
- *pilose:* with soft, clearly separated hairs.
- *puberulent*, or *puberulous:* with fine, minute hairs.

- *pubescent:* with soft, short and erect hairs.
- *scabrous,* or *scabrid:* rough to the touch.
- *sericeous:* silky appearance through fine, straight and appressed (lying close and flat) hairs.
- *silky:* with adpressed, soft and straight pubescence.
- *stellate,* or *stelliform:* with star-shaped hairs.
- *strigose:* with appressed, sharp, straight and stiff hairs.
- *tomentose:* densely pubescent with matted, soft white woolly hairs.
- *cano-tomentose:* between canescent and tomentose.
- *felted-tomentose:* woolly and matted with curly hairs.
- *villous:* with long and soft hairs, usually curved.
- *woolly:* with long, soft and tortuous or matted hairs.

Poinsettia bracts are leaves which have evolved red pigmentation in order to attract insects and birds to the central flowers, an adaptive function normally served by petals (which are themselves leaves highly modified by evolution).

In the course of evolution, leaves have adapted to different environments in the following ways:

- A certain surface structure avoids moistening by rain and contamination.
- Sliced leaves reduce wind resistance.
- Hairs on the leaf surface trap humidity in dry climates and create a boundary layer reducing water loss.
- Waxy leaf surfaces reduce water loss.
- Large surface area provides large area for sunlight and shade for plant to minimize heating and reduce water loss.
- In more or less opaque or buried in the soil leaves, translucent windows filter the light before the photosynthesis takes place at the inner leaf surfaces (*e.g. Fenestraria*).
- Succulent leaves store water and organic acids for use in CAM photosynthesis.

- Aromatic oils, poisons or pheromones produced by leaf borne glands deter herbivores (*e.g.* eucalypts).
- Inclusions of crystalline minerals deter herbivores (*e.g.* silica phytoliths in grasses, raphides in Araceae).
- Petals attracts pollinators.
- Spines protect the plants (*e.g.* cacti).
- Insect traps feed the plants directly.
- Bulbs store food and water (*e.g.* onions).
- Tendrils allow the plant to climb (*e.g* peas).
- Bracts and pseudanthia (*false flowers*) replace normal flower structures when the true flowers are greatly reduced (*e.g.* Spurges).

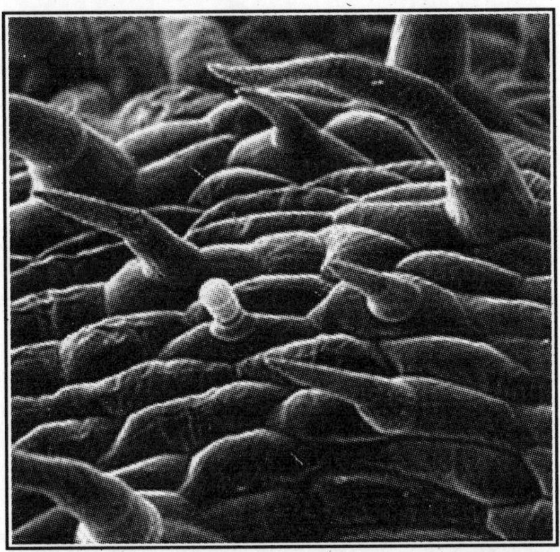

**Scanning Electron Microscope Image of Trichomes on the Lower Surface of a *Coleus blumei* (Coleus) Leaf**

## Interactions with Other Organisms

Although not as nutritious as other organs such as fruit, leaves provide a food source for many organisms. Animals which eat leaves are known as folivores. The leaf is one of the most vital parts of the plant, and plants have evolved protection against folivores such as tannins, chemicals which hinder the digestion of proteins and have an unpleasant taste.

Some animals have cryptic adaptations to avoid their own predators. For example, some caterpillars will create a small home in the leaf by folding it over themselves, while other herbivores and their prey mimic the appearance of the leaf. Some insects, such as the katydid, take this even further, moving from side to side much like a leaf does in the wind.

# Poaceae

Poaceae (formerly known as Gramineae) is a family in the Class Liliopsida (the monocots) of the flowering plants. Plants of this family are usually called grasses, or, to distinguish them from other graminoids, true grasses; the shrub-or tree-like plants in this family are called bamboo (there are also herbaceous, non-woody bamboos). There are about 600 genera and some 9,000-10,000 or more species of grasses (Kew Index of World Grass Species).

Plant communities dominated by Poaceae are called grasslands; it is estimated that grasslands comprise 20 per cent of the vegetation cover of the Earth. Grass species also occur in many other habitats that are not formally considered to be grasslands, including different types of wetlands (*e.g.*, fens, marshes), forests and tundra.

Poaceae is often considered to be the most important of all plant families to human economies: it includes the staple food grains and cereal crops grown around the world, lawn and forage grasses, and bamboo, which is widely used for construction throughout east Asia and sub-Saharan Africa. Civilization was founded largely on the ability to domesticate cereal grass crops around the world.

The term 'grass' is also applied to plants that are not members of the Poaceae lineage, including the rushes (Juncaceae) and sedges (Cyperaceae). This broad and general use of the word 'grass' has led to plants of the Poaceae often being called 'true grasses'.

Poaceae have hollow stems called *culms*, which are plugged (solid) at intervals called *nodes*, the points along the culm at which leaves arise. Grass leaves are alternate, *distichous* (in one plane) or rarely spiral, and parallel-veined. Each leaf is differentiated into a lower *sheath* which hugs the stem for a distance and a *blade* with margins usually entire. The leaf blades of many grasses are hardened with silica phytoliths, which helps discourage grazing animals. In some grasses (such as sword grass) this makes the edges of the grass blades sharp enough to cut human skin. A membranous appendage or fringe of hairs, called the *ligule*, lies at the junction between sheath and blade, preventing water or insects from penetrating into the sheath.

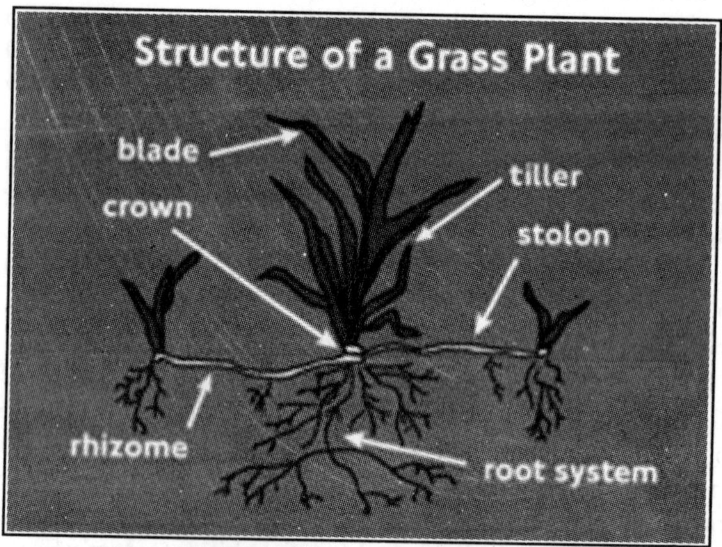


**Structure of a Grass Plant**

Grass blades grow at the base of the blade and not from elongated stem tips. This low growth point evolved in response to grazing animals and allows grasses to be grazed or mown regularly without severe damage to the plant.

Flowers of Poaceae are characteristically arranged in *spikelets*, each spikelet having one or more florets (the spikelets are further grouped into panicles or spikes). A spikelet consists of two (or sometimes fewer) bracts at the base, called *glumes*, followed by one or more florets. A floret consists of the flower surrounded by two bracts called the *lemma* (the external one) and the *palea* (the internal). The flowers are usually hermaphroditic (maize, monoecious, is an exception) and pollination is always anemophilous, that is, by wind. The perianth is reduced to two scales, called *lodicules*, that expand and contract to spread the lemma and palea; these are generally interpreted to be modified sepals. This complex structure can be seen in the image on the left, portraying a wheat (*Triticum aestivum*) spike.

The fruit of Poaceae is a *caryopsis*, in which the seed coat is fused to the fruit wall and thus, not separable from it (as in a maize kernel).

There are three general classifications of growth habit present in grasses; bunch-type (also called caespitose), stoloniferous, and rhizomatous.

The success of the grasses lies in part in their morphology and growth processes, and in part in their physiological diversity. Most of the grasses divide into two physiological groups, using the C3 and C4 photosynthetic pathways for carbon fixation. The C4 grasses have a photosynthetic pathway linked to specialized Kranz leaf anatomy that particularly adapts them to hot climates and an atmosphere low in carbon dioxide.

C3 grasses are referred to as 'cool season grasses' while C4 plants are considered 'warm season grasses'. Grasses may be either annual or perennial.

- Annual Cool Season — wheat, rye, Annual Bluegrass (annual meadowgrass, *Poa annua*), and oat.

- Perennial Cool Season — orchardgrass (cocksfoot, *Dactylis glomerata*), fescue (*Festuca* spp), Kentucky Bluegrass and perennial ryegrass ( *Lolium perenne*).
- Annual Warm Season — corn, sudangrass, and pearl millet.
- Perennial Warm Season — big bluestem, indiangrass, bermudagrass and switchgrass.

## Grass Evolution

Until recently grasses were thought to have evolved around 55 million years ago, based on fossil records. However, recent findings of 65-million-year-old phytoliths resembling grass phytoliths (including ancestors of rice and bamboo) in Cretaceous dinosaur coprolites, may place the diversification of grasses to an earlier date.

## Subfamilies and Genera

*Tragus roxburghii* from Chloridoideae

The most recent classification of the grass family recognizes twelve subfamilies:

- Anomochlooideae, a small lineage of broad-leaved grasses that includes two genera (*Anomochloa, Streptochaeta*).
- Pharoideae, a small lineage of grasses that includes three genera, including *Pharus* and *Leptaspis*.
- Puelioideae, a small lineage that includes the African genus *Puelia*.
- Pooideae, including wheat, barley, oats, brome-grass (*Bromus*), reed-grasses (*Calamagrostis*) and many lawn and pasture grasses.
- Bambusoideae, including bamboo.
- Ehrhartoideae, including rice, wild rice.
- Arundinoideae, including giant reed, common reed.
- Centothecoideae, a small subfamily of 11 genera that is sometimes included in Panicoideae.

- Chloridoideae, including the lovegrasses (*Eragrostis*, ca. 350 species, including teff), dropseeds (*Sporobolus*, some 160 species), finger millet (*Eleusine coracana* (L.) Gaertn.), and the muhly grasses (*Muhlenbergia*, ca. 175 species).
- Panicoideae, including panic grass, maize, sorghum, sugar cane, most millets, fonio, and bluestem grasses.
- Micrairoideae.
- Danthonioideae, including pampas grass.

*Poa* is a Pooideae genus of about 500 species of grasses, native to the temperate regions of both hemispheres.

## Economic Importance

Grasses are, in human terms, perhaps the most economically important plant family. Grasses' economic importance stems from several areas, including food production, industry, and lawns.

## Food Production

Agricultural grasses grown for their edible seeds are called *cereals*. Three cereals — rice, wheat, and maize (corn) — provide more than half of all calories eaten by humans. Of all crops, 70 per cent are grasses. Cereals constitute the major source of carbohydrate for humans and perhaps the major source of protein, and include rice in southern and eastern Asia, maize in Central and South America, and wheat and barley in Europe, northern Asia and the Americas.

Sugarcane is the major source of sugar production. Many other grasses are grown for forage and fodder for animal food, particularly for sheep and cattle, thereby indirectly providing more human calories.

## Industry

Grasses are used for construction. Scaffolding made from bamboo is able to withstand typhoon force winds that would break steel scaffolding. Larger bamboos and *Arundo donax* have stout culms that can be used in a manner similar to timber, and grass roots stabilize the sod of sod houses. *Arundo* is used to make reeds for woodwind instruments, and bamboo is used for innumerable implements.

Grass fibre can be used for making paper, and for biofuel production.

*Phragmites australis* (common reed) is important in water treatment, wetland habitat preservation and land reclamation in the Old World.

### Lawn and Ornamental Grasses

Grasses are the primary plant used in lawns, which themselves derive from grazed grasslands in Europe. They are also provide an important means of erosion control (*e.g.*, along roadsides), especially on sloping land.

Although supplanted by artificial turf in some games, grasses are still an important covering of playing surfaces in many sports, including football, tennis, golf, cricket, and softball/baseball.

Ornamental grasses, such as perennial bunch grasses, are used in many styles of garden design for their foliage, inflorescences, seed heads, and slope stabilization. They are often used in natural landscaping, xeriscaping, contemporary or modern landscaping, wildlife gardening, and native plant gardening.

With 10,025 known species, the Poaceae is the fourth largest plant family. Only Orchidaceae, Asteraceae, and Fabaceae have more species, although with over 10,000 species the Rubiaceae is not far behind.

Biomes dominated by grasses are called grasslands. If only large contiguous chunks of grasslands are counted, these biomes cover 31 per cent of the planet's land. Grasslands go by various names depending on location, including pampas, plains, steppes, or prairie.

In addition to their use as forage worldwide by many grazing mammals such as cattle and other livestock, deer, and elephants, grasses are used as food plants by many species of butterflies and moths; see List of Lepidoptera that feed on grasses.

The evolution of large grazing animals in the Cenozoic has contributed to the spread of grasses. Without large grazers, a clearcut of fire-destroyed area would soon be colonized by grasses and, if there is enough rain, tree seedlings. The tree seedlings would eventually produce shade, which kills most grasses. Large animals, however, trample the seedlings, killing the trees. Grasses persist because their lack of woody stems helps them to resist the damage of trampling.

Grasses have long had significance in human society. They have been cultivated as a food source for domesticated animals for up to 10,000 years, and have been used to make paper since at least as early as 2400 B.C. Also, the primary ingredient of beer is usually barley or wheat, both grasses that have been used for this purpose for over 1000 years.

Some common aphorisms involve grass. For example:

- 'The grass is always greener on the other side' suggests that an alternate state of affairs will always seem preferable to one's own.
- 'Don't let the grass grow under your feet' tells someone to get moving.
- 'A snake in the grass' means dangers that are hidden.
- 'When elephants fight, it is the grass who suffers' tells of bystanders caught in the crossfire.

# References

Evans, L.T. (1998). *Feeding the Ten Billion—Plants and Population Growth*. Cambridge University Press. Paperback, p. 247, ISBN 0-521-64685-5.

Kenrick, Paul & Crane, Peter R. (1997). *The Origin and Early Diversification of Land Plants: A Cladistic Study*. Washington, D.C.: Smithsonian Institution Press. ISBN 1-56098-730-8.

Raven, Peter H., Evert, Ray F., & Eichhorn, Susan E. (2005). *Biology of Plants* (7th ed.). New York: W.H. Freeman and Company. ISBN 0-7167-1007-2.

Taylor, Thomas N. & Taylor, Edith L. (1993). *The Biology and Evolution of Fossil Plants*. Englewood Cliffs, NJ: Prentice Hall. ISBN 0-13-651589-4.

Trewavas, A. (2003). Aspects of Plant Intelligence, *Annals of Botany* 92: 1-20.

Asimov, Isaac (1968). *Photosynthesis*. New York, London: Basic Books, Inc. ISBN 0-465-05703-9.

Bidlack JE; Stern KR, Jansky S (2003). *Introductory Plant Biology*. New York: McGraw-Hill. ISBN 0-07-290941-2.

Blankenship RE (2008). *Molecular Mechanisms of Photosynthesis* (2nd ed.). John Wiley & Sons Inc. ISBN 0-470-71451-4.

Govindjee (1975). *Bioenergetics of photosynthesis*. Boston: Academic Press. ISBN 0-12-294350-3.

Govindjee Beatty JT,Gest H, Allen JF (2006). *Discoveries in Photosynthesis*. Advances in Photosynthesis and Respiration. Berlin: Springer. ISBN 1-4020-3323-0.

Gregory RL (1971). *Biochemistry of Photosynthesis*. New York: Wiley-Interscience. ISBN 0-471-32675-5.

Rabinowitch E, Govindjee (1969). *Photosynthesis*. London: J. Wiley. ISBN 0-471-70424-5.

Reece, J, Campbell, N (2005). *Biology*. San Francisco: Pearson, Benjamin Cummings. ISBN 0-8053-7146-X.

Eames, Arthur Johnson and MacDaniels, Laurence H. (1947) *An Introduction to Plant Anatomy* McGraw-Hill, New York.

Esau, Katherine (1965) *Plant Anatomy* (2nd edition) Wiley, New York.

Lambers, H. (1998). *Plant Physiological Ecology*. New York: Springer-Verlag. ISBN 0-387-98326-0.

Larcher, W. (2001). *Physiological Plant Ecology* (4th ed.). Springer. ISBN 3-540-43516-6.

Salisbury, Frank B. & Ross, Cleon W. (1992). *Plant Physiology*, 4th, Belmont, California: Wadsworth Publishing. ISBN 0-534-15162-0.

Chapman, G.P. and W.E. Peat. 1992. An Introduction to the Grasses. CAB International, Wallingford.

Cheplick, G.P. 1998. Population Biology of Grasses. Cambridge Univ. Press, Cambridge.

# Index

**D**



**E**



**F**

## M



## N

**R**



**S**